No More Baby Daddies

It's time for men to stand-up, man-up, own-up, be fathers and take care of their kids!

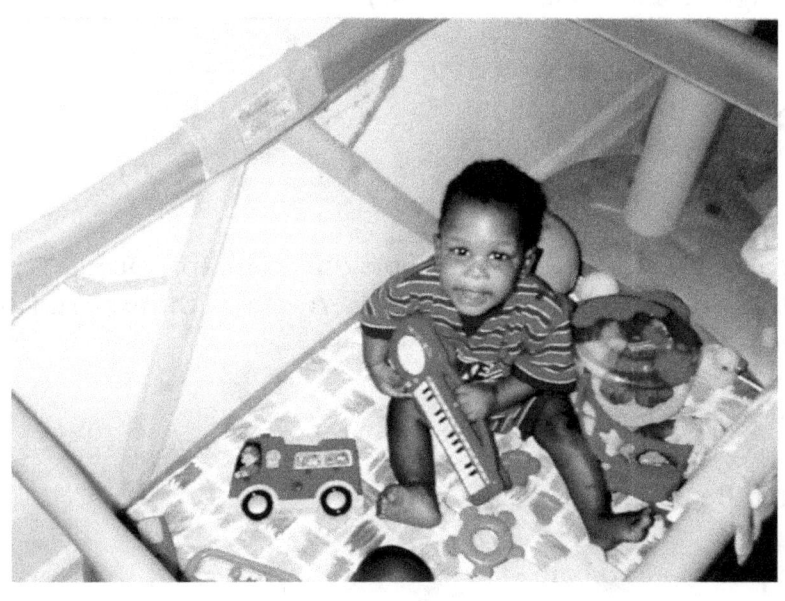

H. Nigel Kassembe

Copyright © 2011 H. Nigel Kassembe
All rights reserved.

ISBN: 0984542809
ISBN-13: 9780984542802
LCCN: 2011925398

No part of this book may be reproduced in any form, except for the inclusion of brief quotations in a review, without permission in writing from the author or publisher.

Nigel Publishing
P.O. Box 5471
Hyattsville, MD. 20782

Nigelpub@Yahoo.com

www.NoMoreBabyDaddies.com

Printed in the U.S.A

This book is dedicated to:

(1.) First to my wife (Sanyambe) for being such a great mother to our kids, thereby making my job as a father that much more easier.

(2.) Second to my kids (Imani, Nigel, and Isaiah) for being such great kids, thereby making my job as a father that much more enjoyable. Thank you guys!

Much love, love you always,

Daddy

Contents

Introduction   ix

1. Damn, she got me   1

2. I can't believe I'm about to become a baby daddy   5

3. You are the father   11

4. Men's lustful nature   17

5. Promiscuous girl   23

6. Fools for love   49

7. Daddy's little girl   67

8. Mama's boy   73

9. Like mother like daughter   83

10. Like father like son   93

11. Parenting 101   141

12. Parenting 102   157

13. Parenting 103   197

14. Parenting 104   217

15. Child $upport   229

16. Where's daddy?   235

17. No More Baby Daddies   249

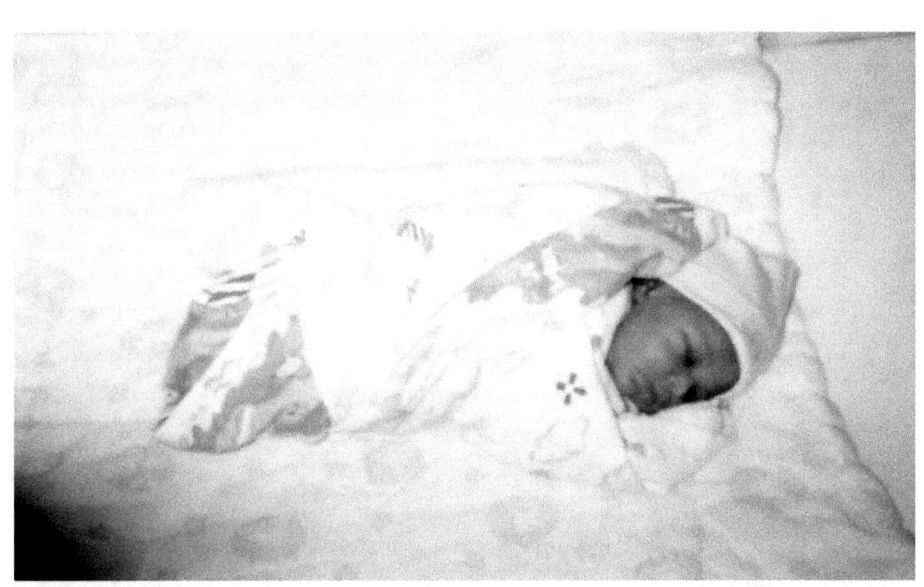

Introduction

When I was younger, I used to wonder why all these athletes and other entertainers always used to say, "Hi mom, this is for you!" You know, whenever they did something spectacular, you know, like scoring a touchdown, or winning a Grammy, or winning a championship of some kind, you know, just accomplishing something special and being recognized for it. I mean, I used to wonder why they would always tend to give a shout out to their mothers and never even give an inch or word of mention to their fathers. I mean this used to really bug my mind as a kid, you know, trying to figure out why they never seemed to show their fathers some love, you know, by shouting them out like how they would for their mothers.

Then I started thinking, well, maybe it's just more fashionable to say "Hi mom, this is for you!", rather than to say "Hi dad, this is for you!" But then that didn't make much sense, because I mean, if you want to honor your parents for the hard work and sacrifice that they had to make in order for you to achieve the accomplishments you are achieving, why would you only shout out your mother and leave out your father in this special moment of your life. And so this is when I started to realize (when I got older and started to put two and two together in solving this "Hi mom" mystery), that the reason why most of these athletes and entertainers tend to say "Hi mom" instead of "Hi dad", or much better, "Hi mom and dad", is because that most of these athletes (like most kids nowadays) tend to come from single parent homes raised only by their mothers, you know, mama was the only parent there because daddy chose to be a deadbeat.

And notice how I said "chose" to be a deadbeat. And this is because really and truly, any guy that really wants to be in their child's life will do whatever they have to do to be in that child's life. And when I say anything, I mean like, if you gotta take your baby mama to court to get some visitation rights, well, then that's what you gotta do. Or, if the court orders you to pay child support in order to get some visitation rights, well, then that's what you gotta do. Or, if your baby mama is giving you much drama and you just can't stand her a$%, that it pains you to have to go to her place to have your twice a week visit with your kid, well, if that's what you gotta do, well then, that's what you gotta do!

And so anyway (back to the "Hi mom" mystery solving answer), when I realized the reason why most athletes and entertainers tended to say "Hi mom" and hardly ever "Hi dad" in their victory shout out was because their fathers were deadbeat dads, I became very disappointed. And the reason for this disappointment is because, if there can be this many athletes and other entertainers who have grown up without their fathers in their lives, just imagine how many more kids out there in the general population there are who are growing up right now without their fathers.

I mean it's crazy, it's disheartening, it's sad, and it's very disappointing. And the reason why it's very disappointing is because, the main reason why there are so many kids growing up without their fathers in their lives is not because their fathers are dead (deceased, passed away) or something, or no, hell no! The main reason (why so many kids are growing up without their fathers) is that their fathers are deadbeat dads, you know, guys who run away from their responsibilities as a father. And I mean, it should be shameful, I mean, these guys should be ashamed of themselves. I mean, I am ashamed for them (as a man), as all men should be ashamed of guys who run away from their responsibilities as fathers. And so this is why this deadbeat dad epidemic is very disappointing to me, because it really doesn't have to be this way, you know what I mean? Because I mean, if we as men truly understood and took the job of raising a kid as an honor and as a measure of us deserving the title of being called a man (a real man), most guys would not so easily run away from their responsibilities as a father. Because I mean to do so would be like giving up their claim to being a real man, which most guys would like to think they are.

And so yeah, this is one of the main reasons why I decided to write this book (on fatherhood), and it's because there are just too many guys out there who are running away from their responsibilities as fathers. And so by writing this book I'm hoping to add my two cents to the "fatherhood" movement (which has already started) that I believe really needs to become the next Civil Rights like movement that the NAACP, Jesse Jackson, Al Sharpton and other notable leaders (like how Bill Cosby has been talking about, in which I loudly applaud, and in which I wish more notable individuals would join him), need to seriously take a lead on. And I mean, President Obama has already given several speeches on the importance of fatherhood (himself understanding the challenges of having to grow up without his father). So really and truly the only thing needed now is an organized effort that will work to encourage guys to take more seriously the role that a father plays in a kid's life.

And so this is the main reason why I wrote this book. And the reason is, there are just too many kids out there who are suffering, hurting, sad, confused, miserable, low self-esteemed, mad, undisciplined, disrespectful, filled with hatred, filled with anger, don't know who to trust, don't know who to love, don't know how to love, ashamed, insecure, unhappy, and it's all because their fathers aren't there to teach them, to show them, to encourage them, to discipline them, to guide them, to hug them, to play with them, and to tell them how special and loved they really are!

See guys, we gotta step up our fatherhood game man, because our kids really need us. Because I mean raising kids is no joke, it's hard work. And so if we really want to call ourselves real men, we gotta stop taking the easy way out and leave the women to do all the work of raising the kids. Because I mean, not only is it not fair, it's really embarrassing to all of us men as male species. And the reason why I say this is because, it seems like nowadays women are actually out fathering us men. And what I mean by this is that, women are actually starting to think and or feel like they can be better fathers to the kids than we men can. And to this I say, come on guys, we can't afford to be out fathered by the females. Because the next thing you know, women will actually start to think and or believe that they don't need a man in the house or in their lives, you know, to help with the raising and fathering of their kids. Oh, wait a minute, I think women have already started to think that they don't need us (men) in their lives, you know, they have already started to think that they can be both mothers and fathers for their children. And to this I say, come on men, we must not allow this thinking to foster and or continue any longer. Because not only is it dangerous in its assumption, but it is also false by nature, therefore we must act fast to squash it from becoming a normal female mentality. And we can do this by becoming better fathers to our kids, so that way the women can go back to being the wonderful mothers to their kids without having to think and or worry about having to play the fatherly role also.

Well my friends, thank you for your support, as I try to encourage guys to stand-up, man-up, own-up, and be fathers to their kids. So go ahead and read the rest of the book, and let me know how you liked it (or not) by e-mailing me at: Nigelpub@Yahoo.com. Thanks again, peace and much love!

Chapter 1

Damn, she got me!

I can remember it like it was just yesterday! So there I was, in my room, just chilling, minding my own business, trying to watch a football game (I think it was the Washington Redskins versus the Dallas Cowboys, and being a Redskins fan, I was really into the game). But then all of a sudden the phone rang (startling me for a second), so I quickly picked it up and said hello. The voice that came back to me (on the phone), was that of the girl that I had been trying to break up with for the past few weeks. But every time I thought I had succeeded (in breaking up with her), she would end up calling me again, and seducing me back to her again, with the offer of sexual pleasure, you know, just one more time for the road. And I mean, somehow she always succeeded in getting my punk behind to go back to her for one more round of pleasure principles, you know what I mean, ha ha ha ha ha!

But then so, after we are done, there we go again, I mean, there I go again, doing the whole thing again, of trying to explain why we can't be together. You know, I gotta try to explain to her again that, besides sex, we are really not compatible in a lot of other areas, you know, like in; spirituality, morality, values, goals, aspirations, education, communication, and so on and so on. And really, I'm just not ready for a serious relationship right now. And also, I really don't want to get you pregnant, so we really need to break up, because the more I'm with you, the more I start to relax, and the more I relax, the more I start to not use a condom, and the more I don't use a condom, the more the chances of me getting you pregnant, and the more the chances of me getting you pregnant, the more the chances of me becoming a father, and the more the chances of me becoming a father, the more the chances of me becoming a baby daddy. And this is because, I know our relationship won't work, then we gonna have to break up, then I'm gonna have to become a baby daddy, and I definitely don't want to be just a baby daddy to nobody. I want to be a daddy and a father when I'm ready to have kids, and right now, I'm just not ready.

Wow, what a mouthful ha! What an explanation ha! And just imagine having to give this same darn explanation to the same person more than three times, in about a month or so. Man, what was I thinking, going back and back for one more last time. Man, the power of the goodies, the power of the goodies! Can someone say, **danger**, ha ha ha ha ha!

And so anyway, every time I finished explaining to her why we couldn't be together, she always acted like she understood what I was trying to say, you know what I mean? But then, one or two weeks later, she would end up calling me and seducing me all over again. So this time (as I'm trying to watch my football game), I prepared myself mentally to say no, no thank you, we are really over, no more pleasure principles for us. But to my surprise, the tone of her voice on the phone sounded different, you know, she didn't sound flirtatious as she usually does. So I was like, "What's up, what's going on?" And she just hit me off the top with it, I mean no warning at all, you know, no warming up to it, you know, no small talk before it, you know, she just hit me up like, "Nigel, I'm pregnant!" Wow, silence, speechless, I couldn't say a word, words were escaping me, running away. Then my jaw got heavy, because I couldn't close my mouth, because my mouth just stayed wide open from the surprise, the shock, the disbelief and the confusion that was settling in my brain. I could hear her on the phone asking me, "Are you alright?" "Did you hear what I said?" "Are you still on the phone?" And that's when I whispered back, "Yeah, I'm still here". Then she asked me if I wanted to talk to her mother, you know, to reassure me that she wasn't lying (cause her mom was there when she took the pregnancy test). I whispered again back, "Nah, nah, I don't need to talk to your mom, I believe you". Then she started laughing at me, while asking, "Are you alright, are you ok, you don't sound right, you sure you ok?" All I could say was, "Yeah, yeah, I'm cool, I'm alright, I'll be fine". Then she said, "Well, I'll call you tomorrow, to check on you", and I said (in a whisper), "Ok, thank you!"

And then as soon as I hang up the phone, I started to feel an intense headache coming on. I couldn't watch the game no more, because I couldn't concentrate. So I got up from where I was sitting, walked myself to the bed, laid down on my back, with my eyes wide open, I looked up at the ceiling (staring at nothing in particular), trying not to think about it. But I couldn't help it, my mind was going crazy, I couldn't believe this was happening, I couldn't believe I got her pregnant!

Damn, is all I could think, as I laid there in bed with my eyes wide open. Damn, is all I could think, as my headache turned into a migraine. Damn, is all I could think, as my migraine turned into a double and triple migraine. Damn, I can't believe this! Damn, I think she got me! Damn, I can't believe I'm about to become a baby daddy! Damn, damn, damn, damn, damn, damn, damn…………!

Chapter 2

I can't believe I'm about to become a baby daddy!

Man, I can't believe I'm about to become a baby daddy! I mean, all this time I have been trying my best not to get any girl pregnant, and then all of a sudden, bang, I'm about to become a baby daddy! Well, I guess that's what I get for relaxing too much, you know, that's what I get for not using a condom every time.

And so there I was, the next day, after having done some soul searching and realizing that my life as I knew it was about to change, after I had calmed down, after I had reassured myself that everything was going to be ok, it's not the end of the world, it's just the end of me being a bachelor with no kids, you know, because now I'm about to become a bachelor with a kid. So I figured, ok, there's got to be a way for me to be a real father and still enjoy my bachelorhood, and also, still go after my dreams. Oh man, my dreams, my aspirations, my goals, my plans, what was I thinking! I wasn't thinking, that's what happened. I got too comfortable, I relaxed, I played house. Damn she got me! What's going to happen now? I can't be a deadbeat dad, I gotta take care of my responsibility. I mean, I was man enough to get her pregnant, now I gotta be man enough to own up to it. And it's like, I have always promised myself that, if I ever get a girl pregnant, I would own up to my responsibility and be a real father to my kid. I mean, I never wanted to be one of those dead beat dads, you know, absent fathers, or to be known as just a baby daddy.

No, not me, just a baby daddy, oh no, I want to be a real father to my kid. I mean, I have always told myself that, when I'm ready to have kids, I'm going to make sure it's going to be with the person that I'm in a serious relationship with, you know, someone that I'm committed to, you know, someone that I'm engaged to, or, better yet, someone that I am married to. Because you know, that way it will give the kid a better chance of being raised with both parents full-time in the household, you know, instead of having to raise the kid one week here and one week there, and all other kinds of crazy arrangements, you know what I mean? Because I mean, I've always figured that, if you are in a committed relationship (especially a marriage), you give yourself a better chance to fight and stay in that relationship, you know, for the sake of the kid. But, on the other hand, if you are just dating (even serious boyfriend and girlfriend dating) and a pregnancy occurs, it is very easy for the guy to run away from the whole situation, you know, because there is no real commitment there, and so the guy might not feel any extra pressure to stick around, especially if he wasn't into her or didn't even like her as much as she thought he did. I mean, he might have liked her a lot, but not to the point where he wants to have a baby with her. See, this is where most girls mess up, because they always get so caught up with the guy that, they start to think, "Mmm, if I get pregnant and have his baby, he will always be in my life, and he will always be mine!"

Wrong, wrong, wrong, ladies! Because for one, he'll probably run away as soon as you tell him that you are pregnant. And for two (if he decides to stay), he will probably resent you for making him a father before he was ready, and therefore y'all will probably end up breaking up sooner than later because of his resentment. And for three, as far as him being in your life forever because you have his baby, well, yeah, he'll have no choice but to run into you from time to time when he wants to see his kid, but as far as him really being in your life, oh no, not at all, because at this point you will be nothing to him but just a baby mama.

And here is where a lot of girls get so mad and start harassing a brother, you know, like calling him and saying staff like, "You are such an ass, you ain't nothing but a dog, you can go to hell, I hope you die!" Man, come on ladies, calm down, let it go, I know y'all mad, I know y'all hurting, I know y'all frustrated, but he wasn't into you like that, because if he was, he would have given you a commitment, you know, like a marriage proposal. But I guess it's hard to let go ha, especially if you have fallen for the guy and the guy has not fallen for you. I mean, I have experienced the pain and hurt of falling in love and having the girl not being in love with me. I mean, it hurts, but you gotta let it go, because maybe it just wasn't meant to be, so there's no reason trying to force it, it will never work. But it's hard to let go, and this is one of the reasons why girls tend to give guys baby mama dramas all the time, because they just can't let go.

So anyway, yeah, there I was, the next day after being told that I'm about to become a baby daddy, the next day after spending the night wide awake reassuring myself that I can do this, you know, that I can be a great part-time father and still go after my dreams. And so there I was, more assured, ready to own up to my responsibility, ready to be the best baby daddy in the world! So I picked up the phone and called my soon to be baby mama. When she picked up the phone, she hit me with a question that I hadn't even thought about. This is what she asked me, "So, what do you think, should I keep it or should I have an abortion?" Wow! I didn't even think about that, I didn't even think about abortion as an option. Actually, I couldn't believe she was willing to give me the option of abortion, because I mean, most girls that want to keep a guy, having his baby they figure is the best way to do it. Then again, maybe she was just testing me to see what I would say, you know, like if I said abortion, she would laugh at me and say something like, "Ha ha ha ha, sorry sucker, I got you, I'm having this baby, I'm having your baby, and you and me are going to have to be in each other's lives foreverrrrrr!" Ha ha ha ha ha, you know what I mean?

But so anyway, my answer to her was very quick, I didn't need much time to think about it, because I have always thought abortions were morally and or spiritually wrong, you know, unless it's a health issue with the mother or something. And also it can be a very traumatic experience, leaving a lot of mental scares that can really affect the mother for the rest of her life. And so my answer to her was very easy, I mean, I just told her, "Look, whatever you decide to do, I will support you, you know, if you decide to keep it, cool, I'll just have to be a man about it and help take care of that little young'n, and then too, if you decide to abort the pregnancy, I will support you and help pay for it, I mean, it's really your choice to decide." I think she was kind of shocked by my answer, actually I know she was shocked because she told me so, you know, she told me she was surprised I didn't jump on the abortion option, you know, as an easy way out of the situation. So of course she chose to keep the pregnancy, and that marked the official beginning of the prelude of me becoming a baby daddy.

But, we never made it, I mean, the baby never made it, because around the third month or so she started having complications with the pregnancy, so I took her to the doctor and the doctor put her on bed rest. Then about three weeks later, I remember her calling me, and panicking. And so I jumped in my car, rushed over to her house and took her to the hospital. But by the time we got there it was too late (the look on her face said it all), she had had a miscarriage. I remember her looking so sad, and I felt so bad for her. I remember driving her back to her house, the drive was pretty quiet, I didn't know what to say. I remember when we got to her house, before she got out the car, she turned, looked at me and said, "Thank you for being there for me, you are not as big an a&%hole as I thought!" With that being said, I turned slightly, looked at her, gave her a slight smile, hugged her, told her to take care of herself, then I drove off.

The drive back to my place was kind of weird, I mean, I was kind of zoned out. I mean stuff was just running through my head,

I was having conflicting emotions. Because it's like, on one hand, I was kind of relived that I won't have to be a father just yet (cause truth be told, I really wasn't ready), but on the other hand, I was really feeling bad for my would be baby mama, because it seemed like she really wanted the baby. And I mean, even I myself had started getting used to the idea of being a daddy. Because I mean, we had gone so far as to picking names for the baby and stuff, you know. I mean it's crazy, because it was like, I would come up with a name, she would disagree with it, and she would come up with a name, and I would disagree with it, you know, that was kind of fun.

And so I mean, without knowing it I was actually starting to get used to the idea of having a baby. But, oh well, you know, it wasn't meant to be. And so, as I got to my place, I went to my room, got my radio, opened the tape deck, put in my Sade tape, pressed play, and then I went to my bed, laid down on my back, with my eyes half closed I looked up at the ceiling (staring at nothing in particular), thinking and saying to myself, "Man, man, man, man, man, that was close, I just dodged a huge bullet, I mean, from now on, I'm definitely gonna have to take extra care to make sure I don't get no other girl pregnant, because I'm definitely not ready to be a father, and I definitely don't want to be anybody's baby daddy!"

Chapter 3

You are the father!

"You are the father!" I think these can be the most terrifying words that any man could ever hear, especially if they are coming from a girl that the guy doesn't even really like. Now, you are probably asking yourself what do I mean by saying, "coming from a girl that the guy doesn't even really like". And what I mean is, most guys only like the girls they are dating just enough to have sex with and not enough to actually want to have a baby with, you know what I mean? Because it's like, well, think about it ladies (because guys know exactly what I mean), why do you think there are so many baby daddies out there? Because it's like, combine a guy's fear of fatherhood with a guy's propensity to get a girl that he doesn't even really like pregnant, and what you get is, a baby daddy (you know, a guy who is no longer with the mother of his kids), or worse, a deadbeat dad (you know, a guy who is not involved in his kid's life at all).

See, this is why I say "You are the father" can be the most terrifying words that any man could ever hear, especially coming from a girl that the guy doesn't even really like. And this is because, not only are guys never really ready to be fathers (unless they are married to their girl), but also the thought of having a baby with a girl that they don't even really like just makes the whole situation that much more unpleasant and even terrifying. And the reason why it's terrifying is because, the guy already knows that not only will his life style (as a bachelor with no kids) take a hit (because he'll have to do some baby sitting and pay some child support), but he already knows that there will be a whole lot of baby mama drama that he'll have to deal with after he dumps her (if he hasn't dumped her already).

And this is one of the reasons why there are so many baby daddies out there, and it's because guys continue to get girls that they don't really like pregnant. Now, notice how I keep saying "girls that they don't really like", instead of just saying girls that they don't like. And the reasons for this is because, even though most guys that get with a girl kind of like the girl to some degree, they tend not to like the girl enough to the point where they actually want to settle down and have some kids with them. Oh no, the kids tend to come by surprise (to him anyway), you know what I mean? Because I mean, if the guy really liked the girl, then he should be happy when the girl comes to him and says, "Guess what, I'm pregnant, and you are the father!" But that is not what usually happens is it? I mean what usually happens (when the girl tells him that she is pregnant) is that the guy will look down and go quiet for a few seconds (shaking his head, biting his lips, looking irritated), and then he will look back up at her and ask her something like, "Are you sure it's mine?", or ask her something like, "So what are you gonna do about it?"

See I told you, most guys don't really like the girls that they are dating. I mean sure they may like them enough to take them to the movies and or spend nights full of passion with them. But, as far as liking them to the point that they want to have babies with them, hell no, I mean, no. Because really and truly (ladies), the only girls that guys don't really mind having kids with are the girls that the guys happen to fall in love with, you know what I mean? And when I say fall in love, I'm talking about head over hills kind of love, you know, in love to the point where he actually starts to think about kids, marriage, and settling down.

Now, you probably want to ask me, "Hey Mr. Nigel (since I seem to know it all, which I do, especially when it comes to why guys do what they do when it comes to relationships), if guys only want to have kids with girls that they are in love with, then why do they continue to impregnate girls that they don't really like?" Well my friends (especially my lady friends), once again I have the answer for you, and I'm going to try to make the answer as simple and as short as possible. And the answer is (drum roll please), and the answer is, because guys become idiots when they are horny. That's it, that's it (ladies), that's why us guys keep impregnating girls that we don't even really like. And it's all because we got horny and instead of using our brains to make sure we don't get the girl pregnant, we instead dive in head first (no pon intended) without thinking about the consequences that can occur from the two and a half minutes of pleasure. Oh, wait a minute, did I just say two and a half minutes? Oh no, what I really meant to say was, two and a half hours, you know what I mean fellas, ha ha ha ha ha! Hey, some of us are studs out here, you heard, ha ha ha, stop playing with all that two minute brother stuff, you know what I mean fellas, ha ha ha ha ha!

But so anyway, yeah, us guys can be very careless when we are horny. I mean it's crazy, but for some reason our brains just get so focused on the pleasure that we are about to receive that it can't bother to worry about the consequences that can result from that pleasure. And this is one of the reasons why the HIV/AIDS epidemic keeps getting worse. And it's all because guys get horny, lose focus, and either forget or choose not to use protection during sex. And so too, this is the same reason why guys tend to end up impregnating girls that they had never planed on having babies with. And it's all because they got excited about the pleasure that they were about to receive that they could care less about using protection at that moment. And so this is why I say guys tend to become idiots when they get horny. And it's all because we tend to lose focus of the big picture (you know, making babies, getting STDs, etc.) that can result from sex. I mean it's crazy, but it takes a lot of focus and or discipline for a guy not to let his horniness control his mind to the point where he allows himself to become a sexual idiot.

And so yeah, guys do not intend to get girls they are not in love with pregnant (which is most girls), they just make a mistake by losing focus and allowing themselves to become sexual idiots. I mean this is why there are so many baby daddies out there. And it's all because guys become sexual idiots and end up impregnating girls that they have no intention of having any sort of long term relationship with, you know what I mean? And some guys are so sexually stupid that they end up impregnating a whole bunch of women, which means they'll end up with a whole bunch of baby mama dramas, which will also mean that there's no way they will be able to be great fathers to all of their kids.

Man it's crazy, but being told that you are about to become a father before you are ready to be a parent is one of the most defeating words that any guy could hear, especially if the words are coming from a girl that the guy has no long term interest in. And this is because not only does the guy know that he's about to become a baby daddy (because he knows that he will be dumping her sooner or later), he also knows that he'll have to do a lot of sacrifices of his life style if he wants to be not only just a baby daddy, but also a real father to his kid. Because I mean, I truly believe that it's still possible for a guy to be a good father to his kids even if he doesn't live in the same household with them. But of course it will require a whole lot more energy, desire, persistence, focus and outmost dedication to succeed. Because it's like, not only will the guy have to be willing to deal with all the baby mama drama that he'll face, but he will also have to be willing to sacrifice a whole lot of his time and money to really make it work. And then off-course, the more baby mamas a guy has, the more difficult the task of being a good father to all of his kids becomes. And this is one of the reasons why when I was younger (early dating age, before I got married), I always hoped, wished, and planned to try my best to have all my kids by the same woman, you know what I mean? You know, this way just in-case the relationship doesn't work out, at least I'll only have one baby mama drama to deal with, you know, increasing my chances of still being a great father to my kids.

I mean I'm telling you, I had the whole thing planned out, you know, trying to date only girls that I knew I wouldn't mind if they were my baby mama if an accident happened, you know what I mean fellas, ha ha ha ha ha! But then off-course I quickly realized that I was missing out on a lot of potential dates by my high standards, to which I quickly decided it's ok to temporary reduce my standards from time to time as needed, you know what I mean fellas, ha ha ha ha ha! Because I mean, good girls are hard to find, and then when you do find them, most of them won't give you their goodies until they are convinced that you are not a player, you know, meaning you have relationship potential. And so needless to say (to my surprise), I was not very good at convincing them (the good girls) that I was not a player, which of-course left them no choice but to give me no play, to which of-course left me no choice but to increase my dating the bad girls (and hoping I don't impregnate none of them), you know, until a good girl comes along and gives me a chance to fall in love with them so that if a pregnancy occurs I can have a good girl as my baby mama, thereby reducing my chances of being just another baby daddy.

Man, I'm telling you, it's just so easy to impregnate the wrong woman. And this is one of the reasons why there are so many baby daddies out there. And it's because guys date girls that they don't really like like that, and get surprised when sooner than later one of them comes to them and says something like, "Hey look here buddy, I'm pregnant and you are the father!" And this is when the guy gets the deer in the head light look on his face and all he can do or say is, damn damn damn damn, what the hell did I just do, damn damn damn, stupid stupid stupid, idiot idiot idiot, I can't believe I got her pregnant, damn I think she got me, damn I can't believe I'm about to become her baby daddy, damn she got me, damn damn damn!

Chapter 4

Men's lustful nature

Oh man, that was close! I almost became a baby daddy! I mean, I was sweating bullets! I just couldn't believe I was about to become a baby daddy. I mean, that whole situation showed me how easy it is for anyone to become a baby daddy. Because it's like, all my life I tried my best to be a very disciplined person, and since I never wanted to have a baby out of wedlock, I tried my best to make sure that I always used a condom. But as you can see, I too slipped on that department from time to time, because that's how I almost became a baby daddy.

And this is one of the reasons why a lot of guys become baby daddies, because they are just not disciplined enough to make sure that they always, always, always use condoms. Because I mean, it's just so easy to not use a condom, especially if the both of you (you and your partner) are extremely heated and are just ready to tear each other's clothes off! I mean, horniness can be very dangerous, especially for guys. Because when a guy gets extremely horny, forget it, he almost goes temporally insane. Because it's like, his brain (the horny part) starts telling him, "I gotta have sex, I gotta have sex, I gotta have sex man!" And this is why you always see guys checking out girls, especially the ones that look easy, you know, easy to get. And this is because, when a guy is horny (which is often), he has no time for playing games, you know what I mean?

And this is why guys tend to look for girls that seem to be willing to poke right away, you know, girls that don't know how to play hard to get. And this is one of the reasons why a lot of girls tend to find them-selves getting dumped not long after they give a guy some sex. And this is because the guy has gotten what he was after and now it's time for him to bounce, you know, because he didn't really like the girl that much, he really just wanted her body.

And so this is why it is very important for girls that want a real relationship to try their best (notice how I say their best, because some guys are very smooth talkers that can really charm a girl into falling in love or falling in lust with him in one night, which can result in her wanting to give up her goodies to him right away) to not give their goodies to a guy so soon, you know, without making him wait at least after a few dates, you know, so as to give herself the chance to get to know him better. Because I mean, it is amazing at how many girls are out there who are willing to give a guy sex without even putting him to the test, you know, the test to find out and see whether or not the guy is really worthy of their goodies. I mean, it is amazing at how many girls are out there that are quick to provide a guy with some sexual healing without even knowing whether the guy really likes them or not. Because I mean, truth be told, when a horny guy needs healing, forget about it, he's ready to poke any girl that says yes. I mean, she could be big, small, tall, short, has some butt, has no butt, has some breasts, has no breasts, looks sexy, don't look too sexy, has some teeth, has no teeth, hey, as long as she says, "Hey big daddy!", shoot, that's it, she's good to go, ain't no time to be picky, you know what I mean, ha ha ha ha, ha, just turn the lights of baby, just turn the lights of, ha ha ha ha ha!

But I mean, I'm I right or wrong? Because I mean, when a guy is horny, his standards for choosing a girl drops tremendously. For example; say he used to like girls that are smart, funny, good looking, and very respectful, but, when he gets horny, all that standard stuff goes out the door, because now, all he'll be looking for is sexiness, that's it, sexiness, as long as she looks kind of sexy, she's good to go. And this is one of the reasons why guys end up with baby mamas that they don't even like, but since the sex was kind of good, they kept going back for more and more, then before you know it, bang, she gets pregnant. And so, there he is, left there thinking, "Damn, I should have never hooked up with her, what was I thinking!" You weren't thinking my friend, you weren't thinking, your horniness had taken over your mind and left you with a one-track mind, and that one-track mind was, to **s.c.o.r.e...** ha ha ha ha ha!

Now, it's funny how girls like to say that guys are dogs, well, I would like to disagree with that, no, guys are not dogs, we are just players, ha ha ha ha ha! I mean, we are not dogs, we just like to hump and move, you know, hump and move on to another girl that is also ready and willing to engage in some sexual healing, you know what I mean, ha ha ha ha ha! Hey, it's not our fault, we were made like that, we were made to hunt, you know, we were made to hunt as much game as we can catch, hey, that's why we were filled with so much testosterone. I mean, we are filled with so much testosterone that we gotta release it somehow, and sex is the best way to release it, because I mean, that's why most guys go to sleep right after sex, because their testosterone has been reduced to a satisfactory level, you know, leaving them feeling relaxed, comfortable and ready for a nap, you know what I mean, ha ha ha ha ha! But I mean (ladies), how does your man look before and after sex? I bet you he looks angry, mad, irritated, uncomfortable, miserable, and just plain all sad, before you give him some sex (even pity sex, ha ha ha ha ha!). And after sex, I bet you he looks relieved, relaxed, rejuvenated, comfortable, and just plain all happy. I'm telling you (ladies), it's serious business when it comes to guys and our need for sex. And this is the reason why guys are dogs (or, wait a minute, did I just say guys are dogs, ops, I meant to say, this is the reason why guys are players, ha ha ha ha ha!), because it's just in our nature. I mean, that's how we were created, we were created to plant our seeds everywhere. You know how the Bible says to be fruitful and multiply, well, us guys, we take that very seriously. No, really, I'm serious! I mean, whether consciously or subconsciously, it's built within us to try and multiply as much as possible. And that's why there's so much lust in us, you know, so as to help us or push us to get with as many girls as we can get with. Because it's like, the more girlfriends we have, the more the chances of us multiplying a lot. And this was beneficial at the beginning of the world, because the world was not that populated. But now of course the world seems to be over populated, but, us men still have the same instinct of multiplying a lot, you know, explaining our lustful nature.

Now, even though we were meant to be fruitful and multiply, it by no means meant for us to be irresponsible. And this is why God created the institution of marriage, so that a man and a woman can join together as one, multiply as much as they can, and also be obligated to nurture, provide, protect, and to love each other. I mean, God knew what he was doing! Because I mean, if a man feels a sense of ownership to his kids, and he feels a sense of obligation to the woman (his wife) that bore him those kids, he will do whatever he can to be the best provider he can be for her and the kids. Because his love for them will be so strong that, he will want to make sure that they are very well taken care of.

Also, the other reason why God created the institution of marriage, is so to help guys suppress their lustful tendencies. Because I'm telling you, the hardest thing that a guy will ever do in his life, is to try to suppress is natural instinct, you know, to try and suppress his desire to plant his seeds everywhere, you know, to try to sleep with every sexy chick he sees. I'm telling you, if it weren't for marriage, guys would never settle down and try to be faithful to their woman. I mean, think about it ladies (because y'all always complaining about, "I don't understand men, why they always gotta be looking at her, her, her and her!"), really, think about it. Because I mean (ladies), what man do you know, given the chance, won't want to have his cake and eat it too. I mean, what man do you know, that would not welcome the chance to have more than one girlfriend? Not too many, right? Hell, if you knew one you would probably be trying to marry him quick, you know, before another girl comes along and shows him her Victoria Secrets, and then take him for herself, right? I mean, that's why girls are so protective over their man, because they know a good man is hard to find, and they know how seductive women can be, so they will be damned before they will let another girl just parade her trifling sexy pretty self around her man, you know, and try to seduce him. Because it's like, women instinctively know how weak men are when it comes to lust, you know what I mean?

So it's like, women know that, give a man the eye, show him some thighs, lick them lips, and then give him the smile that says, "I'm all yours big daddy, just come and get it!", and it's a wrap, another man is about to get trapped and fall, by the power of a woman's seduction. And here is where a guy can find himself in some extra-curricular activity that he would rather not be in (good example; John Edwards, messed up his whole presidential and political career by not only cheating on his wife, but also by fathering a baby from his mistress), but he just could not suppress his nature, and now finds himself lost, lost in lust.

Man, I'm telling you, going against nature is not easy! That's why most guys try their best to avoid commitment and or marriage. But sooner than later, they will have no choice but to commit, because everybody falls in love once in a while in their lifetime. And this is usually when guys are kind of ready to commit and get married, you know, when they fall in love. And this is because the fear of losing the girl will force them to be more willing to commit, you know, more willing to get married and work hard to suppress their lust for others. And that's why marriage is important, because under marriage is usually where guys work their hardest to suppress their instinctive nature, you know, the desire to score with all the sexy mamas, you know what I mean fellas, ha ha ha ha ha, yeah!

Chapter 5

Promiscuous girl

What the hell are girls thinking about these days? I mean, what the hell is going on with these females nowadays? I mean, what's going on in the minds of our young ladies nowadays? I mean, why are our young girls giving up their sex so easily these days? I mean, why are girls so promiscuous nowadays? I mean, it's crazy out there! Girls are going crazy, acting like they just don't care anymore, acting like they have totally lost their inhibitions! I mean, girls no longer wait till guys chase them down, you know, mack them down, you know, throw their little hot rhymes to the young ladies to the point of exhaustion before the young ladies fall in love with them to the point of wanting to give them their goodies.

But no, girls nowadays don't wait for all of that, you know? I mean, most girls nowadays just don't really make a guy work for it anymore. Because I mean (guys), remember how when you were younger and liked a girl and you wanted to do the nasty with her, remember how long it took for you to just get her phone number. And then after you got her phone number, remember how long it took for you to get her to agree to go out with you. And then after she agreed to go out with you, remember how hard it was for you to just get one kiss on her lips. Because I mean, remember how every time you tried to kiss her, remember how she would always tend to turn her head around so as to give you her cheeks for you to kiss. And remember how you would get so frustrated but you would hold your cool, hoping she would be ready to kiss you on the next date. And then finally, after a few dates, remember how she would let you kiss her on the lips, but, she wouldn't let you grab or touch her butt, or feel all up on her body, you know? But then, finally, after numerous dates, and after numerous conversations about life, love, and marriage, and after she has had enough time and information about you to decide whether you are indeed worthy of her goodies, then and only then, that's when she lets you in, you know, that's when she lets you make love to her. And notice how I said "make love to her", because believe me, you will be making love to her. Because it's like, after all this time that she has been making you wait, trust me, you gonna have such a build-up of lust for her, that a quickie just won't cut it, you know what I mean? Because by this time you will be longing for her love so much so that, you are going to want to make love to her all day, all night, the next day again, and the next day, and the next day, and the next day, until you actually start to fall in love with her, if you are not already! I mean it's crazy, but girls used to make you chase them hard, you know, so they can make sure that you really like them before they would give you their goodies.

But nowadays, forget about it, girls are going crazy, they are just giving out their sex like its candy! And I mean, sure there are girls out there who are not promiscuous (even virgins), but the promiscuous girls just seem to out-number and over shadow everyone. Because I mean, think about it, because it's like, when you was in school, elementary, junior high, high school, oh wait a minute, did I say elementary, oh yeah, don't be fooled by those innocent looking little mamas, especially those fifth and sixth graders, I'm telling you, they think they grown! Because I mean, I hear them talking all the time, and I just shake my head in disbelief, because the stuff they are talking about, I'm like, what?! Because you can hear them as you are walking by (especially if you live in an apartment complex, cause they are not very good at whispering), I mean, you can hear them say stuff like, "She ain't nothing but a slut!" "Did you hear who she slept with last week!" "And the whole school knows she's easy!" "And she better not be trying to get with my man cause I'ma smack the………!" And I'm like, did I just hear what I think I heard! And as I turn to look at them in disbelief (they of course keep on talking, trying their best to lower their voices as they notice me walking by with a questionable look on my face), I can't help but think to myself, "Wait a minute, ain't y'all in elementary school, so what the hell are you'll doing talking about sex, shouldn't you'll be talking about homework, and if you'll are going to talk about boys, shouldn't y'all be talking about falling in love, getting married and having a huge wedding, you know, day dreaming about your prince rescuing you with a white horse and taking you away to live with him in the land of happiness forever!" I mean, isn't this what little girls should be talking and day dreaming about! But oh no, not these days! These days girls are just growing up to fast! I mean, instead of playing with barbies, they want to play with boy-friends, and instead of playing nurses, they day dreaming about kissing, and instead of pretending to be singers, they learning to dance like strippers.

I mean, it's crazy, girls are growing up way too fast and it doesn't seem like they are going to slow down anytime soon. Because I mean, do you see how these little girls are dressing these days, I mean, who are they showing their little bodies to? What body anyway? I mean, they wear clothes so small and so tight that they can hardly breath. It's crazy! I mean, this society is so sexualized its ridiculous! That's why it's very important for both parents to be in their kid's lives. I mean, even if the parents are not together anymore, they both still need to be in their kid's lives for reinforcement of discipline and nurture, otherwise this society will corrupt them into making wrong decisions. I mean, it's crazy out there!

Anyway, back to what we were talking about, before I started rumbling on and on and on. Oh man, I forgot what we were talking about! Oh yeah, ok, I remember now, we were talking about promiscuous girls and how they tend to overshadow all other girls.

And this is because promiscuous girls tend to be the most popular girls anywhere they are. Because I mean, when you were in school (elementary, junior high, and high school), which girls seemed to be the most popular, I bet you the most popular girls in your school were the promiscuous ones. I'm I right or wrong? And when you were in college, which girls seemed to be the most popular? I bet you the most popular girls in your college were the promiscuous ones. I'm I right or wrong?

And in your neighborhood, which girls seem to be the most popular? I bet you the most popular girls in your neighborhood are the promiscuous ones. I'm I right or wrong? And also, at your church, which girls at your church seem to be the most popular? And here too I bet you the most popular girls at your church are the promiscuous ones. I'm I right or wrong? What, you don't want to answer the question, why don't you want to answer the question? Come on, I won't tell that you said that there's some promiscuous girls at your church. Come on, don't be afraid, you know which girls you suspect to be promiscuous. You want me to tell you which girls you are suspecting? Ok, I'll tell you. You are probably suspecting that girl that likes to wear her Sunday dress a little extra tight with her cleavage popping out. Or, you are probably suspecting that girl that likes to wear her skirts a little too short and tight, to better showcase her hips and thighs. Or, you are probably suspecting that girl that seems to always be flirting with the brothers in the band, even though she's not in the choir. Is that enough clues, or do you want me to give you some more. Because I mean, promiscuous girls are everywhere, even in church. I mean, why do you think that church girls have the reputation of being the freakiest girls around? This is because most church girls are taught not to date (you know, so they can stay virgins till they marry), but, the problem comes in that, most girls don't like to be tamed (even if it's for a good reason), and so (unless their spirituality is strong enough), one day they wake up and just start rebelling and going wild. And it's like, when a church girl goes wild, she really goes wild as if she's making up for all the years she missed out on dating. And that's why church girls get the reputation of being freaky, because when they decide to start dating, they really date, you know, they date with a heavy appetite. So I mean, I'm telling you, promiscuous girls are everywhere, and it's usually not hard to spot them, because they are usually surrounded by guys (vying for something).

And this is why promiscuous girls seem to be more popular than other girls, because they always have guys following them trying to get dates with them. And the reason why guys seem to be attracted to promiscuous girls is because, guys don't want to have to work hard to get some sex, and so, guys know that if they get with a promiscuous girl, game over, they will be getting it easy, because promiscuous girls tend to give up their sex easily. It's crazy out there! I mean, girls are having sex with guys that they don't even know! I mean, a girl can meet a guy today, and before you know it, she's having sex with him the next day (if not the same day), and all she knows about the guy is, he's kind of hot.

And I mean, this is why there are a lot of girls out there who are not even sure who their baby daddies are. I mean, I'm not kidding you, because just look at day time television shows, and you will see that most of them deal with doing DNA tests to found out who the girl's baby daddy is. I mean, it's amazing, girls just parading guys after guys (they have had sex with) to the stage, trying to find out which one of them is the father of their baby. And some girls bring on five or six guys to the shows (in different episodes), just to find out who is the father of that one baby. I mean, are they serious! Because for them to think that those five or six guys have the chance of being the father of that one child, that will have to mean that, she must have had sex with all those guys in a period of about one month or three weeks. I mean, how crazy is that? It's really trifling if you think about it!

Man, what's really going on? I mean, what's driving our young ladies to be so promiscuous? I mean, what's causing our young ladies to lose their self-respect, their dignity, their morality, their spirituality, and their self-worth? Could it be, that nobody (close to them, you know, like father, mother, brother, sister, uncle, aunty, cousin, etc.) ever told them that they were pretty? Or could it be, that nobody ever told them that they were precious? Or could it be, that nobody ever told them that they were smart? Or could it be, that nobody ever showed them love (you know, unconditional love). Or could it be, that nobody ever gave them spiritual guidance? I don't know, but I think it's all of the above. Because I'm telling you, girls need a lot of attention. And this is because they feel everything, I mean, they got so much emotions that they feel everything hard. And this is also why girls are more readily to shed some tears and cry over anything, no matter whether it's really a big deal or not. And this is because girls feel everything real deep, you know, causing their hearts to feel and ache with pain and or misery so easily. I mean, don't get me wrong, guys have emotions too, and their hearts can feel and ache with pain and misery too, but not as quickly and or easily as girls. Because us guys, we were made to be tough (both emotionally and physically), because we were made to be hunters, you know, breadwinners, you know, providers for our families. And so, you can't be all softy softy and emotional when you are out there trying to hunt for food, you know, because you could get eaten up yourself. And I mean, of course nowadays people don't really go hunting for food anymore, but the same principle still applies, because we do go hunting for jobs, right? So it's like, when you are out there looking for employment, you can't get discouraged and quit looking just because you have been rejected a few times, you gotta keep on looking, because you gotta feed your family. And so the principle applies, because you gotta have tough skin to compete in the job market, because it's a crazy world out there and everybody is jockeying for position to take the same good jobs that will allow them to better take care of their families. And this is why guys were made a little bit tougher, because it was meant for guys to be the breadwinners. But of course nowadays women are forced to take on the position of being the main bread winners (providers) for their families, because the men are not doing what they were meant to be doing, you know, working hard to better care for their families.

And so, this is one of the reasons why a lot of women tend to lose respect for us men, because they see most of us as being softies, you know, because they know we were meant to work hard and bring back the bacon so they can better feed and nurture the kids. But they are right, most of us men are becoming softies (aka lazy), because just give us a little adversity, and we are ready to give up and let our women deal with it. I mean, come on guys, I know we can do better. So let's stop making excuses and let's start showing these women what a real man looks like by working hard and by being the best providers that we can be. Because after all, we are men aren't we?

So anyway, yeah, women are meant to be soft and emotional, because they are nurturers by nature. And to be a good nurturer, you need a lot of emotions, so you can feel everything and so that way you can deal with it in a more delicate manner. And this is why girls are so sensitive, because their emotions get the best of them and they just go crazy or they just shut down completely. And this is why you have to be extra careful what you say to a girl, because she will digest it, chew it over, digest it again, chew it over again, and then finally, after she has felt every syllable of what you said, she will either erupt with extreme joy or extreme pain.

And that's why it is very important for parents to take extra care on how they treat their daughters, because when a girl feels mistreated or unloved at home, her emotions can lead her to make wrong decisions. And this is why there are a lot of girls that act crazy and become promiscuous, because they feel like they are not being shown love at home, and so they go out looking for it elsewhere. Because I mean, I really don't believe that girls become promiscuous just for the hell of it, I mean, I'm sure there's always an underlining reason for it. Because it's really not in a girl's nature to just sleep with everybody, because girls by nature are meant to be nurturers, and so they tend to look for that one guy that they believe will be a good partner to settle down with, have kids with, love and nurture, and live happily ever after as a family.

And this is the reason why girls tend not to have as many boyfriends, as guys do girlfriends. And this is because guys are dogs by nature and girls are nurturers by nature. And so, since nurturing requires a lot of emotions, girls can usually only nurture one guy at a time (you know what I mean, because us men, we can be very hard to please sometimes), especially if she really likes him and wants him to settle down with her, which is what most girls are looking for, someone to settle down with. I mean, I bet you if you ask most girls what they dreamt about when they were little girls (in terms of boyfriends), I bet you most of them will say something like; to fall in love, get married, have a big wedding, and raise a bunch of kids. And then I bet you, if you ask most boys what they dreamt about as little boys (in terms of girlfriends), I bet you most of them will say something like; to have a lot of girlfriends, and, well, there's really no and, because really that's all that us guys really want, you know, a lot of girlfriends. See (ladies), we start being dogs (I mean players), very early in our lives, you know what I mean, ha ha ha ha ha?!

So, if girls were not meant to be promiscuous by nature, what has happened to make them so promiscuous? Well, I think, three things: (1) the over sexualization of society. (2) Increase in sexual and emotional abuse. (3) Neglect. These three reasons I think are the basis of why girls are so promiscuous nowadays. Well, maybe we should just examine each one of these reasons a little bit to see what's really going on.

Now, let's start with the first one; the over sexualization of society. Man, sex, sex, sex, everywhere you look, everywhere you turn, everything you watch, everything you listen to, everything you read, everything you wear, man, it's crazy, and that's why these girls are going crazy! Because all they see, read and hear all day has something to do with sex, and so they start to think that that's what's up, you know, they think that's what you gotta do to be considered cool. And for a lot of young people, the pressure to be cool is very intense. I mean, peer pressure for these young girls nowadays is amazing, especially the pressure to have sex and or to be sexy. And this is because society has turned sex into a cool thing to do, you know, something to have fun with, you know, like there's no real consequences that can occur, you know, both physically and emotionally. I mean it's crazy, because it looks like (nowadays) the idea of being a virgin till marriage has been thrown out the window, you know what I mean? Because nowadays it looks like having sex and being sexy is what is being promoted. I mean, look around you, girls are wearing clothes so small and so tight their bodies look like they are about to pop out!

And please, somebody please tell me, who is the genius that came up with these jeans that girls like to wear these days (**low riders**, I think is what they are called) that do nothing but show the crack of a girl's butt. I mean, come on, are you kidding me! I mean, who the hell thought making jeans that would show the crack of a girls' ass as sexy? I mean, I don't think it's sexy, do you? I don't think most people think it's sexy either! And that's why I say, who ever created these jeans is a genius, them and their marketing team. Because they have succeeded in brain washing these girls to the point that they would allow themselves to wear a piece of clothing that would not properly cover their hips and buttocks. Because I mean, that's what pants are supposed to do, cover your lower body from waist down, right? And that is also why just in case your pants is a little too big and keeps falling down, that's why you wear a belt, right? Because I mean, that's why belts were created, so as to help keep your pants up above your hips, you know, so you don't have your butt all exposed, right?

But no, somebody decided that that's not good enough, I mean, they decided that that's not sexy enough. So what they did is, they chopped off half of the top part of the jeans (you know, the part that goes from the top of the butt crack to the waist), and then added a little bit of design to it (you know, to act like they worked hard to come up with a cool idea), then "Wholla!", there's your knew and sexy jeans ready for the market. But then of course they will have to do some marketing and promotions, you know, to brainwash some young girls into wearing them. So what do they do? They pay some hot celebrities and models to wear them, and then before you know it, bang, it's a hit. And so now every girl wants to wear them, so they too can walk around with the crack of their asses exposed, you know what I mean, thinking it's cool, thinking it's sexy, when in actuality, it's nothing but trashy. I mean it's funny, peer pressure is a mother, because I have seen some girls that definitely should not be wearing these jeans, you know, girls like; the ones that are definitely out of shape, "No baby, leave it alone, you are too much of a lady for these jeans", and girls like; the ones with a big all butt, "No ladies, give it up, those jeans were not made for you, because that's why every time you bend over to pick up something your whole butt gets exposed, you know what I mean?" Because it's like, just today, when I was outside watching my kids play, this young lady walked by with her two little kids, and as she walked by, I noticed that her butt crack was exposed.

So I started to think to myself "Hmm, does she know that part of her butt is exposed!", and then as soon as I was thinking that, she suddenly stopped, bent over to pick up one of the kids (the smallest one, I guess he wasn't walking fast enough for her), and as soon as she bent over, me and some of the boys that were just hanging around (obviously they had been watching her walk by), we almost simultaneously did a lean back kind of motion with our heads, in disbelief that her whole ass was actually staring at us, showcasing that she definitely was not wearing any underwear. I mean, of course she didn't mean to do it, you know, she didn't mean to moon us or show us her butt, but them jeans boy (I guess that's why they call them low riders), them jeans can embarrass you if you are not careful. I mean, they can embarrass you even if you are careful, because as soon as she picked the little boy up, she tried her best to pull her jeans up, but the jeans would not go up beyond the crack of her butt, so she just had to keep on walking with her ass crack all exposed.

Peer pressure man, boy, peer pressure is a mother! Because I mean, why in the hell would anybody want to walk around showing the crack of their butt? I mean I'm telling you, the peer pressure to be sexy for these girls nowadays is crazy! And it's amazing that girls actually think they look sexy wearing these jeans, but in actuality, these jeans don't do nothing but make them look trashy. But that's fashion for you, and girls fall for anything that they think will make them look cool or sexy, even if it's something that exposes their body parts in the most in appropriate way. And this is because most girls think that, in order to be sexy, they have to expose some part of their body. And this is why girls are always exposing some part of their body, you know, like; if they are not exposing their cleavages, they will expose their thighs, and if they are not exposing their thighs, they will expose their waists, and if they are not exposing their waists, they will expose their backs, and if they are not exposing their backs, they will expose their hips and ass cracks, you know what I mean? And the reason for this is because most girls just feel the need to expose something to feel sexy, you know?

And the reason why girls feel the need to expose something to feel sexy is because, that's the image that society has pushed into them, I mean, that's the image that society has brain washed them with. Because it's like, everyday girls get bombarded with images of sexiness, sexiness, sexiness. And these sexy images that they see just so happens to be of girls that are half dressed or half naked, whichever way you look at it. And so subconsciously, girls tend to internalize and equate less clothing as being sexy. And that's why you have all these girls nowadays walking around half naked thinking that they are looking sexy, when in actuality they are looking trashy.

But it never amazes me what girls will do to look sexy, because they are brain washed to do it. Because it's like, they look at the television and all they see is half naked women running around trying to be sexy, I mean, it never fails. Because it's like, from TV shows, to movies, to music videos (music videos are the worse), all the girls that are supposed to be sexy are always wearing very little clothing, and in music videos, forget it, they barely wear any clothing at all. And so, of course girls are gonna internalize all this half nakedness as being sexy, because this is what society promotes as sexiness, you know, exposing your body as much as possible. I mean it's amazing how sex has been commercialized so much so that people have actually become so desensitized to it.

Because I mean, remember when it used to be kind of taboo to talk about sex all in the open? I mean, remember when if you wanted to have sex you would have to really seduce a girl, and then, if she said yes, you would have to wait till she sneaked out the house and met you somewhere where no one knew y'all. And then, after y'all finished doing the dirty, she would have to sneak back to her place (and you couldn't really walk her all the way home, because she didn't want anybody to see you with her, cause then they would start talking about her being a tramp, because she's holding hands with a guy, and everybody knows she's not married yet, but they assume she's having sex, and that was a no, no till you got married), and act like nothing special has happened. And this is because if her family found out that she was having sex, she would be cast of as the shame of the family, you know, because back in the day, virginity was very highly regarded.

Now, when I say back in the day, I'm not even talking that long ago, you know, because I mean, I'm only in my mid-thirties myself, but I do remember it being a very big deal for a girl to have sex back in those days when I was in my early teenage years (mid to late eighties in my case, because after the nineties hit, forget it, because this is when girls really started going crazy, you know, taking a page from Madonna, Cher and all them other so called liberated women), unlike these days, when all you gotta do or say is, "Hey sexy!", and the girl is ready to give you some sex, without giving a second thought to her virtue and or the stigma it may cause.

I mean, it's crazy how sexualized the world has become nowadays. And I mean, sure there are some countries that are still very conservative and demand their women be covered up, and also ban the public display of sexual publications. But for most countries (especially western countries), it's only getting worse. Because I mean, just watch any TV show for just about five or ten minutes, and I bet you a sex scene (or conversation) will appear, and if it doesn't appear in the show (you are watching) itself, then it will appear in the commercial that follows. Because it's like, nowadays it seems like sex is being used to sell just about anything and everything under the sun.

I mean it never fails, because advertisers know how sexualized society is and there for they figure they might as well appeal to people's sexual senses. Because advertisers know that, their commercial is more likely to get more attention if it appears to be sexy, you know, cool and sexy. And this is why every commercial seems to have hot girls and guys in them, you know, so as to exude coolness and sexiness and help sell whatever it is that the advertiser is trying to sell. And I mean, it doesn't matter if the object to be sold has anything to do with sex or being sexy, if it needs to be sold and sold quickly, sex will be used. And that's why TV commercials, TV shows, movies, music and music videos, books, magazines, and etc., that's why they are all filled with so much sex scenes or imagery. And this is because everybody is using sex to sell their products, because everybody knows sex sells, and so, boy are they selling the hell out of it!

Man, it's crazy how society has devalued sex, I mean so much so that they have managed to make girls become more and more promiscuous. Because I mean, girls nowadays don't value their virginity like they used to back in the day, you know, when it used to be a big deal to lose ones virginity. And since it used to be a big deal for a girl to lose her virginity, girls used to be extra picky to whom they will lose it to, which usually would be their husband or their fiancée, because the guy would usually have to promise marriage before the girl would give up her virginity to him. But nowadays, forget it, girls are going wild! I mean, they have been desensitized by society so much that they are starting to treat sex as not being a big deal. Because I mean, you know how they like to say, "Hey, everybody is doing it!" But what girls don't realize is, no matter how much society seems to promote and accept them as being sexually active, guys are still looking for a virgin to marry. And this is because guys don't like the idea of marrying a girl that's been with a lot of other guys, you know, because guys like to put their wife's on a pedestal and think of them as being virtuous. And this is why you will tend to see a guy date a promiscuous girl for a minute, but then, when he is ready to get married, he will tend to look for a conservative girl to marry, you know, because he figures she will be more of a lady, and better represent him as a wife.

I mean it's crazy, but girls are becoming more and more promiscuous these days, and one of the reasons for it is the over sexualization of society, as we have already discussed. And so now, let's talk about the second reason for the promiscuousness of girls nowadays, which is: the increase in sexual and emotional abuse. I mean, it's amazing how many girls get sexually abused as little girls, you know, which can scar them for life. I mean, it's crazy how many girls are walking around with some emotional scars from their childhoods that have to do with sexual abuse of some kind. And I mean, some girls do a better job of trying to forget it and move on with their lives, but a lot of girls just can't burry it, and the abuse just keeps tormenting them for years, until they get help, you know, until they get professional help to help them deal with it, which unfortunately most girls don't.

And so, since most girls don't get professional help to deal with the abuse, the abuse ends up manifesting itself as a dysfunctional behavior causing the girl to act out. And unfortunately, when most girls act out, they really act out, you know what I mean? And this is one of the reasons why a lot of girls become promiscuous, because they let themselves go, using the abuse as a reason to not care about their self-worth, because they feel their innocence has been stolen from them, therefore they feel like they don't have much self-worth left, and so therefore they end up giving up their sex to guys easily.

And actually, most abused girls end up using their sex as a way to get what they want from guys. I mean it's like, it can get so bad for a girl that has been sexually abused to where she can end up putting very little value to her sex that she ends up selling it for money (you know, prostitution, pornography, etc.). And some girls like to rationalize that by getting guys to buy them stuff in exchange for sex is actually smart because it gives the girl a sense of not being used, but in actuality, all the girl is doing is abusing her own self, because she is doing exactly what her abuser did to her, devaluing her worth. And most girls who devalue their worth, find it very had to get into and or maintain a relationship, and this is because they don't feel worthy of love. And so it's like, the moment a guy comes along and actually falls for them and wants to love them (instead of just to have sex with them), they will start panicking and almost immediately sabotage the relationship so the guy can dump them. I mean it's crazy, but some girls are actually scared of being in a relationship, because they find it hard to trust any man. And so they would rather just have sex with a guy, get what they want to get from him (usually it's financial) and just be by themselves.

It's crazy, sexual abuse is very dangerous, because it can ruin a girl's life, because it can be very traumatic! And unfortunately, most girls don't report it or go get counseling for it. And one of the reasons why most girls don't report it is, it's because most of the sexual abuses are usually caused by someone who is very close to the girl, you know, like a relative or a close family friend. I mean it's scary! And this is why most girls don't report the abuse, because (1) they feel ashamed that it happened (2) they can't believe that it happened, they are in shock (3) they can't believe the perpetrator is their own family member (4) they start to think maybe it was their own fault, maybe they deserved the abuse. I mean, it's crazy, but it's very hard for an abused girl to come forward, especially if the abuser is a family member that she has come to know, trust and love as a family.

And that's why sometimes it will take years before an abused person will come forward and confront the abuser, because it takes time for them to find the strength and will power to confront the abuser and let whatever happens after that happen. Because a lot of times, the abused person will not be believed, and so there for they will be left to feel cheap and dirty, like it was their fault for what happened to them.

And the funny thing is, most abused persons know that the odds are really not on their side when they take on an abuser, especially if he or she is regarded as an outstanding member of society, you know, like a priest, a judge, a teacher, or other kinds of community leaders. And this is because, no one will want to believe that this good standing person could do such an immoral act, and not only violate an innocent kid, but also mess up their own good name. No, they won't want to believe that, and so before the abused person can prove their case, they will have to first wear the Scarlet Latter and be vilified. And this vilified part is what most abused persons don't want to go through, because it can be very traumatic (more so than the abuse itself, in some cases). Because not only will people start calling you names, they will also start treating you like a low down and dirty shame, you know, like you are worthless. I mean, people can be very cruel, because it's like, we are always ready to put people down, instead of up lifting them. And that's why it's hard for abused persons to come forward, because by the time they prove their case, and are shown to be telling the truth, their names will have been dragged through the mad so much so that even if the abuser ends up being put in jail, it won't do much good for the abused person, because by this time their name will have been tarnished to the point of despair. And the people who help tarnish their name won't even come to the abused person's aid, as in to help them reclaim their name by offering a public apology or by writing an official apology for dragging the abused person's name through the mad.

I mean it's crazy, it's almost a no win situation. And that's why most abused persons just decide to keep it to themselves and hope the abuser will not abuse them again. Because really, most abused persons would prefer to just put the abuse behind them and try to move on with their lives without having to go through more drama by trying to prove that they are really telling the truth. I mean it's crazy!

And this is one of the reasons why some abused persons just end up killing the abuser, because they just could not take it anymore, you know, because the sight of the abuser just made them sick (physically and mentally), so much so that they ended up going temporarily insane and decided to take matters into their own hands, you know what I mean? And this is especially true if the abuse was a prolonged one, you know, going through years of being abused by the same person. I mean, it's crazy, but everybody has a limit, you know, everybody has a thrash hold of how much injustice they can take before they start to retaliate. And when a person has reached their thrash hold, you better run, you better run and hide real well, because they will be coming to look for you, and if they find you, that's it, it's game over for you. So don't ever think you can just abuse somebody and they will just take it and take it and take it forever, nah, one day they will just snap, and if you are not careful, when they do snap, they could end your life. Because it's like, most people who are being abused, they usually tend to be extremely reserved and or like to keep to themselves, you know, holding everything in while just getting mad, mad, and madder. But then one day you just hear that they have killed someone, and it's usually a family member. And then so everybody starts running around trying to figure out why, what happened, what caused it. Then, sooner than later, it will leak out that, the person that got killed was an abuser (child molester). Because by this time the abused person will have no choice but to tell why they felt like they had to do what they did, you know, end that person's life.

I mean it's crazy, but people get tired of being treated like sh%t sometimes, you know? And the funny thing is, once one person comes forward and accuses someone of molesting them, there are usually more people that will come forward and actually accuse that same person of molesting them also. Because I mean, usually molesters don't just molest just one person, no, they usually make a habit out of it, you know, and leave a trail of victims. And that's why it's important for sexual abuse victims to come forward, that way they can help stop the abusers from continuing with their sick ways, you know, so they don't harm anybody else.

It's crazy this sexual abuse stuff! And this is why a lot of girls who are sexually abused tend to act up and end up being promiscuous, because they just don't know how to deal with it, so they just end up adding more stress to their already low self-esteem. And this is why it is very important for abused girls to get some professional counseling, so that they can help themselves heal, you know, so they won't lose themselves in this crazy world of promiscuousness!

Now, aside from sexual abuse, there's also emotional abuse, which for some reason goes very unnoticed, but can have a huge impact on how a girl feels about herself. And the reason why this abuse (emotional abuse) tends to go unnoticed is because, it rarely leaves physical scars (like physical abuse), but it's emotional scars can be very damaging, almost more damaging than physical abuse. And the reason I say this is because, in physical abuse, the girl can remove herself from the situation (realizing the abuser is an ass), but in an emotional abuse, even if the girl removes herself from the situation, she can't really get away from the emotion. Because it's like, an emotional issue stays real deep in a person's heart, and it doesn't come out quickly even if you command it. And this is because emotions are feelings and feelings don't evaporate overnight. No my friends, feelings just linger on and on and on until they exhaust themselves out, or, until you learn to put them in their proper prospective.

And this is why counseling can be very beneficial, in helping to put emotions in their proper prospective, so you can move on with your life. Because unlike physical abuse (which can be felt right there and then), emotional abuse usually takes a longer time to be felt, and there for, it becomes harder to categorize and be put in it's proper prospective. And the reason why emotional abuse is harder to categorize and detect is, it's because it involves **words**, and words can take a long time to digest before you start to feel it's effects, you know, it can take a while to realize how the words somebody said to you really made you feel. I mean, what I am trying to say is, it's like, for example; someone may say something to you today that is very negative, but you may not think about it too much (you know, you brush it off), but then, when tomorrow comes, like out of nowhere, you start to think about what that person said to you and you start to get pissed off like, "What the hell was their problem, why did they have to say such mean stuff to me, I mean, that was really un called for!" I mean, it's crazy, but words can be very powerful and can linger in our brains for a very long time. Because it's like, someone can say something to you today, but you won't react to it till next week when you have had time to really digest it, process it, digest it again, process it again, and finally come to the conclusion that, that was not a very nice thing they said to you and they have really hurt your feelings. And this is why sometimes you will have somebody come to you and say, "Hey, I did not appreciate what you said to me last week!" And then so, there you are, standing there, trying to figure out exactly what was it that you had said to this person that seems to have made them so mad that they had to confront you with it a week later. Because I mean, by this time you probably thought everything was cool with this person, but unfortunately it looks like you really hurt them by what you said, because obviously it must have bothered them so much so that they had to bring it up a whole week later.

 And actually, a week is not that long for a person to hold stuff that was said to them that really hurt them. Because I mean, some people hold stuff for years, and years, and one day they just can't take it no more, it's got to come out, and that's when you see them either go to therapy or just confront the person that had said these mean things to them that has bothered them for years. And sometimes people hold on to their emotional pain until they die, never having the courage to confront or to go to therapy so they can try to heal from the emotions caused by the words that somebody said to them that were really hurtful. But that's the power of words, they can be very dangerous! And that's why they say words are mightier than swords, because even though a sword can cut you and kill you, words can cut you and kill you slowly, you know, from the inside out, you know what I mean? Because it's like, of course words won't leave you with a physical cut on your skin, but it will leave an emotional cut in your heart. And have you ever felt an emotional cut in your heart, I mean, it almost feels like someone has just opened your chest and has stolen your heart, because the emptiness inside your chest will leave you breathless, like your life is being sucked out slowly from inside out. And this sucking out of your life can be going on for years and years and years, until you either go see a counselor or therapist, or, until you confront this person or persons, or until you die, you know, whichever comes first.

 It's crazy, but words are very powerful, that's why you have to be very careful in how you use them, because you can really hurt somebody's feelings. And I mean, this is why when people are mad at each other they will say some very mean things to each other, and this is because they know those words will hurt that person. And then so, that's also why when the same people that were being mean to each other finally make up, this is why they will try their best to take the words they had said back, you know, so they can try to undo the pain they had just caused the other person. But usually by this time it's too late, because the pain will have been so deep and so ingrained in the brain, that it will take time for it to dissolve, and let the healing process began. And that's why you will tend to hear people say something like, "I'm gonna need some time to heal and get over it," and also, that's why people can forgive but not forget, because the emotional scars can take a very long time to heal.

And this is why emotional abuse can be very dangerous, because it can just tear or torment the person that has been abused (emotionally) for years after the abuse has stopped. And this is why it is very important for parents to be very careful at what they say to their kids, especially girls. And I mean, sure boys can be tormented from emotional abuse too, but girls, girls take it extra hard. And this is because girls are extra sensitive, and so they eat up every word emotionally. And so this is one of the reasons why girls are becoming more and more promiscuous these days, because they are really hurting inside and they need a way to release their pain. And unfortunately, the way most girls choose to deal with the pain is by acting out, and being rebellious, which of course leads them to become promiscuous.

I mean it's crazy, but a lot of girls are being emotionally abused! And the funny thing is, most of this abuse is not coming from strangers, oh no, it's usually coming from the abused person's own family members. I mean it's crazy, but our own families can turn out to be very emotionally abusive to us. Because I mean, it's amazing the number of parents that curse out their kids, you know, call them names and stuff like that. I mean, there are parents out there that actually tell their kids that they are worthless, I mean, are you kidding me! I mean, why in the hell would you want to tell your kids that they are worthless or no good, don't you know that you are damaging your kid's self-esteem when you say stuff like that? I mean, it's like parents don't care, like they don't give a damn about their kids' feelings. Because really there's no excuse, really there's no excuse for parents to say these kinds of ugly words to their kids. Because I mean, kids are kids, so they will do stupid and dumb things sometimes, but it doesn't call for them to be labeled as worthless, stupid, or dumb, because these kinds of labels can be very damaging for a kid. And this is one of the reasons why there's a lot of kids out there who don't have much value or self-esteem for themselves, because they have been called these words so much that they have come to believe that they are indeed worthless, stupid, and or dumb.

And this is why a lot of kids don't aspire to be great in life, because they don't believe they have what it takes to become great at anything. Because it's like, their parents have beaten and ingrained in their heads so much so about them not being able or capable of becoming something great (you know how they like to say stuff like; "You will never amount to nothing!" or, "You are just as dumb like your father!" or, "You are just as stupid like your mother!" or, "I don't know what's wrong with you, you just don't seem able to do anything right!"), that the kid loses his or her self-esteem and start to see themselves as being hopeless. Because it like, kids naturally are born motivated, energetic, full of life, and ready to conquer the world. But parents, parents are the ones that usually put a halt to this motivation, because parents have a tendency of bringing their frustrations, their stress, and their own misery upon their kids. And this is because most parents don't know how to deal with their own mess and frustrations of life that, they just go off, not realizing that they are damaging and bringing misery to their own children, whom they swear they love.

I mean it's crazy, but yeah, parents are usually the ones that bring misery and therefor damage their own kid's self-esteem. Because it's like, no matter how much the outside world or extended family members may try to discourage a kid by saying mean things to them, if the parents are on the ball (doing their best parenting job) and have the kid's back (by showing support and letting them know that they can be or achieve anything that they set their minds to), their kids will not be crushed by any negative thing that someone says to them because they will have a great sense of self-esteem and will be eager to conquer the world. Because it's like, the most sought after opinion and affection that kids seek is that of their parents, and so, if kids feel and know that their parents love them and think highly of them, forget it, it's off to conquer the world, no matter what the world thinks or says about them!

And this is why parents have to be careful and take extra care of how they treat and what they say to their kids, because kids absorb all this negative stuff that is said to them and when it gets to be too much to handle, they either shut down and become depressed, or they start to act out, get out of control and become promiscuous. And this is one of the reasons why girls are becoming more and more promiscuous these days, because they are more and more emotionally abused!

Now, the third reason why girls are becoming more and more promiscuous nowadays is because of, **neglect**, and most importantly, neglect from their fathers. I mean, it's amazing at how many guys are neglecting their kids, their own kid's, I'm talking about their own flesh and blood! It's crazy out there, what's really going on? Because I mean, there's really no excuse! I mean, even if you don't want to be with the mother of your baby (for whatever reason), you can still be in your child's life. Because I mean, even if you have to be in your child's life in a part time basis (for whatever reason), that's fine, just as long as when you do spend that precious time with your child (because it will be precious, especially for them, if not for you also), you make it meaningful, joyous, and memorable. Because what all kids really want from their parents at the end of the day is, **love**, love and a sense of security, you know, to feel protected. I mean, that's it, that's really what kids want! And I mean, sure it's nice and wonderful to buy your kids stuff like; toys, clothes, bikes, skates, and so on and so on, you know, so as to try and show them your love, but, at the end of the day, nothing comes close or compares to just giving them a hug and telling them "I love you".

I mean, I'm telling you, that's all that kids really want! They want their parents to hug them and tell them that they love them, because this reassures them that their parents indeed do love them, because not only did they hug them, but they also said "I love you." And the reason why hugging and saying I love you to your kids is important is because, kids tend to respond more readily to touches and words, rather than on material possessions. And this is why you can buy your kids all the toys in the world, and you can give your kids all the money in the world, but if you never say I love you, and you never hug them, one day they will come to you and ask you "Mommy, daddy, do you love me?" And you are gonna be left there speechless like, "What do you mean, of course we love you!" And then your kids are gonna say something like, "Then why y'all never hug me or say I love you to me?" And that's when you gonna realize that all them toys, money, and other stuff that you were giving to your kid did not equate to love in their eyes, and this is because kids are very good in separating love and toys (material things). Because it's like, to kids, love comes with hugs and kisses, and toys are just material things for them to play with (to take away their boredom), and then when they are done playing with them, or when the toys break, they throw them away and then come looking for daddy, you know, to see if he is not too busy to give them some of his time so that he can take them to the park, you know, so that he can teach them how to play some sports, or teach them how to ride their bikes, or so he can just watch them play, you know, so they can show him how fast they can go through the monkey bars, and the slides, and the swings, and them horse things, and the etc., etc., and etc. I mean you know, kids just love to impress their parents, and kids just love the attention they get from their parents, because that equates to love to them. And that's why kids always seem like they are looking and yearning for attention, because attention to kids equates to love.

And this is one of the reasons why girls are becoming more and more promiscuous, and it's because they are not getting enough attention at home (feeling neglected), so there for they go out there in the world to seek it. And unfortunately for girls, the attention that they mostly seek has to do with love, the desire to be loved, and if they can't get love, then they are willing to settle for like. And this is where the promiscuousness begins, when they realize that giving up their sex makes boys want them, chase them, talk to them, tell them they are sexy, tell them they are pretty, tell them what they want to hear (to make them feel wanted, liked and kind of special), even if it's for the wrong reasons, because it makes them feel loved, even if it's for the moment. And this is what we call "looking for love all in the wrong places". Because it's like, these girls are so eager to feel the passion of love, so they can feel the sense of being wanted and loved, that they end up giving up their sex so easily to the first person that says, "Hey love, hey sexy, what's up princess!" That's it, that's all it takes to get a girl that's looking for love all in the wrong places to give up their sex, because that's all they want, all they want is someone who may be willing to pay attention to them, no matter if that person is right for them or not.

And that's why a lot of girls end up with guys that are absolutely not good for them, because girls who are neglected at home, who are not being told that they are special, who are not being told that they are beautiful, who are not being told that they are smart, who are not being told that they are princesses, who are not being told that they are daddy's little girl, who are not being shown love with hugs and kisses, will tend to fall for the first guy that says, "Hey sexy!" I mean it's crazy, but girls will fall for the wrong guys, get dumped, then fall for the wrong guys again, get dumped again, and again and again, until it becomes clear to her that all that the guys she had been dating just wanted one thing and they got it. And not only did they get it, but they also left her with a reputation of being easy (aka promiscuous). And it's like, once a girl gets the reputation of being easy to get, the flood gets open, and all the boys start maneuvering to try and get a turn, you know, get a piece of her too. And so the poor girl is left there caught in an undesirable position of being everybody's flavor of the month, which means she's being viewed as a sex toy, not a relationship hopeful, which is bad for the girl, because guys will just use her and leave her, instead of loving her and cherishing her.

And this is why it is very important for parents to pay attention to their kids, so they won't have to go out there into the world to look for it, because the world is full of predators who are always on the lookout for venerable prey that they can lure and take advantage of. And this is why it's important for fathers to be in their daughter's lives, so she won't have to throw herself in the arms of men that don't deserve her time and love, but she gives it to them anyway because her father wasn't there to teach her, to show her and to tell her that she's special and that only a special guy can have her hand in marriage, so she need not waste her time with these lousy guys, because they ain't nothing but dogs trying to get a bone, you know what I mean? Hey, take care of your daughters y'all, because its crazy out there, and all girls should be made to feel like a princess, instead of just the flavor of the month!

Chapter 6

Fools for love

I think it's women's fault that there are so many baby daddies! And the reason why I say this is because, women these days are no longer waiting until men marry them before they give them babies. I mean, it used to be that a woman would make a man chase her hard, you know, play hard to get until either he quits (then she will know that he wasn't really serious about her) or perseveres until she gives in. And of course before she gives in she will have to put him to the test, you know, to find out if he really likes her or just her body.

And this is how the test usually goes; first, after numerous phone conversations with him (you know, to kind of get to know him a little better), she will finally agree to go on a date with him, but, she won't let him get to close, you know, she won't let him be all up on her, you know, hugging up on her, or feeling up on her, you know, stuff like that, and, at the end of the date, she will only let him kiss her on the chick. And then, if the first date went well, she will agree to a second date, and this time she will let him get a little bit closer to her and actually let him kiss her on the lips (at the end of the date, as he's saying good night to her).

And then so, as he starts to feel secure about his chances of getting the goodies, she ups the ante, you know, so she can find out whether he's in love with her, or just in lust with her. And so what she do is, she invites him to her mama's house, you know, so he can meet her mom, and too so she can see if her mom will take a liking to him, you know, because they say moms usually have a sense of knowing whether a guy is good, or just a waste of time. And then so, if the guy passes the mommy test, it's then time to meet daddy. Now, if the guy really loves the girl, here is where it will show, because guys don't usually like to meet a girl's father. I mean, I don't know what it is, but when a guy has to meet a girl's father, he starts to get nervous. I mean, his chest starts to beat hard, he starts to sweat, and he starts to think, "Damn, why do I have to meet her daddy? I mean, it's not like we are in a serious relationship! Oh man, could it be, oh man she's the relationship type!" That's it, that's the reason why most guys don't really like to meet fathers, because they know that once the girl introduces them to her father, they know that the relationship has taken a serious turn. Because it's like, usually girls don't introduce guys to their fathers unless they are very serious about the guy.

And this is why a lot of guys get nervous when they have to meet the girl's father, and this is because they know that her father will be sizing them up, you know, to see what their intentions are with their daughter. Because I mean, guys know that when they meet the girl's father, most likely than not they will have to answer some tough questions like; what are your career goals, where do you see yourself in five or ten years, do you believe in marriage, so do you love my daughter or are you just wasting her time?

Now, you see why guys seem so nervous when they go meet the girl's father, because they know they won't be able to bullsh*t their way into the father's good side by charming him or any other crap like that. Because, to begin with, fathers generally are skeptical of any man that is dating their daughter (because they understand a man's nature, you know, a man's lustful nature!), and this is because they just don't want to see their daughter taken advantaged. I mean, you know, because they still remember how they used to take advantage of other people's daughters. And this is why it's hard for fathers to except boyfriends, because to them, their daughters are princesses, you know, daddy's little girl and only a prince is suitable to be with his daughter. And this is also why it usually takes fathers a very long time to be comfortable with the man in their daughters lives, because the man has to prove himself worthy (by his actions, you know, by how he treats her and stuff like that), for the father to give his approval. And this is why it is important for girls to bring their boyfriends to meet daddy, you know, so daddy can try to weed out the potential heart breakers who are out there for only one thing, and that one thing is, to score!

Now, this is also the reason why it's very important for fathers to be in their daughters lives, that is so that their daughters can bring their trifling little boyfriends (who think they are grown) to their fathers, and so the fathers can size them up and grab them by their trifling saggy jeans (if they have to) and throw them out the door, you know, before them trifling little boys hypnotize their desperate little girls into falling in love with them, you know what I mean? Because it's amazing how many girls fall for these trifling boys, you know, falling for these so called thugs. I mean, they straight up lose their minds! And it's not just young girls that fall for bad boys, grown women fall for them too! And when I say fall, I don't mean just infatuation, oh no, I'm talking about straight up lose your mind kind of love, you know what I mean? And that's why you will tend to see a good girl or a nice woman in a relationship with a bad boy, because they are just so infatuated with them. And also, the reverse of this is also true, you know, good boys falling for bad girls. Oh yeah, guys get infatuated too! And that's why you will also tend to see a good guy in a relationship with a bad girl, you know what I mean? And that's when you will ask yourself, "What the hell does he see in her?" "She doesn't even seem to be his type!" I'm telling you, infatuation is a beast! Because it's like, a good boy and or a good girl can find themselves in a relationship with a bad girl and or a bad boy and know that it is not the best thing for them, but, they won't leave, instead, they will result in trying to change their partner, you know what I mean? Because it's like, you know how girls like to say, "Girl, I can change him!" No, you can't! And guys always think, "Man, I can change her, watch!" No, you can't! Nobody can change anybody, unless that somebody wants to change themselves. And most bad boys and bad girls don't want to change, because they enjoy too much the attention that they get from being bad. And this is because people just seem to gravitate to them for some reason. And I mean, I think I know the reason why people are drawn to them. And the reason I think is because, bad boys and bad girls tend to lead a more reckless life style, you know, they tend to throw caution to the wind and do whatever they want to do without worrying too much about consequences. And this sense of recklessness seems to exude some sort of excitement about them (whether real or false) that draws people to them.

And that's why the most famous people tend to be guys and girls that have that badass moniker associated with their names (for example; Paris Hilton for girls, and Lil Wayne for boys). Because I mean, that's why everybody wants to be around Paris Hilton or Lil Wayne (not counting their money), because they want to be around excitement, and these people exude excitement (whether real or false). So to take it back to regular everyday folks, everyday people want excitement too, but the only difference is, everyday people want excitement but they don't want the consequences that can occur by being too reckless.

And so yeah, this is also why bad boys and bad girls seem to be more popular in school and other places, and it's because they seem to let their inhibition lay out in the wind, which causes other boys and girls to think that they are so cool. And this is also why bad boys and bad girls tend to be a lot more promiscuous. And it's because, not only are they being courted by other bad boys and bad girls, but they are also being courted by good girls and good boys. Because it's like, not only are bad boys being pursued by bad girls, they are also being pursued by good girls too, so it's like double the whammy, you know what I mean? And so too, vise versa, it's like, not only are the bad girls being pursued by bad boys, they are also being pursued by good guys too, so it's like double the whammy here too, you know? And that's why bad boys and bad girls tend to be a lot more promiscuous, because they tend to be a lot more reckless, combined with having plenty of potential sex partners chasing after them.

And this is also why, bad girls and bad boys tend to have more baby mama and baby daddy dramas, because they poke everyone, and then can't remember and or figure out who is the baby's daddy (until DNA is done). I mean, I'm telling you, there are a lot of trifling people out there y'all, be careful, otherwise you might find yourself becoming a baby mama or a baby daddy to someone that's not even worth your time.

Anyway, so, what were we talking about again, before I started rambling on and on about bad assess? Oh, I remember! We were talking about bringing the boyfriend to daddy, so daddy can size him up, and if he finds him to be trifling, he can throw him out the door before the boy causes unnecessary heart ache and pain to the girl. And so, continuing, let's assume that the boyfriend passes daddy's test, or actually let's assume that he semi passes daddy's test (because no boy will pass a girl's daddy's test the first time, it takes time, more like years, to prove himself worthy in the daddy's eyes). And then so now, the girl will feel more secure in the fact that the guy must really like her (even love her), because he was willing to endure her father's grilling of him, you know, serious questioning. So now, three to six months after they started dating, and after him meeting her mother and father, she finally feels comfortable and secure enough to let him make love to her, because she knows his interest in her is genuine. Because I mean, if a guy is not that interested in a girl, he will not subject himself to an uncomfortable situation (like meeting the parents), because guys just don't like meeting the parents, because it becomes too personal. Because it's like, now, not only are they going to be dating the girl, now they are also going to be accountable to her parents. Which means that, he's going to have to be extra careful of how he treats their daughter, because he knows she will be reporting on his behavior, and if she has any ugly things to say (of how he's treating her), they know who he is, and so if need be they can come looking for him, you know what I mean?

And this is why it's important for girls to introduce their boyfriends to their parents, so that not only will it force the guy to think about his intensions, but it will also help the girl take her time before feeling and succumbing to the pressure to have sex with him (just because she likes him) without even knowing if he truly likes her or not. And if he truly likes her, by her making him wait, it forces him to really get to know her, and by him really knowing her, it forces him to start to love her.

And this is where girls should want their man to be (in love with them), before they give him a baby. Because if you give a guy a baby before he is ready, he will feel like you trapped him, because guys are never really ready to be fathers, unless they are in love. Almost like females, right! I mean it's like, when a girl falls in love, she's usually always eager to have the guy's baby. And the reverse is true, when a guy is in love, he's usually eager for the girl to have his kids. I mean, I'm telling you ladies, when a guy is in love with you, he will be excited when you get pregnant, because he will be happy to know that the girl he loves is the girl that's gonna be the mother of his kid. Because it's like, just like females, guys like to multiply themselves with the person they love, you know, have babies with the girl that they are in love with. And that's why it is important for ladies not to give a guy babies before he marries her, because most often times than not, the guy is gonna feel like he got trapped (you know how guys like to say; "She trapped me man, she knew I didn't want no baby, but she went ahead and let herself get pregnant, I'm telling you, she is trying to trap me!"), and then resent it and then split (you know, leave). And this is because guys are just not ready to have a baby when they are not even in love with the girl that they happen to be seeing or dating. I mean, I'm telling you (ladies), trust me, guys are never really excited about having babies unless they have fallen and are deeply in love with the girl they are with.

Now, you are probably asking yourself, "If guys are never ready to have babies until they fall in love, then why do guys always seem to get girls they don't love pregnant?" Well, simple, easy answer, I mean the answer is so simple that I almost don't want to say it. Well, ok, fine, I'll say it! And the answer is (drum roll please!), and the answer is ladies and gentlemen, the answer is, **"lust"**, that's right my friends, that pure unadulterated emotion, lust! I mean, lust is so powerful that a lot of people confuse it with love. I mean, when two people are in lust, they become so into each other that they start to think that they are in love. And this is especially true for girls, because girls soak up all that emotion, intertwine it with theirs, and before you know it, they are in love. That's why girls fall in love so quickly, because they got so much emotion in them.

And this is also why girls usually end up falling for the wrong guys, because they are quick to interpret a guy's lust as love, and then they let their own love go, and then before you know it, they end up in a relationship that has no love in it. But by this time it's too late, because she's already pregnant, with his second baby. And so she figures she might as well stay with him, and hopefully he will grow to love her, but he never does, so they end up breaking up sooner than later. And so, this is why it is very important to take your time (ladies), before you give a guy a baby. Because guys are full of lust, and they can fool you to think it's love. I mean, you know how guys are, I mean, you know guys will do and say anything to get some (goodies). I mean, calm down ladies, and take your time! I know you want love and relationships (ladies), but having a guy's baby won't make him stay, worse, it will push him away, you know, it will make him ran before he even gets a chance to really know you, you know, before he even gets a chance to really love you!

And so, this is one of the reasons why I think it's women's fault that there are so many baby daddies, because women are just fools for love. I mean, a woman will meet a guy, have sex with him, fall in love with him, and then before giving the guy a chance to prove his love for her, she lets herself get pregnant, and gives him a baby.

Now, I know what you are probably saying to yourself right about now (ladies). You are probably saying to yourself, "Nigel, you are full of sh%t!" "What the hell do you mean it's women's fault that there are so many baby daddies?" "What the hell do you mean we just let ourselves get pregnant?" "It's not our fault that y'all men are dogs!" "It's not our fault that y'all men don't want to take care of your responsibilities!" "Hell, it's not our fault that y'all men don't like wearing condoms!" I bet that's what you are saying right about now. I'm I right or wrong? And I bet you, you are probably saying it with your neck and head moving back and forth vigorously with a snap to it. I'm I right or wrong? Ha ha ha ha ha! It's ok, I understand, you don't want to agree with me, but think about it. Because I mean, it's like, you already know that men are dogs, and you already know that men don't like wearing protection (oh, you didn't know, you didn't know that men don't like to wear condoms? Well, now you know! I mean, that's why some men will say they are allergic to condoms, that's so the girl won't force them to wear one. And this is because guys just have a strong desire to feel the thrill naturally, you know what I mean?), and you already know that men don't fall in love easily (because we hate settling down, because settling down to us (men) means, the end of freedom to indulge our nature, you know, to get down and dirty with different women), and I mean, you already know that men can be very irresponsible, you know, like deadbeat dads. Then why in the hell would you allow yourself to get pregnant when you are not even sure whether the guy you are sleeping with (and not using protection with) really loves you or not? And that's why I say it's women's fault that there are so many baby daddies! Because I mean, in these days of so many contraception options, you know, so many birth control stuff out there, there is no reason why women should be having babies before they are ready.

    I mean, come on ladies, you know if you really don't want to get pregnant there's stuff you can do or take to make sure you don't get pregnant. Because I mean, if you leave it to the guy to look out for you and not get you pregnant, forget it, you gonna end up pregnant. Because guys are just not that careful. I mean, sure he will use a condom the first, second, third, and forth time, but when it gets to fifth, six, and seventh time, forget it, the condom is going to be hard to find. And then, not only is the condom going to be hard to find, but he also going to start coming up with excuses to why he can't wear the condom anymore. You know, he'll start to say things like, "Am, I don't like this brand of condoms!" or "This condom is too small for me!" or "Man, this doesn't feel right, I can't feel anything!" or "You know what, I think I'm allergic to condoms!" See, leave it up to guys, guys will say anything to stop wearing condoms. Oh, I forgot, here is one more excuse that guys will use to not wear a condom, "Come on baby, you know I love you, come on baby, let me take this thing off so I can feel you naturally, you know, so we can really connect, you know, come on baby, you know I love you!" I mean, there are so many excuses that guys use to not wear a condom. But I think the last excuse that I listed, you know the "I love you" excuse, I think this excuse is the most powerful. Because, boy, I'm telling you, ladies love to hear those words. I mean, just try it, just tell your girl "I love you", and see what happens. I bet you, first she's gonna turn around and look at you stunned, like she can't believe you actually had the courage to say I love you. Because women always complain that men just don't like to say those words, which is true. And the reason why guys don't like to say those words is, because they make you sound so girlish, you know, they make you sound so soapy. I'm sorry, I just don't know how to describe it, I mean, wait a minute, I think I got it, I think I got the best way to describe how it makes a guy feel. And the answer is, **soft,** that's it, it makes a guy feel soft, you know, un-macho, when he says, "I love you". There, it's true, I could feel myself feeling soft when I just said it as I was writing it. Because I mean, guys are macho, you know, tough (as we would like to think), and those words are just a little bit too softy for us to say. I mean, we need tougher words to express how we feel.

But, or well, I guess we are just going to have to make do with what we got. Because the ladies love those words, I mean, they are just perfect for them. And so, since us guys love the ladies, we are just going to have to get used to saying those words. And actually, those words can be very beneficial and come in handy in certain situations, you know, like; when you are in need (you know what I mean guys), and or, when your woman is mad at you (right guys!).

Oh man, those words can be very beneficial and come very handy, especially when a guy is in need, you know, of some sexual healing. Because all you gotta do here is, whisper slowly in your woman's ear like, "Hey sexy, I love you!" Shoot, not only will she know what you want, she will also feel some heat waves traveling through her body all the way down to the appropriate spot, you know, indicating that she's ready, willing, and able to grant you your wish. Because the next thing before you know it, she will be all over you, you know, giving it to you straight, no chaser, you know what I mean, ha ha ha ha ha!

And so yeah, those words are very beneficial and can come in extremely handy, even when your girl is mad at you too, to the addition of you being in need. Because all you gotta do here is (of course this has to come after she has finished talking, you know, after she has finished telling you what's bothering her, and how you haven't been helping or supporting her. And so now it's your turn to talk, you know, to explain yourself), well this is what you gotta say, "Baby, you know I love you, right?" And then she's going to say something like, "Come on, I'm trying to be serious here!" But, her face and her mood will have softened up a bit, giving you a better chance to advance with your powerful words. And so you gonna continue like this, "Well babe, first I want to say I'm sorry!" Heat waves will have started creeping in her body. And you continue, "I know I have been very un-attentive lately". Heat waves, heat waves! "I have understood what you have just said, and I promise to be better from now on." Lots and lots of heat waves will be circulating within her body right about now! And so this is when you go for the finishing punch line, you know, by saying, "Come on baby, you know I love you!" Bingo, game over, heat waves have hit the spot! Because now, before you know it, she's ripping your clothes off, throwing you into the bed, and proceeding to give you some sexual healing, you know, even though she knows you ain't really understood all of what she was trying to tell you, but, because of them heat waves (caused by your powerful sensitive words), she couldn't help but want to lose herself in your love, you know what I mean, ha ha ha ha ha, yeah, real talk baby, holler at your boy, yeah, ha ha ha ha ha!

See the power of "I love you!" But, you have to be careful not to abuse it, you know, in terms of saying it too much to your partner that they become desensitized to it. What I mean is, be careful how you use it, when you use it, and how often you use it. Because if you over use it, then the words become part of everyday conversation and they lose their luster, you know what I mean? I mean, your partner will be so used to hearing those words that, when you do have a special occasion and you really do need to use the words, your partner will just brush you off as just you being you and they won't take you too seriously. I mean, they won't mean to brush you off, it will just be that, they have heard you say those words so much that they are just used to it, you know, like it's no big deal. And so it's like, if you are not the type to throw those words around casually, when you do say them, they will have a huge impact on your partner, because they will not be used to hearing them, and so when you do say it, it will touch them deeply.

And this is one of the reasons why when I used to be out there dating (I'm married now), I was very careful not to say those words unless I meant it. Because those are very powerful words! And girls eat those words up like it's candy, you know, they eat those words up, chew them, digest them, and then store them right inside their heart, to feel the sweetness of it. And that's why girls feel so bad and get so depressed when their hearts get broken, because their chests feel like they have been ripped open by the pain of lost love that they were storing in their hearts. And that's why I was always careful to whom I said I love you to, because I just didn't want to bring pain and misery to anybody that I dated and I knew our dating wasn't serious. Because if you go around saying I love you to people (you are dating) that you are not serious about, all you are doing is misleading them to thinking that there's potential here, when in actuality you are just having fun. But to the other person, they will think you are serious and start investing them-selves into you a lot more than they should. That's why I used to try to be as real as I could with the ladies, so they can realize that I'm up to no good, that way they can decide whether they still want to chill with me, or just let my sorry behind go. I mean, I tried to be as real as it gets, you know, I would just tell them, "Look, I'm not looking or ready for any serious relationship right now, but if you want to have some fun, hey, we could chill! I mean, straight up as I could say it, that's how I said it. And I think a lot of the ladies appreciated my direct talk, that way they had the option to still roll with me, or too just let my sorry ass be as I be, you know what I mean, ha ha ha ha ha!

And of course I lost a lot of dates with my up-front approach confessions of my interest in them, but I also scored some favorable dates too. And actually I think my up-front approach kind of made some of the ladies like me even more, because I think they noticed a sense of honesty in me. Oh, wait a minute, could it be, could it be that my truthfulness approach backfired on me a few times. Because I did have a few girls that did try to turn me into their boyfriend. Come to think of it, two of them did succeed in turning me into their boyfriend, damn it! I just hate it when my plans don't succeed, you know what I mean, ha ha ha ha ha! Hey, at list they didn't succeed into making me their long-term boyfriend right, you know, by turning me into their baby daddy. And then again, one of them almost did succeed, in trying to turn me into a baby daddy, right, ha ha ha ha ha! Man, I'm so glad that I'm married now! Because it's just too much work, that whole dating thing, you know, it's just too much emotion suppressing and un suppressing and all kinds of crazy stuff that takes place. I mean, it can get very tiring after a while, I think so anyway. Or, maybe I just wasn't a true player as I thought I was. Come to think of it, I know I wasn't a true player, because I couldn't juggle more than one woman at the same time, you know, because I would always call the right girl by the wrong name. I mean it's like, I would call the girl that I wanted to talk to, but I would ask for her by the name of the girl that was on my mind for whatever reason. I mean, I kid you not, it has happened to me more than a few times. And the feeling when that happens is awful, and you know right away that you have no shot with her, because the phone will hang up as soon as she asks, "Am, who did you ask for?" or "Who did you just call me?" Knowing that she recognized your voice, all you can say here is "Am, I mean…" And before you even start trying to explain you hear, "And don't ever call me again, a$$hole!" And then clique, the phone hangs up, and I have just lost another date. I guess that's what I get for trying to be a player hah, ha ha ha ha ha!

But yeah, that love word boy, it gets a lot of people in trouble. Because a lot of people use it without much caution. I mean, most guys use it just to get what they want (you know, the goodies), and girls fall for it all the time. I mean it's like, girls just walk around waiting for the first person that says I love you, and they are ready to give up their goodies, and they are also ready to give him some babies.

I mean, it's amazing how much girls crave for the love thing. And I mean, sure guys crave for the love thing too, but it's just not as intense as females. I mean don't get me wrong, guys do fall hard in love sometimes (you know, head over hills), but most of the times, we are able to think subjectively and control our emotions. And this is why guys are able to go from girl to girl to girl and not get caught up, you know, fall for love. And that's why a girl can tell a guy, "I love you", and the guy can still dump her next week. But, tell a girl "I love you", and I bet you she will hold on to the guy she's being thinking about dumping for a few more months (if not years), you know, hoping that he will change.

It's amazing, it's amazing how much emotions females have. But that's their nature, I mean, that's how they were made. Because women were made to be nurturers, that's why they were given so much emotions (so they can feel everything), so they can better take care of their babies, you know, using their maternal instincts. But, these same emotions and instincts that help females to better nurture their kids, don't seem to help them much when it comes to picking mates. And this is because their emotions just runs all over their subjective minds, rendering them unable to think clearly, because their emotions get in the way and clouds their judgments. And that's why you will see a nice girl involved with a guy that everybody knows that he's not good for her. But you won't be able to tell her nothing, because her emotions will have clouded her judgment to the point that, all she can see is love, even if that love is not good and or not healthy for her.

And this is why it's very important for girls to introduce their boyfriends to their parents. And if they can't introduce them to their parents (for whatever reason), then they should at list introduce them to someone that's very close to them, you know, someone that they trust, and someone that they will listen to when given advice and or opinion about the guy, you know, someone like a brother, sister, cousin, aunt, uncle, or a best friend that knows them real well, you know, that way they can help her get rid of any guy that's not good for her, before she falls hard in love and starts to say stupid stuff like, "But I love him, and deep down I know he loves me too, he just doesn't know how to show it!" Or they will say something like, "He just loses his temper, he doesn't really mean to hit me, he's just going through some rough times right now, it's really my fault for making him mad!" I mean, these are some of the excuses that girls make for guys they have fallen for. I mean, even if the guy is controlling, abusive, disrespectful and just plain all mean, she will still make excuses for him, thinking he will change, thinking she can make him change by loving him well. And this is why women stay too long in an abusive relationship, because they always think the guy will change or they can change a guy.

Sorry ladies, sorry to inform you that guys don't really change unless they really want to. And unfortunately, most guys don't want to change, because they are so used to being the way they are that, any mention of faults that they may have can be misconstrued as an insult to their manhood. And this is because, us men, we can be very stubborn that, you can't tell us nothing. I mean, we can be so set in our ways and so full of ourselves that, it's either our way or the highway for you. You know, it's like, either you take me as I am, or you can leave me the hell alone kind of deal.

I mean, some guys don't know how to compromise, and compromising is one of the bases of any good relationship. Because people are different, and their perspective on things can be very different (mostly based on how they were raised, and how they see the world). So if you are in a relationship with someone who does not know how to compromise (without feeling slighted), you can find yourself in a very frustrating relationship, which soon or later will cause you to be resentful of them. And this is because you will be doing all the compromising and the other person will just be taking, taking, and taking you for granted to the point where you just can't take it anymore, leaving you with no choice but to dump them.

    This is why I say, it's very important for ladies to take their time when looking for mates, because you can find yourself with a guy that you don't really want, no matter how hot or cute he looks. Because girls always tend to easily fall for the so-called cute guys, even when their instincts tell them "No, this dude is a player!", they still let themselves fall and fall hard. And then, then they get surprised when the guy leaves them and starts dating their best friend. I mean, I'm telling you, some guys can be hard core players!

    I mean, a guy can date the girl, her friend, her sister, and her mother (if she don't watch out), and then get all of them pregnant, then realizing the situation he has put himself in, he will ran and remove himself from the mess, get with a new girl, and start with his trifling mess all over again. Hey, I'm not exaggerating, why do you think there are so many trifling talk shows about messed up relationships out there? It's because there are a lot of girls and guys that are very irresponsible out there. I mean, that's why some guys have so many baby mamas, because they just hit and run, hit and run, and hit and run again, and everywhere they run from they leave babies. And this is why it's important for girls to take their time before they give a guy a baby, because they can end up finding themselves with a guy that has so many baby mamas. And if a guy has so many baby mamas, having a relationship with him can be very challenging, because not only will you have to deal with his trifling self, you also gonna have to deal with his trifling baby mamas.

And this is another reason why I think girls have to be extra picky when they are looking for mates, because you don't want to end up with so many baby daddies. But, a lot of girls just never learn, I mean, you would think after one baby daddy situation they would calm themselves down and wait until they are in a real relationship (like a marriage) before they birth another baby by somebody else. But nope, they jump from one relationship to another without the blink of an eye. And before you know it, she ends up with three baby daddies and one more on the way and no sign of marriage in sight, and she's already in her thirties. I mean, it's amazing, it's amazing how women are no longer waiting until they are married before they have children. I mean, it's crazy! What are women thinking? Or maybe they are just not thinking straight, I mean, are they that desperate that they are willing to settle with just anybody, and they think giving that person a baby will make him settle? I mean, it's crazy!

And it's funny how ladies never learn that the more kids they have, the harder they make for themselves to find true love and happiness (you know, a long term relationship), because most guys do their best to stay away from women with a bunch of kids. I mean, a guy may have interest in you, but as soon as he finds out that you have a bunch of kids (meaning more than two kids and never married), he'll do his best to be out of there in a hurry. Because guys just don't want the extra luggage of having to take care of somebody else's kids. I mean, they are probably having a hard time trying to take care of their own kids, so the thought of taking care of additional kids (that they had no part in making) does not really appeal to them. And also, the guy will figure (whether true or not), that the women is probably not that responsible, because to have a bunch of babies with different daddies does not really show much sense of being responsible, and guys for some reason want their women to be responsible, even if they themselves are not.

That's why I like to say, take your time ladies! I mean, I know they say there's a shortage of men out there, but wouldn't you rather take your time and find that one good man, rather than go through a catch and miss approach to finding a man? And really, there's not that much shortage of men out there, you know, especially if you are willing to expand your mind and date people from other races. I mean, you never know, cause real love knows no color or nationality, you know, cause love is love in any language and race. And I mean sure we all would like and or would prefer to stay within our races and nationality when it comes to relationships, but man, love is love, and when you get to know someone real well, and when you get to caring about that person real well, their race or color becomes mute and all you start to see is a person that you are in love with, and a person that's in love with you also, you know what I mean?

And so yeah ladies, by you taking your time with the love thing and not having too many babies too early in your life, not only will you increase your chances of finding true love (by not scaring off men with all of your baby daddy dramas), you will actually be giving yourself time to finish school and start chasing your career goals without the extra responsibility of taking care of babies. Because I mean, taking care of babies is hard work, because babies need your attention twenty four seven.

And this is why most single mothers who have babies early never really finish school, and if they do finish school, they hardly ever go to college. And this is because they just find it hard to juggle work (because they'll have to work pretty much full time to better able take care of the kids), the kids, and school, all at the same time, I mean, they'll never sleep. That's why a lot of single mothers drop out and never finish college, because it's just too hard to juggle all that responsibility, especially if they have to handle all of it alone, which most often times will be the case. But then, the problem comes in that, they find themselves having a hard time finding a good job, because they don't have that college degree, which is like absolutely necessary in today's world if you want to get a good or even just a decent job.

And this is why most single mothers live under the poverty line, because they can only find work that pays them at or just above minimum wage (which is actually poverty wages in today's economy). That's why it's important (ladies) to take your time and get your career going before you bring a baby into the world, because most likely you will be raising it by yourself, unless you find a guy that's responsible. But why gamble on that, because you will only really know if a guy is responsible if he is willing to marry you before you get pregnant, you know, because this will not only mean that he is willing to commit to you, but it will also show that he really does love you and not just marrying you because he got you pregnant.

So ladies, take heed and take care of yourselves, because good guys are out there and they are definitely looking for good women to fall in love with (cause you do know that men do complain that a good woman is hard to find). So take care ladies and do make yourself a good woman (without baby daddy dramas), and men will be rushing to sweep you off your feet. So then now, you will be in control of your destiny when it comes to love, because you will be dating real men, not just boys who want to have fun. Oh yes ma'am, you will be the lady that every real men wants, you know, a freak in the bed and a lady in the streets, you know what I mean, ha ha ha ha ha, yeah!

And this is one of the reasons why I like to say it's women's fault that there's so many baby daddies, because women are just not taking their time to see if the guy they are dating is really compatible with them or not. You know, they don't examine whether the guy has the potential to be a good father or not. I mean, if women took their time, and were extra picky with whom they will have kids with, there would be less and less baby daddies running around, because there would be less and less babies popping up everywhere. I mean, ladies don't understand the power that they have in reducing the chances of them becoming just somebody's baby mama. But hey, what can I say, some girls just won't understand, I mean, some ladies just won't get it, I mean, some women just won't be patient or picky enough, and they will just let themselves fall for the wrong guys, and they will just let themselves become, fools for love!

Chapter 7

Daddy's little girl

It's amazing how much girls get so attached to their daddies, I mean, almost so much more than they do their mommies! And this is where I think the term **daddy's little girl** comes from, because girls seem to get so attached to their daddies. And this attachment is not hard for me to fathom, because it's like, the first man that a girl usually gets to know and love is her father, and there for it's only natural for her to get attached to her daddy. And also the other reason why girls seem to be attached to their daddies more than their mommies is because, well, it's because daddies just have a habit of spoiling their girls (you know, daddies little girl).

I mean it's crazy, but fathers will be so hard on their sons, but when it comes to their daughters, forget it, they become as soft as marsh mallows. I mean, I see it all the time, and in myself also, with my daughter. Because it's like, I will try my best to be tough on both my son and my daughter equally, but somehow, I always seem to soften up very quickly when it comes to my daughter than my son, and my son is only five years old and my daughter is eight. I mean you would think by this time I would be harder on my daughter than my son, because you know, I mean, my daughter is the oldest one and so she should be a little be more responsible and understanding of what's right and wrong than my son. But nah, softy me, she always seems to get me! Because it's like, she will blink her pretty little eyes as if she's about to cry (sensing and knowing that I'm mad at her for something she has done), and I just get soften up tremendously that I become unable to render her discipline and or punishment appropriately. But then of course, if the matter is of serious tone and her mother sends her to me, no amount of tears will soften me up, because I know, if her mother needs me to talk to her, then it's a big deal and I really have to deal with it. But usually small stuff I tend to let her mother deal with it, because I probably will be too soft and just let her get away with it by saying something like, "You know what you did wrong right, ok, cool, just don't do it again!"

It's crazy, but girls just seem to have their fathers wrapped all around their fingers, as the saying goes. But it's all right though, just as long as fathers don't let their daughters ran over them and get away with everything. Because girls will test their daddies and try to manipulate them, you know, so they can get away with stuff. Because it's like, if the mother says no, to whatever the girl wants or wants to do, she will go to daddy and try to get daddy to say yes and over rule her mother. And this is why a lot of times you will see mothers and fathers arguing over whether or not to let their daughter do or get whatever it is that she wants. And that's why fathers have to be extra careful in not spoiling their daughters, because the daughter can get so used to daddy saying yes and over ruling the mother that it can start to cause friction between the parents. Because it's like, when it comes to parenting, both parents have to be almost at the same level, you know, see things almost eye to eye. I mean, what I mean is, it's like, if one parent says no, then it's no, the other parent should not over rule it. But of course sometimes parents will over rule each other (with the other parent's understanding and acceptance hopefully) if the situation is small and no big deal, but most often, no has to mean no.

So, yeah, girls are daddies little girls, and we do like to spoil them. Because it's like, to a daddy, his daughter is very precious to him, I mean, a son is very precious too, but us guys tend to be a little bit over protective over our daughters than our sons, and this is because we tend to see our daughters as being a little bit more venerable than our sons. And so, this is why we tend to see our daughters as being a little bit more delicate, as in needing us (fathers) more than our sons might. I mean don't get me wrong, boys need their fathers greatly too, but girls, it seems to me like girls desperately need their father's in their lives. Because it's like, it seems to me that girls desperately need that fatherly love, you know, a manly love, you know, an unconditional manly love, you know, the kind that only a father can provide. And so, this is also why a lot of girls who don't have their father's in their lives tend to feel incomplete, because there's a void there in their heart that has not been filled. And I mean, sometimes this void becomes so huge that no other man can ever fill. And I mean the void can be so huge that not even a stepfather, a grandfather, an uncle, a brother, a boyfriend or a husband can fill it. I mean, the void can be so huge that no matter how much love she might be getting from her mother and other people around her, her heart can still be aching for her father's love.

It's amazing how much girls crave for their father's love, I mean they just have to have it! And the reason why they have to have it is because, girls want to feel special, they want to feel wanted, they want to feel precious, they want to feel loved, and the person that they really want to feel all this love from is, their fathers. Because it's like, for girls, their father's love is the greatest love of all! And I mean, sure their mother's love is the greatest also, but their mother's love is not a manly love, you know, a father daughter love. And this is because girls tend to worship their fathers, you know, they tend to see their fathers as being the greatest man alive. And I mean, of course their father is probably not the greatest man in the world, hell, he's probably not even the greatest man in their neighborhood, and worse, he could probably be the worse man around, but to her, forget about it, he's the best, and she wants his love. And that's why some women have a hard time trying to convince their daughters that their father is really not a nice and loving man, because daughters just never want to see and accept that their father is a no good man, because daughters just want to love their fathers and their fathers to love them in return.

And this is one of the reasons why daughters would tend to give their fathers more of a chance to change and be in their lives (unlike sons), you know what I mean? Because it's like, when it comes to sons, if their daddy messes up and keeps messing up over and over again (you know, making promises and not coming through with it, or not even trying to help take care of them or be in their lives), sons are ready to kick their fathers to the curb and move on with their lives. Because it's like, sons just don't have the patience to deal with a bunch of bull, cause sons are realists and they come to conclusions quick. And so it's like, when sons see a situation that doesn't seem to be working, they are quick to detach themselves from it so that they can go ahead and move on with their lives. But daughters, oh no, they are never ready to move on, because it's like they feel like they are owed love from their fathers and gosh darn it they will get it one way or another! And that's why girls will spend years begging and hoping that their fathers will change and come to their senses, you know, so that they can once again (if they had ever been) be in their daughter's lives and shower them with love by just being there and saying "I love you" to their daughters.

I mean it's crazy, but girls just have a hard time detaching from their fathers. I mean it can be a very devastating life-long problem for a girl not having her father in her life. And this is why some women go through life depressed and unable to maintain relationships. And this is because they don't feel precious enough or worthy enough to be loved, because they feel as though, if their father (who is their flesh and blood) did not have enough love for them to be in their lives, then how can a stranger ever have enough love for them. And this is why some women never get comfortable or relaxed enough to enjoy their relationship with a man, because they are always on guard and wondering whether the man will leave them or not, you know, just like how their father did. I mean, just ask a few ladies whom their fathers were never there or where in and out of their lives, just ask them how the lack of a relationship with their father is affecting them now, in terms of being in a relationship and their views on men. And I bet you most of the answers will be negative, as in, they don't trust men, and they don't really feel comfortable in relationships. And this is one of the reasons why a lot of women tend to not want to be in relationships anymore, because they just don't trust men, because it seems like all the men that supposed to love them have a tendency of leaving them. And so they tend to equate this leaving (of the men in their lives), as a sign that either they are the problem, or that there's no good men out there, including their fathers.

I mean, it's crazy, but it's serious business! And this is why it is very important for fathers to be in their daughter's lives, because daughters need them for their self-confidence and to learn and to see what a good man and what a real man looks like.

So daddies, please make sure you are in your daughters lives, because daughters need their fathers, because there's nothing like a daughter's love for her father, and there's nothing like a father's love for his daughter, you know, **daddy's little girl**!

Chapter 8

Mama's boy

There's an epidemic going on, and this epidemic is very hard to notice at first sight. I mean, it's everywhere you look, it's everywhere you don't look, but it's there, just chilling, not doing a damn thing, unmotivated, all it wants to do is lazy around and be given stuff instead of going out there in the world and bust ass and make something of them-selves. It's crazy, but this epidemic seems to be affecting more and more people (especially males) each year. Because it's like, it seems like guys don't want or don't have the motivation to work hard anymore, you know what I mean? I mean, it's like, this epidemic is causing boys to not want or to not have the desire to become strong independent men who can provide for their families. I mean, this epidemic is causing men to become lazy and irresponsible.

Now, you are probably still wondering what the hell I'm talking about, right? Well, I'm talking about men, and men who seem to have been over protected by their mothers, you know, men who have been pretty much spoiled by their mothers, you know, **mama's boys!**

Man, so many mama's boys, mama's boys everywhere! I guess this is one of the reasons why women are having a hard time finding a suitable man to settle down with. Because it seems like nowadays a lot of men are nothing but grown up mama's boys, you know what I mean? And what I call mama's boys is guys that, instead of working hard to make a living for them-selves, mama's boys tend to just be satisfied with getting by and of course live with and depend on their mamas. I mean, sure not all guys that stay home with their mamas are mama's boys, because sometimes a guy will stay home with his mama just so to help her out with extra income. Because in today's hard crazy world, retirement can be a mother....., because inflation keeps going up and wages stay the same, so most people generally need two incomes just to catch up to the cost of living and to try and maintain a decent lively hood. And also, some guys will choose to stay home with mama a little longer than they should because they may be trying to save some money so that they can go back to school or start a business.

But really, most guys that are still living at home with their mamas and are over the age of twenty-five are nothing but mama's boys. Because it's like, by the time a guy is twenty-five, he's usually or should pretty much be independent. Because I mean, most guys usually by the time they turn eighteen they are ready to split, you know, get out the house, be on their own, so they can do their own thing and try to conquer the world, you know what I mean? Because I mean, generally most guys are go getters (meaning, they are not afraid to work hard to earn a living), but there are a few, a lot few (I know, I know, I can't say a lot few, it's not proper speech, as my wife likes to tell me, and as my English teachers used to correct me, because I like to and have the habit of mixing up verbs and adjectives and even make up words sometimes just to fit what I'm trying to say, especially if it sounds good and cool, ha ha ha ha ha! And so, **a lot few** sounds good and cool to me, so I'm gonna use it and I don't care if it's not proper speech, ha ha ha ha ha! "I'm sorry Ms. Gailliurd, I'm trying my best not to write as I speak, but I just can't help it, because it just feels and or sounds so good the way it comes out of my mouth that I just gotta use it. I mean, I'll try my best not to over-do it though, I promise, ha ha ha ha ha!" Excuse me y'all, but I just had to send a shout out to my 8th grade

English teacher and perhaps the first person to recognize, mold and take interest in my writing abilities. Because I mean, she actually used to challenge me creatively, and once she even had me submit one of my essays for some kind of publication competition, which I ended up winning!

So I mean, I never really took writing very seriously before, I mean, even now I still don't take it that seriously, I mean, you know, I don't like worry about whether my grammar and sentence structures are correct all the time, because really I'm just trying to have fun and enjoy my writing and hopefully someone else will also enjoy and appreciate what I have to say. I mean, it's not rocket science! But I guess there's nothing wrong and it takes a little bit of talent to be able to express yourself properly so other's can understand what it is you are trying to say. So for that, I want to say thank you to Ms. Gialliurd for showing me that I had an ability to be a good writer if I really applied myself. So, much love, and I hope this book finds you, or I just might have to find you myself and give you the book personally. So anyway, let's continue with what we were talking about before I started wondering off the subject matter. Oh man, I forgot what we were talking about! Oh, wait a minute, ok, I remember now, we were talking about **a lot few**, you know, not the majority of guys, but a lot of them), that just don't seem to be motivated to do much. I mean, rather than go out there in the world and struggle to make it, they are resigned to just sitting at home with mama and mooching off of her.

I mean it's crazy, but a lot of guys nowadays run away from hard work, they want easy jobs, you know, they don't want to sweat, they don't want to work long hours, they don't want to work two jobs, you know, they don't want to struggle to make it. And I mean, sure we all would love to have easy jobs that pay us a lot of money, but that is not the reality of things, because it's tough out there, and if you want to get yourself a good job, you are really gonna have to get out there, bust your ass, get your priorities straight, and go for it. I mean, there's no easy way out, because it's like, if you really want to make something of yourself, you just going to have to push, push, push, and push it until doors start to open for you. I mean, matter of fact, you pretty much are going to have to actually kick some doors open yourself, you know, and let yourself in the game, in whatever career or industry that you want to be in.

I mean, it's crazy, it's just crazy how this generation and the next generation of men (who are teenagers now) just don't seem to want to work hard, I mean, we are becoming just plain all lazy (us men). Because I mean, it seems like nowadays that, women are working way harder than men. Because it's like, every time I turn and look around, it's women that I see (out numbering men) who seem to be on the go, who seem to be in a hurry, who seem to have a goal, who seem to be determined to achieve something. I mean it's crazy, but just look around, just take a few seconds to pause and be observant, and I bet you will notice that, there's a lot more women than men that seem to be working longer hours, working two or three jobs, and basically seem to have more of a fight to make it than men do.

I mean it's wild, but women nowadays just seem to have much more of a focus and determination to make it in this world than men do. It's crazy, I mean, what happened to us men? Why have we become so lazy? Why are we letting our women out work us? Why are we forcing our women to work and struggle so hard? Because I mean, we are the ones (men) that are supposed to struggle and work, work and work hard, you know, so we can provide for our families. Because it's like, really, men are the ones that are supposed to go to work and bring in the bacon, you know, be the provider. And women are supposed to stay at home and be the nurturers, you know, take care of the kids. I mean, that's the way God intended for it to be, isn't it? I mean, isn't this the reason why back in the old days men used to work from sun up to sun down, and have two or three jobs so they can be the best providers for their families? Because it's like, back in the old days, you would not be considered a real man unless you worked hard. I mean, people would actually look down on you, and you would actually feel ashamed and feel like you are being less than a man. But nowadays, there are so many people that don't like to work hard that the shame factor is not there anymore. I mean it's like there's a shame support network for people who don't want to work. Because it's like, they tend to like to congregate together.

I mean, it's true, I'm not making it up, you can see them for yourself, because they are everywhere, just hanging out, waiting for nothing. I mean, I see them all the time, all around, as I'm driving around. I mean, it never fails, it's like, there they are, hanging around the corner, doing nothing in particular, just shooting the breeze, wasting time. And there they go, another group, walking around the block, going nowhere in particular, just shooting the breeze, wasting time. And still, there they go, another group, sitting on some steps, in front of a house, doing nothing in particular, just chilling, shooting the breeze, wasting time. I mean it's crazy, it's scary, and it's disappointing at how men are becoming more and more lazy nowadays. I mean it's almost becoming an epidemic, if it isn't already!

Man, it's almost saddening the state of us men nowadays, because it's almost like we have lost our pride, you know, it's like we have lost the pride of working hard, the pride of taking care of our kids, and the pride of self-respect. Because it's like, back in the day, men were proud to be considered strong providers for their families. I mean, they gave extra effort to make sure their kids, their wives, and their extended families were taken care of. And this is because back then, your respect as a man was based on how well you provided for your family. I mean it was serious business, laziness was not acceptable, unless you didn't mind to be looked upon as a girly man, you know, a softy! But nowadays, forget it, people don't have strong prides anymore. I mean, it's like people don't have the motivation to aspire to be great anymore. I mean, it's like we are ready to give up at the first sign of an obstacle. I mean it's crazy, and it's sad at how lazy this generation of black men have become. I mean, it's like we have given up hope or something. And I mean, don't get me wrong, there are a lot of black men that work hard and strive to succeed, but the lazy ones just seem to over shadow them.

And I mean, of course other races have their laziness problems too (because I have seen and worked with some of them), but us black people, oh men, it's like we have taken laziness to the next level, like how we like to do with everything else, you know what I mean? Because I mean, there's really no excuse for not trying to be productive and succeed in something (especially in this here good all U.S.A.). I mean sure things are not easy, and I mean, sure things are tough, but such is the world, and such is life, life is tough. But so what, so what if life is tough, that only means that you gotta be tough too.

Because I mean, you really can't afford to lose, especially if you've got kids, because the kids will be depending on you to take care of them until they can take care of themselves. And this taking care of kids can be a very long and strenuous journey, especially if your financial situation is handicapped by your laziness and/or fear of hard work. Because I mean, kids require a lot of attention and a lot of financial obligation from their parents until they are grown and able to provide for themselves. And so, if the parents are not in a good financial situation, they can find it very strenuous to raise their kids properly. And this is why it is very important for parents to not give up on hard work, because your kids are depending on you for their survival and lively hood. And this is also why it is very important for parents to try to get their careers straight before they have kids, because it will help them better enjoy the process of raising their kids. And this is because the financial part will have somewhat been taken cared of, and there for it will not be a burden, or an issue, or a handicap that can affect the raising of their children properly.

I mean, life is tough, but there's no real good excuse for not trying to succeed or to be productive in your life, especially in a free country like the United States. Because it's like, the U.S. is one of the few countries in the world that opportunities to advance your life still exists. I mean, even in this time of wars, recession, inflation, corruption, loss of jobs, natural disasters, increase in poverty, low minimum wages, home foreclosures, and etc., etc., and etc., there's still opportunities for people to make something of themselves, especially if they are willing to work real, real, real hard. Because I mean, that's what this country requires, it requires a lot of sacrifice, it requires a lot of education, it requires a lot of natural talent, it requires a lot of discipline and planning, it requires a lot of risk taking abilities, it requires a lot of understanding of the flow of money (the economy), and finally, it requires a lot and a lot of patience. Because I mean, it's like, in an extreme capitalist country like this, it's really all about the money. And so, if you can recognize and understand how the system works, opportunities will start to jump out at you, and dreams will start to appear more visible and feasible to achieve.

And so I mean, sure life is tough, and sure good jobs are hard to find, but that still is not a good reason for not trying to succeed in this world. Because I mean, all of us face obstacles from time to time, but that's not a reason to give up and ran back to mama's house. I mean, sure we all might have to retreat to our mama's house once or twice in our lives to get a fresh start on life, you know, after we have failed in an endeavor or we have lost a job. But, this retreat should not last for more than six months, otherwise we will become endangered of becoming a mama's boy, you know what I mean? Because I mean, isn't this what mama's boys usually do every time they are met with an obstacle or challenge? I mean, don't mama's boys always seem ready to ran back to their mama's house every time their life gets tougher, you know, instead of just muscling through the situation? And the funny thing is, their mothers actually let them stay and mooch off of them without forcing them to go out there and find a job.

And really, this is not a surprise for mothers to let their sons mooch off of them, because for some reason mothers tend to be so soft on their boys, you know, they tend to let their boys get away with almost anything, you know, they tend to let their boys ran all over them. Because I mean, if this was their daughter that was mooching on them and laying around the house without a job, their mama would actually start to call them lazy and start pressuring them to go get a job so they can become independent. I mean, I don't know what it is, but when it comes to mothers and their sons, forget it, because mothers would rather spoil their sons than discipline them. I mean, it's almost like, actually it's exactly like how fathers are with their daughters, you know, because fathers would rather spoil their daughters than discipline them.

And this is one of the reasons why it's very important for fathers to be in their children's lives, so that they can balance out the mother. Because it's like, mothers tend to be harder on their daughters than they are on their sons, and fathers tend to be harder on their sons than they are on their daughters. And so the balance helps, because kids need to feel a sense of both love and discipline, because too much of one and not enough of the other can affect a kid negatively. Because it's like, if a kid is getting too much love and not enough discipline, they will tend to end up spoiled and lazy. And vice versa, if a kid gets too much discipline and not enough love, they will tend to feel neglected and unloved. And so, this is one of the reasons why it is very important for fathers to be in their kid's lives, so they can balance out the mother.

And this is one of the reasons why there are so many mama's boys running around today, and it's because their fathers are not in their lives. And so mothers are left there to have to try to raise and man-up the boy, which can prove to be a very monumental task. Because boys by nature are very hard headed, you know what I mean? And so it's like, if you really want a boy to learn something, your best bet is to teach him by example, you know, like if you want him to know how a real man looks and acts, you gonna have to show him a real man so he can easily process and imitate that.

And I mean, this is why a lot of kids imitate the rappers or other older guys they see in the streets, you know, because they think this is how a real man is supposed to act and or look like. And the reason for this is because the kids just don't know any better, and nobody has really taken the time to teach them and or show them how a real man acts and looks like. Because see, it's like this, kids are visual creatures and imitators, and so what they see is what they believe and what they believe they imitate. So when they see the rappers on TV, they don't understand that most of those rappers act and behave the way they do just for show, you know, just for the cameras, you know, because they are entertainers, but when the camera is off, most of these guys are pretty quiet and very respectful. And I mean, sure there are some rappers who are just plain all trifling all the time, but most of them are pretty humble and try their best to act normal (off screen). But the kids don't know that, and so they end up imitating the rappers and thinking that's what a real man looks and acts like. And this is why it is very important for fathers to be in their sons lives, so they can take their time and teach them and show them what a real man looks like and acts like, you know? Because I mean, kids need to know that real men respect themselves and others, you know? And they need to know that real men know how to speak properly, real men are proud to work hard and take care of their families, and real men love and cherish their kids. I mean, this is what a father's responsibility to his son is, to teach him how to become a mature and responsible adult, you know, to teach him how to become a real man!

Man, it's crazy, but this is one of the reasons why there's so many mama's boys running around nowadays, and this is because their fathers are not there to men them up, you know what I mean? So come on guys, we got's to do better in our fatherly duties, especially when it comes to our young men, because if we don't, most of our boys are going to turn into mama's boys who are good for nothing but to be some poor girl's baby daddy. And Lord knows we have already got enough of those kinds of guys, ain't I right (ladies)? And the congregation says, "Amen!"

Chapter 9

Like mother like daughter!

They say that history has a funny way of repeating itself, and I say that's true, especially when it comes to mothers and their daughters. I mean, it almost never fails, daughters always seem to follow in their mother's footsteps (whether it be good or bad). And this is understandable, because a girls first role model is usually her mother, and so, whatever habits or traits her mother has, the daughter will consciously or subconsciously pick up. Now, this can be good or bad, it all depends on how her mother is as a person. Because it's like, daughters tend to pick up so much of their mother's character, you know, their mother's behavior.

And so, this is why it is very important for mothers to watch how they behave, because their daughters are watching and will copy everything their mothers do (whether consciously or subconsciously), you know what I mean? And so, it is very important for mothers to try their best to be great role models for their kids, because kids are watching, and whatever they learn at home is what they will take to the world. And being that the world is as crazy as it is nowadays, daughters need strong and positive role models to follow, otherwise the world can corrupt and force them to make wrong decisions for their lives. I mean it's crazy, but daughters need their mother's to take extra care in teaching them and molding them, so that they can in turn grow up to be mature and responsible women.

So I mean, yeah, like mother like daughter! Because it's like, daughters always seem to follow in their mother's footsteps, you know? Because it's like, for example; if the mother is an educated woman, then the daughter will tend to grow up to be an educated woman, and also too, if the mother is a hard working responsible parent, then the daughter will tend to grow up to be a hard working responsible parent. Now, the reverse of this example is also true, you know, like; if the mother is not an educated woman, then the daughter will tend to grow up to be un an educated woman, and also too, if the mother is not a hard working responsible parent, then too the daughter will tend to grow up to not be a hard working responsible parent.

I mean, it's crazy, but daughters take so much of their mother's characteristics that if mothers are not careful, their daughters will end up just like them, good or bad, and we hope it's good. Because I mean, there are so many bad mothers out there that it's scary! I mean, I see them, in a regular basis, all the time, because they are everywhere, and it looks like they don't even care who sees them being bad mothers. I mean I'm sure you have seen them too, because they are not that hard to spot, because their true trifling inner selves always seems to come out, even without being provoked. I mean, I see and hear them all the time, walking around, looking mad and angry, like someone has just pissed them off, you know, and when they speak, nothing but negativity comes out their mouths. And it's like, you start to feel sorry for their poor kids, because you know it must be hell in the household. And the poor kids will have no choice but to absorb all this negativity that is unleashed by their mothers in a daily basis.

I mean it's crazy, but I hear mothers shouting and cursing at their kids, I mean even their little kids, and even their babies! I mean, are you kidding me, what kind of language is that to use with a little kid? And to curse at a baby, I mean, what does that say about you, what does that say about your character? I mean, what are these parents thinking, or maybe they are not really thinking? Because I mean, I really don't think that any parent who knew what kind of damage they might be inflicting to their kids by their behavior would continue in their trifling ways, but then again, maybe they would. Because I mean, it just seems like a lot of parents are very ignorant to how their own behavior can affect their kids. And this is one of the reasons why a lot of parents spend years being trifling in front of their kids and then act surprised when their kids start acting out and start getting into trouble. Because a lot of parents just don't think that their kids are watching them, and not just watching them, but also copying them. And that's why you have kids whose mothers are trifling, act trifling themselves. And that's why you also have kids whose mothers are mature and responsible, act mature and responsible themselves. Because it's like, you know, like mother like daughter, I mean, it almost never fails!

But then of course, there's always an exception to the rule, you know, sometimes somehow girls just refuse to follow in their mothers footsteps (whether it be good or bad, and we hope it's the bad one). Because it's like, sometimes a girl can have a very caring, responsible and hard working mother, but the daughter can end up being trifling. And then vice versa, a girl can have a trifling mother, but she can turn out to be a very mature, responsible and a hard worker. I mean, some girls just refuse to be trifling, even if that's all they see at home. And these are the girls that seem to be embarrassed when they are out and about with their mothers, you know, hoping and wishing that their mothers don't embarrass them by saying or acting stupid, or should I say, by acting ghetto. But of course these girls who refuse to be trifling like their mothers are far and a few, because most girls just follow in their mother's footsteps, you know, if the mother is trifling, then the girl is gonna be trifling too, and also too, if the mother is mature and responsible, then the girl is gonna be mature and responsible, you know, like mother like daughter!

And so, this is one of the reasons why it is very important for fathers to be in their daughter's lives, you know, so they can reinforce the good things that the mother is teaching their daughter, and also too, they can dispel the bad things that the mother is teaching their daughter. Because I mean, sometimes kids just need a second opinion, you know, a second ear that will sit down with them and listen to their problems and help them, and teach them about life. And I mean, who better to be that second ear than the girl's father? Because I mean, sometimes or should I say, a lot of times, mothers and daughters just don't seem to get along, you know, they just tend to clash a lot.

I mean, I don't know what it is, but it's just amazing how much mothers and daughters just seem to piss each other off. I mean, actually, I think I might know why this is so, why they tend to get in each other's nerves so much. And the reason for it is, **sensitivity**, you know, that whole emotional thing that women have, you know, so touchy feeling, you know, so sensitive. I mean, it's the same reason why women tend to not have so many female friends, because they tend to get on each other's nerves so easily. And so, when it comes to mothers and their daughters, not only are they both emotional, they are also pretty much just one and the same, you know, like mother like daughter, you know, they tend to have the same habits. And so, since they are pretty much one and the same, their sensitivity and temperament tend to be at the same level, which can make it hard for them to communicate effectively without one of them catching feelings, you know, get emotional.

And so, this is another reason why fathers need to be in their daughters lives, you know, so they can act as a buffer between mother and daughter. I mean, because it's like, sometimes mothers and daughters just need some time apart, you know, they need a breather from one another before they piss each other off (especially if the mother is very domineering, and the daughter is very rebellious). And so, here is where a father who is in his daughter's life can come in and have a talk with his daughter about what her mother is upset about, and also, he can go to the mother and tell her what the daughter is upset about. Because sometimes the situation or problem can be very small, but since the girl and her mother are not communicating well, a small situation can end up being blown all out of proportion, causing unnecessary riff between mother and daughter.

I mean, it's crazy, it's scary, and it's weird how mother daughter relationships can be. Because it's like, sometimes mothers get along so well with their daughters that, they actually hang out together, you know, actually enjoy each other's company. Because it's like, most often times, mothers and daughters do their best to stay away from each other's faces, you know, avoid each other. Because it's like, the mother feels as though the daughter will say or do something that will irritate her, and the daughter feels as though the mother will do or say something that will irritate her. And so, instead of spending quality time together and or talk through some problems or misunderstandings, most mothers and daughters just choose to avoid each other, instead of facing each other.

And this is why there's a lot of disconnect between mothers and daughters, because mothers just don't take the time to deal with their daughters so they can find out what's really going on in their daughters lives. Because I mean, girls go through so much changes (both physically and mentally) that they need that extra attention and extra patience from their mothers, so that way they can have time to adjust and get comfortable with themselves, so their journey from childhood to womanhood can go a little bit smoother than otherwise would. Because it's like, it seems like nowadays mothers just don't take the time to properly talk to and teach their daughters about life and about womanhood, you know, teach them how to be a lady. And this is one of the reasons why there are so many girls nowadays running around being very un lady like, you know, being just plain trifling. I mean, they just don't know how a real lady acts or looks like, for that matter. And it's all really because no one has ever taken the time to teach them and or to show them how a real lady looks like and acts like.

I mean, it's crazy! And it's getting to the point where, most girls are starting to associate being a lady as being weak, you know, a sign of weakness. I mean, it's crazy, but it's understandable. Because it's like, nowadays girls are growing up so fast and so rough, you know, they are growing up in rough and or bad environments (outside and inside the household), that they feel the need to be and or act tough, you know, because their environment demands it, you know what I mean? And so, because they feel the need to look and act tough, being and acting like a lady is the farthest thing from their minds, because they are too busy making sure that nobody is trying to step all over them, you know, making sure nobody tries to mess or take advantage of them.

And so, this is another reason why it is very important for fathers to be in their daughters lives, you know, that so they can give their daughters a sense of protection (from both the inside and outside the household). And so, by giving their daughters this sense of protection, it will allow their daughters a chance to relax, you know, to be less defensive. And then so, by them being less defensive, they will feel free to concentrate on being a lady, instead of concentrating on being a tough girl that no one will want to mess with. I mean it's crazy, but I understand why a lot of girls behave the way they do, and it's because the environment that a lot of our young ladies are growing up in these days is very rough and chaotic. And so just imagine how hard it must be trying to be a lady living in an atmosphere like that, of chaos and insecurity. Because I mean, the environment that we leave in tends to have a lot of influence on how we act and or behave. Because it's like, if everyone around you is not behaving properly or acting right, then the chances of you not behaving and acting right is very high. And this is because, we as human beings have a strong sense of desire to belong, you know, fit in. And so in doing so, we tend to accept and conform to the behavior of our environment, and there for we begin to act and behave just like everyone around us, even if the behavior is not proper or desirable. I mean, this is where that menacing peer pressure thing comes in and rules everything. Because I mean, this is why a lot of people fall for and become un able to escape their environment, and it's because of that peer pressure thing, you know, that peer pressure that forces them to accept and do as everybody else does, you know, even if they don't really want to.

And so, this is another reason why it is very important for fathers to be in their kid's lives, because that peer pressure thing is very strong. I mean, that peer pressure thing can be so strong that if you are not careful and if you are not extra diligent in raising your kids, you can come to find your kids succumbing to peer pressure, you know, you can come to find your kids picking up on a lot of the bad habits of society, you know, like; drinking, smoking, stealing, sexing, cursing, drugging, gang banging and on and on. I mean, that peer pressure thing can be a monster to deal with, that's why it is important for fathers to be in their kid's lives, so they can help the kid to try to stay away from all that bad habits and behavior. Because I mean, sometimes (actually, a lot of times) it's just too much for the mother to try to keep the kids in the straight and narrow, you know, out of peer pressure's grips, you know, keep them from succumbing to peer pressure. I mean, it's hard enough to raise kids with both parents in the household, so just imagine how hard it must be to raise kids in a single parent home. I mean, to tell you the truth, I have no idea how single mothers do it! Because I mean, me and my wife find ourselves tired and exhausted all the time (as we are trying to be the best parents that we can be), and it's two of us in the household parenting, you know, taking turns to teach and discipline the kids. And so, I can just imagine how hard it must be for a single parent, because it's just one person trying to be the best parent they can be. I mean, it must be very hard having to do everything that a parent has got to do to make sure that the kids are properly raised so they can grow to be mature and responsible adults, and to do it all by yourself, man, it's got to be tough!

I mean, I guess this is why a lot of single parents just let their children run wild, you know, because they are just too tired and exhausted (after work and everything) to be chasing their kids around. And this is why there's a lot of kids walking around all over the place looking lost and bewildered, you know, confused. And this is because their mothers are just too tired to give them proper attention, you know, their mothers are just too tired to take time to teach and or give their kids some directions for their lives.

And so, this is another reason why it's important for fathers to be in their children's lives, because sometimes (I mean, a lot of times), mothers just get tired, you know, they just get exhausted and need a helping hand. And so, this is where the father can come in and take the kids out for a while (or for the weekend, if the father and the mother are not together anymore), so that the mother can get some well needed rest and relaxation, that way she can be rejuvenated and ready to properly nurture and or deal with the kids. Because I mean, raising kids can be very challenging, especially if you have to do it all by yourself. So fellas please help the ladies out, because I'm tired of seeing all these women looking tired and mad all the time. So please help them out, because your kid's well-being is depending on them. Because let's face it, most kids nowadays are being raised in single parent homes (usually with the mother). And so, it's like, the kids' happiness and future depends on the mother's ability to stay sane in the mist of stress and fatigue from life and from having to raise the kids by herself. And so fellas, if we want our kids to grow up and have bright futures, we gonna have to make sure we are in their lives, you know, so we can help with raising them (even if we are not in a relationship with the mother anymore). I mean, we just gonna have to force ourselves to be in our kid's lives, even if the baby mama is a headache to deal with, we just gonna have to deal with her, you know, because she's your kids' mother, and your kids definitely need you, especially if the mother is slacking and or is just having a hard time of taking care of the kids by herself.

I mean, it's crazy, and it's wild how fathers just don't seem to understand how much their kids need them, especially their daughters. Because a lot of girls nowadays are just not getting enough attention from their mothers, you know, because their mothers are just too busy working and just too tired to teach and or help their daughters to navigate through life.

And so, this is also why it's good for a father to be there for his daughter, so he can help pick up the slack, especially if the mother is not a very good role model for the daughter. I mean, you know, because it's like, some mothers are just trifling, you know, very un lady like. And so, if fathers are not careful, these trifling mothers will teach and forward their trifling ways to the daughters, you know what I mean? Because it's like, a lot of girls tend to follow in their mothers' footsteps, you know. I mean it's like, for example; if the mother is a smoker, then the daughter will tend to grow up to be a smoker, and or, if the mother is a drinker, then the daughter will tend to grow up to be a drinker, and or, if the mother sleeps around, then the daughter will tend to grow up to be promiscuous also, and still, if the mother is used to living on well fare, then too the daughter will tend to grow up and end up depending on well fare also, you know what I mean?

I mean, it almost never fails, daughters just tend to follow in their mothers footsteps, whether good or bad. And this is why it is very important for mothers to try their best to be the best role models for their daughters, because their daughters are watching them, you know? And so it's like, whatever the mother does (good or bad), the daughter will incorporate it in her own behavior and run with it, you know what I mean?

So ladies, take care of your daughters, because after all, they are representing you, you know, like mother like daughter!

Chapter 10

Like father like son!

They say history has a funny way of repeating itself, and I say this is very true, especially when it comes to fathers and their sons. Because I mean, it almost never fails, how sons have a tendency to follow in their fathers' footsteps. I mean, it's just amazing how a lot of sons end up being just like their fathers, you know, take after their fathers' character. And sometimes sons will take after their fathers so much that it's almost un believable! And this is why you will tend to hear a lot of mothers say to their sons something like, "You are just like your father!", and she means that literally, because it's probably true.

And so, this is also why a lot of women who are not with their baby daddies tend to get so mad at their sons sometimes for almost no apparent reason, all because they are mad at the daddy and the son just happens to look so much like him. And so they end up taking it on the son, just because he happens to look and or act so much like his father, to no fault of his own, but the mother just can't stand it, because it keeps reminding her of her ex, whom she's trying to get over and forget. I mean, it can get down-right nasty sometimes how mothers treat their sons, and it's all because the son strongly resembles the father. I mean, come on ladies, leave the boy alone, he is not his father, he just looks and acts like him. I mean, he can't help it, he's got his father's genes in him. So I mean, of course he's going to kind of or strongly resemble his father, it's only right.

So please ladies, try your best to leave your sons alone, because God knows they've got enough stress and peer pressures coming to them from outside the household that they don't need any-more coming from inside the household. And also too ladies, please stop telling your sons that they are just like their fathers, especially if their fathers are not in their lives, and or, if their fathers are not being productive with their own lives. And the reason why I say this is because, it can really scar a son to be told that he is just like his father, especially if his father is not a well to do man, you know, not a successful man. Because it's like, heck, if his father is a successful man, you can go ahead and tell him that he's just like his father all day and it won't really bother him much. Because in this instance, being like his father won't carry such a negative connotation as opposed to if his father is or was a bum. Because in this instance (his father being a bum), being like his father will be the biggest insult you could ever tell your son, even if it's true, actually, especially if it's true. Because it's like, in this situation, telling him that he is just like his father is like telling him that he will never amount to nothing, you know, just like his father. I mean, being told this can be very detrimental to a son (especially when it comes from the mother), because he can take it to heart and his self-esteem can really be crushed. And so, after a while he will really start to believe that maybe his future is really doomed, you know, maybe he really is like his father and wont amount to nothing.

And this is one of the reasons why a lot of boys give up on try-ing to be better than their fathers, and it's because someone has told them that they will never amount to nothing, you know, just like their fathers. I mean it's crazy, but being told that you are just like your father can have a very powerful effect in a kid's life (whether good or bad). Because it's like, after a while, boys can start to believe it (the statement) and they can start to lose their motivation for even trying, you know, just like how their daddy did. I mean, it can be a very defeating statement!

So ladies, please don't destroy your boy's self-esteem and or cause him more pain by talking about his daddy. Because I mean, he has only got one daddy, so just let him enjoy his daddy until he is old enough to detect, to understand, to conclude and or to realize by himself that his daddy is not being as productive with his life as he could be, or that his daddy is just plain all trifling! And so, please ladies, I beg you, please don't give your sons' unnecessary scars (mental) or stress that they will have to live with, because you can be sure the world is going to give them those, you know, stress and headaches. I mean, sure ladies, I know it can be very challenging to raise a son (especially if the father is not helping), but talking negatively about his daddy and then comparing him to his daddy can only do one thing for him, and that is, it can only bring him down, when what he really needs is to be brought up, you know, encouraged to strive for success, no matter what his daddy's situation is.

So anyway, yeah, sons do tend to take a lot after their fathers. And it's only right, because, not only are they carrying their fathers genes in them, but also boys tend to like to copy and imitate their fathers. And so this is one of the reasons for example, this is one of the reasons why you will tend to see a boy walk and talk like his daddy. And also, this is also the reason why, if the boy's father is a gentleman, the boy will tend to grow up to be a gentleman also, and then too, if the boy's father is a thug, the boy will tend to grow up to be a thug also. I mean, it almost never fails, and this is because, a boy's first role model is usually his father. And so, whatever the father does, the son will usually try to copy and emulate. And this emulation can happen consciously or subconsciously as the son watches and studies his father's habits.

And this one of the reasons why it is very important for fathers to watch how they behave in front of their kids, because kids are like parrots, they copy and imitate everything you do or say. I mean it's like, they are trying to learn how to be a man by watching and studying you. Because it's like, to kids, their fathers are the most manly man around. I mean, you know, because to kids, as far as they are concerned, their fathers are the strongest, the coolest, and the smartest people around. And so, being that their fathers are their first role models, sons tend to copy everything their fathers do, and this is because they want to be just like their daddies, you know, cool, smart, and strong, you know, like their daddies.

I mean, it's just amazing how much little kids admire their daddies, because it's like, to kids, their daddies are the greatest! And it's like, this is why sometimes you will hear little kids in a heated debate over their daddies, you know, arguing over who's daddy is better. I mean, they'll be very serious about it too, you know, and all of them believing that their father is definitely the coolest, the strongest, and the smartest of them all. I mean, kids just admire their fathers, and I mean, so much so that, they almost start to see their fathers as being superheroes, you know what I mean? Because it's like, sometimes you can catch them saying stuff like; "I bet my daddy can beat up your daddy!" or " I bet my daddy can jump higher than your daddy!" or "I bet my daddy can run faster than your daddy!" or "I bet my daddy can lift a car all by himself!" or "I bet my daddy can pull the whole train with one finger!", and on and on and on. And this is because, kids just admire their daddies so much, and it's only right, because daddies are usually a boy's first role model, so of course he is going to admire his daddy.

It's just so amazing how much kids admire their fathers, and I mean, this is because kids just like to put their fathers in a pedestal, you know, they like to view their fathers as being faultless. And this is why sometimes mothers will just go crazy over how much their kids just love their daddies, especially if she's not with their father anymore and he's not really helping out financially, you know, not paying child support and stuff like that. I mean, it can just drive the mother crazy sometimes. Because it's like, there she is, mad at the daddy for not helping out (financially), and so, since she thinks the worse of him, in retribution she doesn't really want him to see the kids. But, she knows the kids really love their daddy, and every time he comes to pick them up or see them, they seem really happy. And so, since she loves seeing her kids happy, she don't dare take their joy of their father away from them (as any real caring mother shouldn't), so she goes ahead and let him see and enjoy his kids, even though she is so disgusted with him.

And so, yeah, kids just love and adore their daddies, you know, until they get to be old and wise enough to realize for themselves that maybe their daddy is not as cool as they thought he was. And perhaps they may even come to realize that their father is just way too trifling for them to be around him. Because I mean, kids eventually do get older and start to see and view their fathers for what they really are, but until then, kids just want to have their cakes and eat it too (meaning, they want to know their fathers and enjoy him too!).

But then also of course, if the daddy happens to be real mean and abusive to the kids, the kids will definitely pick that up quickly, and there for, instead of them having adoration and love for their father, they will instead have hatred and be scared of him. And so, in this situation, definitely mothers gotta do whatever it takes to keep the father far away from the kids, because they definitely don't need this kind of ugliness in their kid's lives. But, other than that, let the kids have and enjoy their daddies, because kids just love their daddies, and they don't care what the two of you are having problems with, that's for you and him to deal with, because kids just want to be happy, and having their daddies in their lives is part of the happiness process, I mean, believe me or not, it's the truth.

And so anyway, yeah, kids just adore their daddies! Because I mean, I too can remember my own admirations of my father from when I was little. I mean, I can still remember it like it was just yesterday! Because it's like, I can still see him in his coolness, you know, with his shades on, his Saturday best on, and his spit shined polished stylish dress shoes on, you know, walking down the street on his way to the restaurant/bar where he used to like to hang out, you know, mix and mingle with his friends. I mean, I can still see it and I can still see him, you know, because I was right there beside him a lot of the times, you know, trying my best to keep up with him as he took those long strides, forcing me to have to run and walk, run and walk, off and on, you know, so I can catch up to him. And sometimes what I would do is, I would just run a few steps past him, you know, so it would take him longer to pass me, you know, so I wouldn't have to run so much. And so, yeah, I used to like to watch him walk, you know, and of course I would try my best to imitate his walk. I don't really remember how he used to walk (because that was a real long, long time ago), but Shaft keeps coming to my mind as I think of it. And this is because, I can kind of still see my dad's shoes as he used to walk, because they were always polished and kind of shiny. And so, as he walked, his feet didn't seem to be touching the ground too much, I mean, his feet seemed like they were just gliding in the air. And so, I guess he probably walked that way so as to try to not get his shoes dirty, but to me, I just thought his walk was just so cool, and so I did my best to copy it.

   I mean, those were the good old days, because he would always take me to the restaurant/bar with him. And this was during the time when it was just him and me in the household, you know, just me and him living together. I mean, this was after his first wife had left (my step mom from hell), and before I had to start living with different relatives, as he was looking for a new job. But yeah, during this time, when it was just me and him, oh yeah, that was a great time. Because it's like, for the first time in my little six/seven years of life, that was the first time that I had ever had a chance to feel like a kid, because before that, forget it, my step-mother from hell just would not have it. I mean, she just made sure that I stayed miserable. I mean, she was like a one-woman torture chamber, you know, just bent on bringing hell to my little ass, for whatever reason. I mean, it just never failed! Because it was like, if it wasn't a slap, then it would be a pinch, and if it wasn't a pinch, then it would be the pulling of the ears, and if it wasn't the pulling of the ears, then it would be being yelled and cursed at, and if it wasn't being yelled and cursed at, then it would be being denied food, and if it wasn't being denied food, then it would be being denied to go outside and play (which was the worst, because to a little kid, going outside to play is what they wake up to do).

I mean, it just never failed, because she would always accuse me of doing something or not doing something. I mean, it was crazy, it's like she would always find a reason to punish me. And the worse part of it was, whenever I would have the guts to tell my dad that she hit me or something, it seems like it would just make the situation worse for me, because as soon as my dad would step out the house to go somewhere, she would come straight to where I was and just let me have it, you know, whoop my little ass again. I mean, I just could not win!

And I can still remember this one occasion when, as soon as my dad got home from work and ask me how I was doing, I just straight out told him that she hit and pinched me that afternoon (and I think I had the marks to show him), because I can still hear them in the bedroom arguing. I can't really remember exactly what was said, but I can still hear the shouting (mostly her), as my dad was trying to plead with her to leave me alone. But then, as soon as the argument ended, and as soon as my dad had to go somewhere, and as soon as he slammed the door to leave, there she was, like out of nowhere, coming straight at me, looking really pissed (I mean, I can still see her face from that day even now as I'm writing this), and all I could do was to braise myself for the fury of pain that she was about to unleash on me for telling on her. And so, without hesitation she consumed to whup my little ass while saying stuff like; "Oh, so you think you can tell your daddy on me ha, what you think he's gonna do, he can't do nothing, your little ass is mine, I can whip you anytime I want to!"

Man, those were some of the worse days in my life! And also, to make it even worse still, she had gotten her kids (my step brother and sister) to not like me either. And the funny thing is, I don't remember ever playing with them. And I think the reason why I don't remember is because their mother never really let me go outside to play, and I can remember them always being outside and playing.

And I can vividly remember this one time, this one time that I really wanted to go outside with them, actually, they were going swimming at the neighbor's house, and I was set to go also. I mean I had my towel and everything. But, just before I stepped out the door, their mother grabbed me and said no, no I couldn't go, I couldn't go swimming. Man, I was crushed! Because it's like for the first time it seemed like I was actually going to get to go swimming with them (unless they had planned on drowning me or something, which at that time I wouldn't have put it pass them, because that's how mean they were to me), but as usual, here came another chore that she had for me to do. And I mean, I was the youngest (and only about five or six years old), and they were the oldest, by at least three or four years. But it never failed, because it's like, whenever there was a chore, it seemed like I was the only one called upon to do it, while they were allowed to go play. And so, on this one occasion, I just had had enough of it, I mean, I was just straight out pissed, so much so that I couldn't hide it. Because I mean, there I was, so close to going swimming, you know, finally I'm about to get a chance to go play in the water, which my step brother and sister had already done numerous times. But no, oh no, that would be too much fun for my little ass I guess. I mean it's like, "Oh no he can't have no fun, oh no he can't just be like the other little kids and go outside and play, oh no he must suffer, he must suffer just like me, oh no he must feel the wrath of my own damn misery", that's probably what she was thinking, you know what I mean?

I'm sorry y'all, I just had to let that one out, cause I still get pissed every time I think of it, because it was just so stupid and painful. So excuse me y'all, I won't do it again, but then again, that kind of felt good, you know, letting it out. Hey, I guess Dr. Phil, Oprah, and my wife are right, you know, you gotta talk about your issues so you can let the pain out. I mean, I think I have done pretty good to heal myself so far, I mean, I'm still kind of sane, I mean, I think so anyway ha ha ha ha ha! Anyway, yeah, my wife says I gotta talk about my issues, even the ones from long, long time ago that I think I have already dealt with myself, you know, through prayer and forgiveness. And so, being that I've got so much stuff inside of me, I have no choice but to try this expressing yourself thing, because I'm just not very good at talking about myself. And so, I guess I'm just going to have to force myself to talk about myself, especially now that I have kids, because they too will have to learn how to talk and express themselves, so I guess I'm just going to have to set the example for them, that way they can feel free and comfortable to talk about stuff, instead of just keeping it all boarded up inside. See, I'm doing good already in this book, talking about myself, my wife will be proud, or embarrassed at how much I have shared or will be sharing with y'all when it's all said and done with the book, right, ha ha ha ha ha!

And so anyway, what where we talking about again? Oh yeah, we were talking about me being mad and pissed for not being allowed to go swimming at the last second, because she (my stepmother from hell) decided to find another chore for my six year old self to do so that I couldn't go swimming, which up till today (about 27 years later), I still blame her for me not knowing how to swim, you know? Because I mean, if she had just let me go swimming even just a few times, I'm sure I would have been a swimming champion by now, you know what I mean, ha ha ha ha ha! And then again, maybe it was a blessing in disguise that I didn't get a chance to go swimming with her kids that day, because being the way they were back then, they would have probably drowned my little self, you know, and I wouldn't have gotten a chance to complain about not going swimming like I'm doing right now, you know what I mean, ha ha ha ha ha! But hey, that's life and that's how it goes sometimes, you know, because life sometimes is just so shitty and there's nothing you can do about it, especially when you are just a little kid.

And so anyway, or, wait a minute, do you want to know what the chore was that she wanted me to do? Ok, I'll tell you! She wanted me to watch the fish dry, you know, well, maybe you don't know. See, it's like this, you clean the fish, then you put them outside in the bright sun for a few hours till they are hard and dry, (I mean, this was common practice were I'm from), and you kind of had to sit there and watch out for the birds, you know, so they won't come and swoop up and eat the fishes. But the problem here was, the sun was already kind of starting to set, and I was already set to go swimming, so I tried to beg for her to let me go swimming, because I had a feeling that she was pulling the fish chore thing just to stop me from going. Because really, if she really wanted to get the fishes dry that day, then she would have brought them out during the early afternoon, you know, when the sun is at its' full beam. But of course I lost my plea, and so I had no choice but to watch them damn fishes dry. So anyway, there I was, mad as hell, and I can see her peeping at me from the window in the house, you know, making sure that I was still there. And so as I sat there (foaming at the mouth), I started to pray and hope that a bird would actually come and get one of them fishes, you know, just to get back at her. And I wasn't really worried about the whupping that would definitely fall upon me, by her hands. Because at that point, I had just had enough of her antics, and also, by now, I had pretty much had gotten used to physical pain, you know, I had learned how to deal with it. I mean, I was so used to it that tears were very hard for me to find in my eyes anymore. I mean, I think I had cried them all out by this time, you know, because I felt like I had no more tears to shed (and I was only about six or seven years old).

And so, as I set there beside the fishes, and as my step mother (from hell) would peep out on me from time to time, from the corner of my eyes I saw this big bird starting to fly low, low and lower, descending and circling coming towards me. My heart skipped for a second as I came to the realization that a beating will be mine indeed if I do go through with my plan to let the bird come and swoop one of the fishes away.

And so, there I was, just watching the bird come lower and lower, and usually by this point I would have already shushed and chased the bird away. But I was still thinking and deciding whether the beating and or any other punishment would be worth it or not. But then, as the bird got even closer, I looked at the window and looking back at me was my step-mother, and she had this look like, you better not dare let that bird get those fishes. So there I was, looking at the bird coming even closer, and then glancing at the window and seeing my step-mother also looking at the bird coming closer. And at that exact moment, when I started to think maybe I should just shush and chase the bird away, I heard the voices of my step brother and sister coming loud and clear from the neighbor's house enjoying their swimming as they laugh and splash water everywhere. At that moment my decision was made, they can all go to hell, so come on birdie, come and get you some fish, and I'll just have to take my beating like a man!

And so, the bird noticing that I was not chasing it away, obliged my offer of fish, and came and smoothly and gently grabbed himself a thick juicy delicious looking fish. And oh man, you should have seen the look on my stepmother's face, it was priceless, well worth the beating I got. And I mean, really, I don't even remember the beating, because I was just so delighted in the fact that I was not scared of her anymore. Because I mean, sure she could beat me or deny me food, or talk to me like I was a bastard child, but I had become hard headed enough to not let her get to me, you know, not let her get inside my head. I mean, it was like a protective mechanism, you know, it's like, sure she could abuse my body, but I won't let her abuse my mind.

And so, that night for dinner she made me sit in the kitchen (by myself) and eat the hard part of the rice from the pot, you know, the part that's in the bottom of the pot that's hard to scrape out. But unbeknownst to her, I had come to enjoy the hard part, you know, from having to eat it all the time. But the problem was, this time the hard part was a little bit extra hard, so I needed a little bit of sauce to put on top of it. But she wouldn't even let me have some sauce, because she said the sauce had fish flavor in eat and since I wasn't getting any fish to eat, I couldn't get no sauce either. So I looked at my dad, trying to get his attention (because they were all sitting at the dining room table), but he didn't look up, so I knew I had lost the argument. So I just went back to the kitchen and tried my best to enjoy the dried up hard as hell plain rice, which I think took about ten years for it to finally digest through my stomach, you know what I mean, ha ha ha ha ha!

So yeah, anyway man, life was rough during my stepmother from hell period. But I think I managed to come out of it not too scarred as otherwise I could have been (by the grace of God of course). Because there are a lot of people who were abused as little kids or kids period and find themselves psychologically messed up as adults. You know, it's like they just can't get over the physical and or emotional scars from the abuse to allow themselves to move on and lead healthy and productive lives. I mean, this kind of abuse and any kind of abuse for that matter, can be very devastating for people to deal with, especially children. And unfortunately there's a lot of children in this world that are being abused both physically and or emotionally every day.

I mean, it's crazy, there's just to many mean people out there in the world. And the funny thing is, it's not strangers that poses the biggest capacity to abuse your kids, oh no, most abusers will come from your own family or close friends. I mean, I myself got caught up in a second extreme abusive situation, and this was just a few years (like two or three years) after the step mother from hell situation had ended after she left, and during the time I had to stay with relatives while my dad was looking for a new job. And so I ended up staying with one of my aunts, whom I hardly knew, you know, they just told me that that was my aunt and I just said, ok, cool, that's fine with me (like I had any choice in the matter, right?). And so I mean, the aunt was cool, you know, as long as you did as you were told, she pretty much just left you alone, you know, she let you be a kid. But her daughter, oh boy, I don't know what the hell her problem was, because she was just so vicious, you know, straight out mean. I mean, the only time that she was nice to me was when she needed me, I mean, to put it more correctly, the only time that she was nice to me was when she needed me to send out a massage to one of her boyfriends, or acquaintances, or something. I mean, I don't know what the hell those guys were to her, but all I know is that, I just got really sick and tired of having to walk a few blocks to some dude's house and pass a message about money. And some dudes would give me money to give to her and some wouldn't. And for whatever reason she would be mad at me for not collecting the money, you know, like I didn't do a good job of convincing the guy that he really need to pay up or else. I mean, I was only about eight or nine years old, and so my voice and my little body was nowhere near developed enough to be trying to threaten anybody, let alone a mean looking dude.

    I mean, I used to hate it, you know? But she usually always succeeded in using me, until one day I just had had enough of it and just refused and told her she could go ahead and hit me if she wanted to, but I ain't doing it no more. Because I mean, most of these dudes looked plain all scary to me, because they hardly smiled and their eyes always looked blood shut red. And most of the times they wouldn't even let me finish my sentence, because as soon as I would say her name, they would tell me to leave immediately and to go tell her to go f@%k herself. And so I would leave and walk very slowly home as I'm trying to think of a better way to put and tell her what the man had said. But of course she would go off and blame me for not collecting some money, like it was my damn job to do so. I mean, it's not like she was giving me a cut off of it (besides buying me a soda once in a while after yelling at me for not collecting all of the money that they owed her), which I think she should have, because it was really scary having to face those dudes.

    I mean, sometimes these dudes did try their best to be nice to me, you know, smiling, saying what's up little man, shaking my little hand, and even give me a little money for myself, but most of them, they looked like they didn't know how to smile. And I can remember this one time (vaguely though, because it was such a long time ago), I knocked on this one guy's door, and when he opened the door, he was only wearing a towel around his waist and he looked really sweaty and was breathing very heavy, and as he opened the door a little wider, I could see two women half naked in the back, kind of looking to see who it was. Oh man, I was really scared! I don't think I managed to say anything, I just remember running, running as fast as I could to get away from there. Man, those were tough times, and they seemed to be lasting forever, as I waited for my dad to come and get me. But she was really mean, and she said and did a lot of mean stuff too, but I won't get into them, or maybe I'll just have to tell them to Dr. Phil one of these days, you know what I mean, ha ha ha ha ha! But I mean, it's crazy how people are just so willing to abuse other peoples' kids. And during that time (when I was so tired of the abuse), that is when I started shutting down more and more, and more and more. I mean, I just became a hard core loner, you know, happier when I'm by myself.

And this is when I started becoming very hard headed, because I had just had enough of people picking on me, you know, and treating me like a bastard child. And this is the time that I started becoming more and more of a day dreamer, you know, be in my own little world, as I'm waiting for my dad to come and take me with him, after he finds and secures a new job.

But so, yeah, those were really tough times, and I just could not believe that I had become a victim of another abusive situation. Because I mean, I had just came from an abusive situation with my stepmother (from hell) just about two years before, and I just couldn't believe that I got caught up in another one just so soon. I mean, I started to feel like this was going to be my life, you know, I was just going to have to endure being abused until I got old enough to either be on my own, or fight back, you know, whichever came first.

I did get a chance to stay with other relatives from time to time though, but I guess most of them did not have enough room for me or something, because I always ended up coming back to my aunt with the mean daughter. I mean, she had older brothers whom I would hang out with from time to time, but she was more in charge of me, because they were too busy with work and staff, and her mom (my aunt) seemed to always be at work, or just too tired to be bothered. And so, she pretty much had me to herself to do as she pleased, and she didn't really care of who said what, I mean, she was just out of control. Because I mean, sometimes her brothers would tell her to ease up, you know, to leave me alone, but no, she would even curse them out, I mean, she was totally out of control.

Because I mean, I can still remember this one time when one of her brothers was trying to tell her something (I don't remember what it was all about exactly, because they always went at it, actually she went at it, because he was one of those quiet types, you know, the ones that will only say a few words to you, and then if you keep yapping at the mouth, they will without additional warning, they will consume to whup your ass till they get tired), but as usual, she just kept yapping at the mouth, I mean, cursing and insulting him real bad, and I mean, I could see him starting to turn red, real red, I mean, I could see it in his eyes and everything, but she's still going at it, yelling and saying stuff like; "You ain't nothing, what you think you gonna do, you ain't nothing but a punk, that's why you can't find a real job, that's why you still living at home, ain't you too old to be living at home with your mama, I bet you don't even have a girlfriend do you" (actually this part was actually a little bit harsher, because I kind of remember her saying something about his manhood, you know, suggesting that he might be gay or something). I mean, she just let him have it, and I was standing there like, oh no, you done did it now, because the next thing you know, he started to beat the sh%t out of her, I mean, he really let her have it.

It was crazy, because I had never seen him that mad before, I mean, I don't think anybody else did either. Because I mean, he was just such a quiet and nice guy, and so nobody thought he would lose his cool, because a lot of the other times when they argued, he would just walk away and let her get away with it. But I guess not this time, I guess this time he had just had enough of her nonsense, because he just started beating her down, I mean, he beat her like she was a man, you know, straight punching and kicking her, I mean, he was whupping her like she stole something, I mean, she started bleeding and everything. I mean, dude had lost it, and she was gonna feel every personal pain that he was keeping inside. Because he just kept beating her, and beating her and beating her, and she just kept screaming and crying for help, and nobody would help her. I mean, people were just standing around watching (I guess that's what happens when you are not friendly to people, you know, they won't help you in your time of need), you know, with the look of, oh well, that's what you get for being so mean.

And she was really mean, and not just to me, but to almost everybody around her, you know, other people in the neighborhood. I mean, it didn't matter whether you were a guy or girl, she would curse you out just the same. I mean, it seemed like nobody in the neighborhood liked her, because she would always be having shouting matches with somebody. It was crazy! I mean even her own mother could get cursed out by her, you know? I mean I don't know what her problem was (I'm suspecting not having her father in her life might have something to do with it), but she was just straight out of control.

But I couldn't take it anymore, I mean, I actually started to feel sorry for her, because she was crying so hard and looked so helpless that I started to worry, you know, I started to fear that he might kill her! I mean, really, I thought he was gonna beat her to death. Because by this time she was on the ground and everything, but dude just kept beating her, you know, kicking her and everything. And so, there I was, praying that someone will stop him, because I couldn't do it, I mean, I was only about eight years old, and he was about nineteen or twenty I would guess, and she was about eighteen or nineteen I would guess, and I was scared he might beat me up by accident, you know, because he seemed to have so much rage in him. But so, sooner than later, a few guys realizing that dude just won't stop beating her, they rushed in and pulled him away from her. But they had a hard time pulling him away, because dude was bent on still beating her, I mean, it was crazy, they had to hold him for a long time to make sure he had truly calmed down. I mean, I felt sorry for her, as she laid there crying and bleeding. I mean, dude beat her so bad that she had to go to the hospital, I mean, it was crazy! But then of course, when she got better, she went back to being her old mean self. But one thing for sure, she never ever dared to disrespect her brother again, and if she did, she did it from very far away, you know, out of his reach.

But yeah, those were crazy times man, and unfortunately for me, I was the only kid staying there at the time (well actually there was her little sister, but she was way too young, and plus, she was her sister, unlike me, I was pretty much an outsider who just happened to be related to her), so of course I would have to bear the brunt of her evilness. I mean, it just never failed, it seemed like I couldn't do nothing right, I mean, I just couldn't win!

And this is when I started to think more and more about my mother (you know, my birth mother), you know, just wondering where she might be and why they won't just take me to go live with her. And then I started thinking, oh man, maybe she doesn't want me to live with her, you know, because I'm sure they could find her if they really wanted to, you know what I mean? But I now know that I couldn't go stay with her, because the dude she was married to didn't really want me there, you know, he didn't want to feed and or take care of a kid that wasn't his. And I mean, I don't think he even wanted or did a good job of taking care of his own kids (two of them being one of my sisters and a brother from my mother's side who happen to not be talking to him, you know, and actually, they don't even want to see their own father any more, I mean, it's crazy and I gotta find out what their beef with him is exactly, one of these days).

And so, my mom couldn't really take me in, so I just had to wait for my dad to get situated and come and get me from where I was staying. And I mean, all this stuff I have just come to find out not that long ago, you know, in my adult years, as I have come to know my mother and my other brother and sisters from my mom's side, who are doing their best to fill me in on their lives growing up. Because I really don't know them like that, you know, I mean it's like we are still kind of still feeling each other out, you know, just sharing little by little.

And I mean, even with my mother, I really don't know her that well, really, I feel like I still don't know her at all, you know, besides knowing her face, her name, her voice and stuff like that, you know what I mean? And so, really, I still have a lot of questions for her, which I know one of these days I'm going to have to ask her, because I just got to know some things, you know, so that way I can feel more comfortable around her, and so that way I can feel free to enjoy her more, you know what I mean? Because it's like, right now, when I'm around her, or talking to her over the phone, I don't really know what to say, you know, because I just don't know what buttons to push or not to push, you know what I mean? Because there are some things that I would like to ask her and to talk to her about, but I just don't know how to start, you know, because I just don't know what and or how much pain she might be holding inside. Because I can kind of sense that she has some pain inside, you know, because it's like, whenever I hear her voice, or whenever I see her and look into her eyes, I can kind of sense that she has a lot of stuff that she would like to tell me and or ask me, but, she too is having a hard time trying to bring a serious conversation on. And I think all this is because we just don't know each other well, you know, we just don't know how each other's lives has been before we found each other again. And so now, being that we don't have the opportunity to see or talk to each other much, the little time that we get to talk, we take the easy way out and talk about casual stuff, you know, nothing heavy, you know, nothing about the past. And come to think of it, we have never really talked about anything regarding the past, and I think this is because we both know that we might end up crying, because whenever I get a chance to go visit her, when it comes time for me to leave, I can see her trying her best to fight her tears back, which makes me wanna cry also.

And also, whenever I finish talking to her on the phone, just when I'm about to hang up, as I'm trying to say good bye, my voice will usually start to crack, you know, I become unable to speak, you know, because I'm fighting back tears. I mean, it happens to me almost every time, and that's why I don't like to call her too much, because it usually takes me a couple of hours (if not days) to calm my emotions and put things back in perspective so I can concentrate on my daily duties as a father and a husband. But I know one of these days I'm just gonna have to sit down with her and just ask her a bunch of tough personal questions and force her to talk, talk and talk, even if we'll have to cry ourselves a river afterwards, you know what I mean? And I mean, I think I'm do myself a cry, because I mean, I haven't cried in so long that my wife keeps telling me maybe I should try to cry sometimes. I mean, my wife thinks that I'm holding a lot of stuff inside, and so maybe crying may help relieve whatever pain that might be inside of me. But I keep telling her that, I just don't think that I have any more tears in my eyes, you know, I just think all my tears were finished when I was around six years old, you know, when I was living with my step mother from hell. Because I remember I used to just cry to myself in my room until I fell asleep a lot back in those days when I was little, as I would be thinking and wondering where my mother was and why I couldn't just be with her.

But anyway, yeah man, living with my aunt and her mean daughter was rough, especially since I was by myself, you know, with no sister or brother to lean on. I mean, I do remember two of my cousins coming to stay there for a while, which helped to take away some of the abuse, but I still felt lonely, because I really didn't know them. And then too, I do remember my brother (from my dad's side) coming to stay there, but I still felt lonely, because I hardly knew him either. And I remember thinking to myself then, when he was dropped off, why in the hell are they bringing him into this hell hole, you know, because I mean, he has a mother, and she doesn't live that far. But I guess his mother wanted him to go and stay with his father, but at that time our dad did not have a place of his own yet, so I thought that was very mean for them to bring him there, because I knew he was gonna have to experience some of her evilness, which can be very cruel. And so, sure thing, her evilness did reveal itself to him, and as soon as his mother found out, she came and got him. And to my surprise, she took me too (which my father had arranged, which to this day I appreciate her for taking me in), which was a welcoming relief for me, because I was ready for a change of scenery, you know, a change of environment, you know, so I can kind of catch my breath and get some room to breathe a little, you know what I mean?

And so anyway, yeah, going to stay with my brother's mom was a welcoming relief for me, because it gave me a chance to be a kid, you know, to feel free to play. But the problem was, by this time, I had already become so much of a hard core loner that, I just didn't know how to play with the other kids in the neighborhood. I mean, I just didn't know how to make friends. Because it's like, a lot of times some of the kids would see me sitting in the front porch doing nothing in particular, and so they would try to get me to play with them, but most often than not, I would refuse, preferring to just sit there and just day dream (which I was very good at).

I mean, I don't know what it was, but I just could not relate to other kids, you know, I mean, I just didn't know how to play and not worry about nothing. I mean, I remember how I used to watch them other kids play and think to myself, "Man, they sure look like they are having a lot of fun!", but for some reason, I just could not bring myself to join them, because I just never felt comfortable, you know, I just never felt comfortable enough to play with them.

And I mean, sure sometimes I would force myself to go and play with them, but this would be actually only when they were playing sports, because when it came to sports, forget it, that was my first love, and I was very good at it. And so, as soon as the neighborhood kids found out that I was kind of good in sports, whenever they needed an extra player, they would always come looking for me, which was cool, because I really enjoyed playing sports. Because it's like, when I used to play sports, all my problems would for a few minutes or hours they would just disappear, you know, I wouldn't be thinking or day dreaming about a better life. I mean, when I used to play sports, those were the most enjoyable moments ever, I mean, the thrill of competing and losing myself in the game was just so sweet and really refreshing to my soul. I mean, and the fact that I was kind of good I think helped me enjoy playing even more, because it gave me the chance to get the ball more often and to score more often, which was great. But as time went on I started to refuse to go and play with the other kids more and more, and this is because the games just started to get too rough, especially when we would go and play kids from the other neighborhoods. Because it's like, it almost never failed that a fight would break out, either during or after the game. I mean, it just never failed! And so, I just started getting tired of all the fighting after the games. And actually, the fighting would usually start during the game, usually towards the end of the game, when the other team would start to cheat because they realized that they were about to lose the game.

I mean, what sore losers they were, you know, because they just couldn't take losing like a man, they just always had to start something. And the funny thing was that, we were usually the youngest neighborhood team, you know, we had the youngest players (ranging from 11 to 16 years old, while most of the other teams averaged around 13 to 16 years old), with me usually being the youngest at 11 years old. And so, when the fights would break out, I usually felt helpless, you know, because my little self, if I wasn't careful, I could find my little self getting whupped. But usually I was very aware of what was going on, and so, whenever a fight broke out, I was usually ready, you know, to either run or stand beside the biggest kid on our side and try to land some punches of my own (you know, with my little fists). And also, if a fight happened to break out before I was ready or aware of it, the big kid on our side would always come looking for me in the mayhem and tell me to stand right beside him as we either made our escape and ran, or just stood there and tried to fight. But a lot of times though we would end up running, because we almost always played in the other team's neighborhood, and so, we usually always got out numbered in the fights because not only would we have to fight the players, we would almost always have to fight their fans too (you know, the other kids from their hoods).

I mean, it just started to get to be too much, and dangerous also! Because I mean, people started bringing chains, sticks, rocks, and even 2 by 4s (you know, those wooden sticks that were very popular back in the days, you know, back in the 80s and early 90s, you know, before carrying knives and guns became normal facts of life in our society today). And I can kind of remember someone pulling out a knife, a knife! I mean, sure nowadays pulling out a knife is not a big deal, because people don't fist fight anymore nowadays, you know, rather they just shoot each other like crazy, I mean, it's crazy, it's stupid, I mean it's like people don't value each other's lives anymore, it's scary!

But back in those days, people would look at you like you were crazy if you pulled out a knife. Because it's like, back in those days, nobody was trying to kill anybody, I mean, oh no, not at all, you know? Because I mean, back in those days, it was all about fist fighting, you know, hand to hand combat, you know, to see who can punch faster and harder. And I mean sure, chains, sticks and other stuff would come into play in more serious situations, but knifes were rare, because nobody really wanted to kill anybody, you know, they just wanted to hand you a good ass whupping, you know, and make sure that you knew about it. But these days, man, it's crazy! I mean, people just don't fist fight anymore, and if they do, they have to watch out for the person that they just fought with doesn't come back and shoot them with a gun later on, especially if they gave the person a good ass whopping, you know what I mean?

I mean it's crazy, it's scary, and it's very dangerous in these streets nowadays, because people are just killing each other like it's nothing, you know, and they are killing each other over really stupid stuff too. I mean, it's just so crazy and I just don't get it, I mean, I just don't understand how someone can shoot and kill another person just because that person somehow had disrespected them. I mean, are you kidding me? And the funny thing is, this disrespect can be as simple as stepping on someone's shoes, or, bumping into them, or, talking to their girlfriend by accident (you know, seeing a pretty girl and going to talk to her not knowing or noticing that her boyfriend is around there somewhere), you know, simple innocent mistakes like that, and these are what people are calling disrespect and killing each other over. I mean, it's just stupid, it's just so stupid!

And I think the reason for all this stupidity killings these days is because there's just too many guns out there in the hands of the wrong people, and actually really, there's just too many guns out there period. Because I mean, anybody can make an irrational decision (when over-heated or over-come with rage) and end up shooting and killing someone over a stupid situation when they have a gun handy. I mean, it's doesn't take much when you have a gun in your hand to feel the urge to use it, because there's just so much stressful situations that you can find yourself in on a daily basis. And that's why it is better to just not carry a gun if you don't really have to, because you will end up using it sooner than later, and most often times you will end up using it for the wrong reasons, especially if you are very temperamental.

But so anyway, yeah, I was so tired of those fights after the games that I just started not participating in the games too much, because the fighting would always ruin the joy of the game for me. But of course, once in a while I couldn't resist but to go and play, because it seemed as though everybody in our surrounding neighborhoods wanted to play us. I mean it's like word was spreading that those young'ns from our neighborhood (us) are pretty good. I mean, we had everybody trying to play us, I mean, even far away neighborhoods. Because I remember this one time we went to play this one neighborhood that was a pretty good walking distance away, and I remember thinking to myself, "Man, where in the hell are we going?", because it seemed pretty far. And I also remember thinking, "Oh man, there's no way I can run all the way home from here if a fight breaks out, and these dudes could leave me behind to get beat up!" I mean, we had walked a long way, and I was only about eleven years old, and the other kids with me were between thirteen and sixteen years old, and so, I was afraid that if we had to run after the game, I was afraid that I wouldn't have been able to keep up with them. But I went ahead and played the game and I remember it being a very good game, but I don't remember if we won or lost, because it was such a long time ago. And I also don't remember if a fight broke out or not, most likely it didn't, because I'm sure I would have been able to remember if it did, especially if I had to run a long way home, you know what I mean, ha ha ha ha ha!

And so anyway, yeah, those were the good old days, when I used to live with my brother's mom. I mean, it was ok to live there (in terms of household stress and what not), because his mom pretty much treated me just the same as she treated them, you know, she didn't show them too much favoritism over me, which was cool. The only problem was, I was just so miserable most of the time during that time. And the reason why I think I was so miserable is because, I think I was just missing my own mother tremendously during that time, you know. Because it was like, you know, they had their mom, and so I was thinking, hey, why can't I be with my own mom. And their younger brother used to remind me from time to time that their mom wasn't my mom, you know, like when he was mad at me for something (you know how little kids are). And so he used to run to his mom to tell on me (on stuff I did or didn't even do, or when I would threaten to kick his butt for messing with me), and while running to his mom he would say stuff like, "Oh, I'ma tell my mama, I'ma tell my mama!", you know, and just for a few minutes there I would be reminded that their mom is not my mom also, you know what I mean? But other than that, staying with them was pretty ok, because I had plenty of time to be by myself and do what I really loved to do, which was, to daydream of course. I mean, I would daydream and I would daydream and I would daydream and I would daydream! I mean, it was great, and I was pretty good at it, especially when it can to dreaming about being rich, oh man, I think if I had a dollar for every time I day dreamed about being rich, I think I would definitely be rich by now. And I mean, I'm not just talking about any kind of rich, oh no, I'm talking about majestic kind of rich, you know, royalty kind of richness!

And I mean, sure almost every little kid that grows up poor dreams of becoming rich when they grow up, but I'm telling you, they had nothing on me. Because it's like, not only was I daydreaming about being rich, but I was also trying to plan of how I was gonna become rich. I mean, I'm talking about serious stuff here (you know, as far as my little eleven year old mind could think of), trying to come up with ideas, you know, besides a lemonade stand. I mean, it was serious business trying to brainstorm an idea, you know, a great idea. But I found it very hard to come up with an idea, so one day I asked this dude, this man, our next door neighbor whom I had befriended, so one day I just asked him (during one of our many talks that we would have, actually it used to be more like, me asking him questions and him answering the best way he could for my eleven year old self to understand. I mean, I would ask that dude a bunch of questions, you know, about any and everything, and the poor guy would do his best to answer them), so one day I just asked him, "Hey, what do people do to become rich?" And the poor guy looked shocked for a second, because he gave me this quizzical look, you know, trying to figure out whether I was serious or just wondering. And then so figuring that I was serious with the question, he gave me a very good answer (which I am still chasing almost twenty two years later, I'm still waiting for the chance to implement it), and the answer was, "Well, if you want to become rich, really rich, you gonna have to start your own business and work hard to grow it until it gets to be big, big and real big, and then you will be rich!" And so that was it, that was the formula that I needed to be rich, you know, start a business and grow it until it's real big and then bingo, I'll be rich! And so, this is the formula that I have been waiting to implement my whole life. I mean, ever since then, I have soaked up any and everything that has to do with business. And when I say everything, I mean everything, you know, like books, tapes, videos, newspapers, infomercials, school classes, college classes, and my own entrepreneurial failures so far. I mean, this business ambition of mine has been driving me crazy for years, from when I was eleven years old till now.

 I mean it's crazy, especially when I think of how long it's taking me to get started, you know, to find a way to get started without proper financing. Because I have come to understand that, it takes money to make money, you know what I mean? I mean, I have come to understand that, the bigger your dream is, and or, the more complex your dream is, the more money and the more energy and the more patience you will need. Because see, in my early years I just figured that I was smart enough to just wing it, you know what I mean? I mean, it's like, I just figured that I was smart enough to just start something and without proper planning or capital, I thought I would be able to just figure a way through obstacles that lack of capital and lack of planning would have prepared me for. I mean, you know, I just thought I was smart enough to out-smart the system, you know?

And so, the rude awakening that I encountered in my first ambitious venture was very educational, I mean, I learned so much about business, about myself, and also about other ambitious people in general. I mean, that kind of education you can't buy in a classroom, because it goes on in your head even when you are sleeping. I mean, it's like a twenty four hour tutorial that just won't quit, unless you yourself quit first and say "No mass!", because you just can't take the stress no more, or, the business tells you no more by failing because you ran out of money to sustain it, you know, you ran out of money to sustain it until you start to make a profit. I mean, business is no joke, it can actually really ruin you financially and mentally if you don't know what the hell you are doing. I mean, it ruined me a little bit (as far as credit cards and other little liability stuff that messed up my credit, but it could have been worse), but the good thing for me was that I didn't have that much money to lose as opposed to others that I know about. But it wasn't that much of a big deal for me (the failure) because I kind of knew that I was just winging it, you know, to try and test the system and see if I could out smart it.

So really I wasn't surprised when I failed, I mean, I just took it as a learning experience and better luck next time kind of approach to it. Because I definitely now know that I can do it, and do it good, you know? Because as I analyze where I went wrong the first time around, I can clearly see my faults and the fact that I trusted other people too much, you know, to do their part. And also, the lack of financing and planning were huge obstacles to overcome, no matter how hard or smart I tried to maneuver around it. But hey, I learned a lot from the experience and my college professor used to remind us all the time that, entrepreneurs fail at least three times before succeeding. So I guess I can count that as my first failure, but I for sure don't want to go through any more failures before I finally succeed, and that's why this time around I have made a conscious decision to really take my time and do it right, you know, especially since I'm doing it without a lot of financing again (because them damn banks won't give me any money, them punks, ha ha ha ha ha!).

But yeah, it was a good learning experience, especially when it comes to learning about other people and their fake ass ambitions. I mean, I never knew that there are so many fake people running around thinking they want to do business or chase a dream. I mean, I never knew how many people out there are sleep walking through their daydreams. I mean, what I mean is, I never knew how many people out there don't have a clue to what the hell it means to be ambitious. Ok, I don't think I'm doing a good job of explaining myself here, because what I'm really trying to say is, I can't believe how many fakers are out there, you know, people who are all talk and no action. I mean, my goodness gracious! Because it's like, when I used to have my office and I used to meet with people for various reasons, a lot of them were very good talkers, you know, telling me stuff like, "Oh yeah Nigel, don't worry about a thing, I got you, I'ma hook you up, it's a done deal, I got connections, I know so and so and so and so!"

I mean, these people can really talk, and if you are not careful, you will think you have just hit the jock pot, you know, they'll have you believing that you have met the person that will help you take your business or career to the next level. I mean it's crazy, and that's why to this day I definitely don't trust fast talkers. I mean, I never trusted fast talkers before, but now, forget it, if you talk to fast around me, the chances of me trusting you will be very hard, even if what you are saying is true. So if you are a fast talker by nature, if you ever find yourself having to tell me something very important and or serious, I would suggest that you try your best to slow down your speech so that my subconscious defensive mechanism is not triggered.

Hey, it's hard out there, and so you definitely have got to know what the hell it is that you are doing or trying to do, because if you don't, you gonna crush and burn, just like I did, the first time around, you know what I mean, ha ha ha ha ha!

But so anyway, yeah, this business thing has been with me ever since that dude introduced it to me when I was eleven years old, when I was staying with my brother's mom, and spent most of my time day dreaming to be rich. And I think that dude was really my first role model, because I remember I was so impressed watching him conduct his transactions with his retailers (he made and distributed lamps), you know, because he used take me with him from time to time. Because really I had nothing else to do, and he would always see me sitting in the front porch looking bored as hell, so he would just ask me if I wanted to go watch him conduct some business, because he knew I was all into that business stuff. And so of course I would always jump at the opportunity to go watch business people handle their business.

And I mean, that whole business stuff fascinated me, and from that day on I definitely knew that is exactly what I wanted to be when I grew up, you know, a businessman. Or, and also, I remember him even letting me carry and deliver some of the lamps for him to his retailers, which was cool, because he would actually pay me some money. I mean, he didn't pay me a lot, but for an eleven-year-old kid, back in the early to mid-eighties, it was good money. Because not only could I buy some sodas (yes more than one if I wanted to), but I could also by some chips and some candy if I wanted to and still have some change left over. I mean, I would have probably done it for free if he ask me to, but I appreciated the money and you bets believe I was saving almost every penny of it, you know, because I had a business to open in a few years I had figured, not knowing how much money it would actually cost me to open a business, but hey, dreaming is good sometimes, and for me, it kept me focused and sane, as I waited for my dad to come and get me.

But yeah, those were some good moments, especially when I would be hanging out with dude (I have kind of forgotten the guy's name, and this is why I keep referring to him as "dude", just in case you are wondering), because he would always be talking about business to me, and I would just be soaking up everything, you know, because I didn't want to miss a thing. And then he started teaching me how to make lamps, oh man, I was so excited, because I was right there in the shop, standing next to his twin nephews, learning right along with them, and they were at least four or five years older than me.

And so I was just enjoying learning how to make them things, but they looked like they didn't want to be nowhere near there. And then I remember one day, in front of his nephews, dude announced that he was planning on expending the business, and also open a storefront, and guess who he was gonna let help in running the storefront (along with the nephews of course), that's right you guessed it right, he was gonna let yours truly, little self me, the day dreamer, the business craver, he was gonna let the ambitious little me help in making sure the store runs smoothly. And of course I had no idea what making sure the store runs smoothly really meant, but I didn't care, because all I cared about was that I was finally gonna be right there front and center doing and learning business first hand.

Man was I excited! The twins though didn't look too happy with the idea of me being included in the mix of things, I think they kind of felt like their uncle was kind of showing me too much favoritism. And actually come to think of it, maybe he did kind of show me a little bit more favoritism over them, or maybe it's just that he kind of expected more from them than he did from me, because hell, I was only eleven years old. Or maybe he truly did see something special in me, because I kind of remember him always saying that honesty and hard work will take you far, and as far as I can remember I have always done my best to be honest and I'm never afraid of hard work. Anyway, whatever it was that made him take a liking to me I really appreciated, because God knows I did need someone to pay me some attention during that time of loneliness. And come to think about it, he is the one that helped kind of shape a lot of my thinking and out-look on life and spirituality for that matter. Because it's like, I remember that I used to ask him a bunch of questions about life and God and stuff like that. I mean, he did a pretty good job of answering a lot of my questions, and the ones he couldn't answer I think he just told me I will understand them when I get older. I mean, to tell you the truth, now that I think about it, dude actually became more like a father figure to me during that time, which was cool, cause he kind of looked out for me.

And so anyway, yeah, I was very excited about working at the store when it opens. But, as the store was nearing its' completion, and as my dream of working there was about to become a reality, I got word that my dad was ready for me (and my brother for that matter) to go and stay with him. Oh man, what a mixed emotion I had that day! Because in one hand, my dad was finally ready for me to go and stay with him (which I had been waiting for), and on the other hand, my dream of working at the store and learning business first hand was just about to become a reality. Oh man, I didn't know what to do! I mean, it was so bad that I almost thought about running away so that I wouldn't be sent to my dad, you know, so I could get a chance to work at the store. I mean, that's how intense the emotions were, I mean, I came so close to running away! But of course I didn't run away, and so I had to go tell dude that I wouldn't be able to work at the store because I'm about to be moving away and go live with my dad. And I kind of remember the dude looking kind of sad when I told him. And so that was it, you know, it was time for a new chapter in my life. But I wasn't really ready to start over again, you know, I wasn't ready to refocus and redirect my life in a new place and or environment, which of course I had to do. And the sad part about the whole situation for me till this day is, I never again was able to find that dude. I mean, I did try to go and see him at the town that we lived in at the time (when I lived with my brother's mom), but I think they had already moved by then. And I couldn't even tell if the store was ever really used or opened at all, because for some strange reason, it kind of looked a little bit unfinished, just like the same way that I had left it about five years earlier. So I don't know, but I do feel some kind of void not knowing whatever happened to that dude and his businesses. But, I guess that is life right, you meet people, you get to know them, you get to befriend them, and then, as the world turns, you may never see them again. But hey, that is life, and life is very unpredictable! And so I guess that's why they say enjoy people while you have them, because you never know what curve balls life will throw your way or their way to cause disruptions of acquaintance, communication, and or tranquility. But hey, that's life, and life demands that we move on!

Anyway so, yeah, I never got a chance to work in that store, because it was time to go and live with my dad again, you know, after about three or four years of living with various relatives. And as I think about it now, those three or four years did a lot to set my personality now as a man. Because as I think about it, with all the stuff that I went through during that time, I really didn't have anybody who was close enough for me to lean on and find some strength in. I mean, sure they were my relatives, but really to me they felt like strangers, because I really did not know them before I went to stay with them, and so, even though they were introduced to me as relatives, to me, they were strangers. And I think the other thing that made it harder for me to fit in was that, I usually was the only kid my age in the household (except for when I stayed with my brother's mom), which made it hard for me to find someone to play with or to share my burdens with. And when I went to stay with my brother's mom, even though him and his other brother and sister where more my age, it took me a while to relax and feel comfortable to play with them because to me they were strangers. I mean, I had known my brother a little bit from the short time that he had come to stay with my dad a little bit, but we were way too young, and so I never really got to know him like that, you know what I mean?

And so, it's like, since I didn't have anybody else to confide in, most of the times I just found myself having to confide in myself, which was kind of hard to do sometimes because it took a lot to try to convince myself that I was tough enough to take it and that whatever I was going through was only temporally, you know, this too shall pass. But it was hard, I won't lie, but I knew I was tough enough to deal with it, I mean, I was just too determined not to let anything or anyone break me, you know, I was just too determined to stay sane. And during this time is when I started to think to myself, "You know what, sometimes life can deal you a bad hand, but you don't have to except that bad hand, and sure you might not be able to do anything about your situation right now, but soon enough you'll be grown enough to lead your own life and make yourself happy!"

    I mean, I kid you not, these are the types of thoughts that were going through my head as a little kid, you know, trying to figure out the meaning of life. I mean, I did so much thinking when I was little, that my childhood just passed me by. I mean, I just didn't know how to be a kid, because I was just too consumed with growing up and leading my own life, you know, so I could make myself happy, you know? Because by that time I had figured that, well, it looked like all the grown-ups in my life had failed to bring me a sense of happiness, so I figured that I was gonna have to be the one to bring my own sense of happiness in my life. And so, of course I had to wait until I was old enough to be on my own, you know, and lead my own life. But as soon as I was on my own, oh yeah, I started right away working on my happiness. And to tell you the truth, I think I have done a pretty good job of it so far. Because I mean, sure I don't have much money (actually I'm still pretty broke), and sure I'm still living paycheck to paycheck, and sure I still pay my bills a few months late, and sure my credit is messed up, and so on and so on, but, I'm still going after my dreams, and I have a wonderful wife and kids, and I am very secure about myself.

    And so, all and all, I am very happy with who I am as a person, and I'm very happy with how my life has turned out so far. I mean, sure I haven't reached my dreams and aspirations yet, but I am happy that I am still chasing them. Because I mean, I have seen and know a lot of people who have dreams, but for whatever reason they have stopped chasing them, you know, they have just settled for something else, you know, either for the money or just because it's easier. But one thing I know, these people just never seem happy in their lives, you know, they just look down right miserable.

I mean, this is why there are so many miserable people in the world, because a lot of people just settle, you know, they just accept their situation as is, you know, they just don't fight for what they want. Because really, you gotta fight for what you want in this world because nobody is gonna give you nothing, you know what I mean? I mean, you gotta work hard and smart to get what you want, you know? I mean, you gotta put in a lot of work, a lot of sacrifice and a lot of determination to earn what it is that you want to get out of life. But what I have realized is that, most of these people who quit or never go after their dreams is because, (1) either their parents or people close to them never went after their own dreams, and so therefore they do their best to discourage them from venturing into risky or hard to get into careers, you know, like; sports, music, acting, modeling, and so on and so on. And then, (2) the other reason why a lot of people quit or never go after their dreams is because, they are just to damn scared of failure! And actually I think reason number two is the biggest reason why people never go after their dreams, because they are just too scared of losing, you know, they are scared of losing everything they own and or they are just too scared of having to start their lives all over again from scratch, you know what I mean? And really I don't blame them, because it can be very traumatizing to realize that you have just ruined your finances, your life style and or your relationship (because when you run out of money, you can easily find yourself without your mate, you know, who swore they loved you, you know, ha ha ha ha ha!). But yeah, I was really determined to be a happy person when I grew up, and I think I'm doing a pretty good job of it so far.

And so anyway, yeah, I finally reunited with my dad, you know, went to live with him after four years of growing up fast, you know what I mean? Because it's like, by the time I reconnected with my dad again, I felt like I was already grown, you know, just waiting for my age to catch up to my mind. I mean, I was so set in my ways that I think it made it hard for my dad to figure me out. And also, him being a hands off kind of parent (you know, the kind of parents that are not really into or know how to interact with their kids, you know, the type that are good at providing food, shelter and clothing, but when it comes to interacting with their kids in a more personal note, nah, that they just don't know how to do), it kind of also made it harder for us to get to know each other better, you know what I mean? I mean sure we knew each other as father and son, but we did not know each other in a more personal note, you know, like, what are our likes and dislikes, or like, what are our views on life, you know, the deep stuff that make us unique as individuals. Because I mean, after four years, I had changed, but I think my dad still saw me as that little happy go lucky kid that he had known from when I was about six, seven years old and living just me and him. But now, I was eleven going on thirty-five and had become an extreme loner and somewhat defensive. And so, I don't think my dad knew how to read me very well.

And also, this is when I realized that we didn't have much in common, you know, in terms of likes and dislikes. Because it's like, all I really liked to do was to play sports, and I realized that my dad wasn't really into sports and sports was me and I was sports. And also, since my dad wasn't a talker (you know, touchy feeling kind), and since I wasn't a talker either, I think that hindered our chance to get to know each other better. And also I think that us not knowing each other better was a cause for some of the frictions that we went through in my teenage years. Because I mean, now that I think about it, really most of what we went through in our little father son frictions were based on misunderstanding of each other, you know what I mean? Because now that I think about it, most of the situations could have been resolved very easily if we had just taken the time to sit down and talk about it. But hey, when you have two headstrong personalities (hey, like father like son right?), I guess nothing will be easy, and so conflict is bound to happen, especially if you all don't know each other that well and don't have patience either.

I mean it's crazy sometimes, how father and son relationships can turn out, because the two of you are pretty much one and the same, you know what I mean? Because it's like, most sons have their father's personalities one way or another, and so, depending on how your relationship was with your dad in your youth, when you grow up, the two of you will either be really close (you know, talking and or even hanging out often) or y'all be some- what distant (you know, only talking and or seeing each other during the holidays). I mean, this goes for girls too with their dads, because girls go through situations too with their dads. I mean it's crazy, but it's just so amazing at how most fathers are just not so good at relating to their kids. And I mean sure, some of it is because of the generational gap, but most of it I believe is because fathers just don't take the initiative or have the patience to sit down and get to know their kids, you know, in a more personal note. And I think the reason why most fathers are like this is because, their own fathers were like that to them, you know, hands off parents. And so, like father like son, when the boy grows up, he tends to follow in his father's footsteps and becomes a hands off parent as well, you know, the ones that don't really get too involved in their kids daily activities, you know, like; checking homework, talking about school, talking about their feelings, and on weekends taking them to the park to play, or taking them to the movies, you know, and so on and so on.

I mean, it's very important for fathers to be in their kid's lives, you know, and so that way when the kid starts to act strange or out of his or her character, the father can notice it right away and be able to render assistance without hesitation. Because what I have realized is that, a lot of times, it's not like the father doesn't want to help or intercede in his kid's life when he notices them going through a rough situation, it's just that most fathers don't know how to start the conversation with their kid, because he has failed to establish an open relationship with his kid and therefore he finds himself in difficulty trying to talk and help his kid because he just don't know where or how to start the conversation.

And the reason why I say that the father has failed to establish an open relationship with his kid is because, I believe it's the father's responsibility to establish the communication channel with his kids, you know, so that way his kids can feel free to come to him and talk to him about any and everything that's on their mind. And because, if you leave it to kids to be the ones to establish openness with their parents, forget it, they will never do it. I mean, because really, kids already don't like for their parents to be all up in their business, no matter how small or serious the situation is, you know what I mean? And this is because kids just don't want their parents to form an opinion about them that might be kind of negative, you know?

And so, being that kids are already defensive by nature, parents have to take extra measures to make sure that their kids understand that it is ok to talk to them about any and everything that's on their minds. I mean because, kids have a lot of stuff on their little minds, and believe me or not, some of these stuff is very serious and can even be very dangerous. Because I mean, in today's society, there's a lot of negative and evil stuff out there that can really mess up a kid's mind. And so, if a kid doesn't have a positive channel to discuss whatever it is in their mind, they can lose themselves to the world and find themselves involved in troublesome situations.

And this is why sometimes you will hear in the news parents crying about their kids after their kids have gotten themselves in serious trouble with the law or even killed, but the parents just don't understand how their kids could have been involved and or why their kids were involved. I mean, it can be very serious stuff when it comes to kids and parent communication, because all kids go through situations that they need someone to tell it to and or to talk about it with. And this is also why some kids result in desperate measures to deal with their problems, you know, like, suicide and or homicide. I mean, it can get very serious when it comes to kids. I mean, this is one of the reasons why a lot of kids act out, take drugs, drink alcohol, and just wild out, because parents are just not doing a better job of communicating with their kids so that their kids can feel free to approach their parents with a problem before it manifests itself as a serious problem.

I mean some parents are just so clueless in what their kids are involved in. I mean, some parents are just so not involved in their kid's lives that the kid ends up doing whatever they want, which most often times is negative. And this is because kids are just much more attracted to the negative stuff of life than the positive stuff, and this is because most kids just follow what their friends are doing, you know, just so they can be part of the in crowd, you know, so they can feel like they belong. I mean it's crazy, but yeah, kids desperately need their parents to pay more attention to them, especially their fathers, and especially in this day of age!

And so anyway, yeah, father and son relationships can be very tricky, because in one hand, fathers tend to be very tough on their sons (you know, very authoritative), and on the other hand, fathers would like to be their sons best friends (you know, little mini me). And so, a lot of times, fathers just don't know how to navigate between being authoritative and curving out a friendship with their sons (and daughters too for that matter). And so as a result, most fathers just tend to end up either being more authoritative or more friendship. I mean, a lot of fathers just have a lot of problems trying to balance being a strong disciplinarian for their kids and also being a close friend to their kids. And this is why some fathers just leave a lot of the discipline stuff to the mother and they just spoil the kids. And the vise versa is also true, you know, where the father becomes a hard core disciplinarian and leaves the mother to be the friendly one to the kids. But the problem is, fathers that are hard core disciplinarians run the risk of alienating themselves from their kids, you know, because the kids will just be too afraid to be in their father's presence, and therefore they will try to avoid him completely if possible. And so, yeah, it can be very tricky for fathers as they are trying to be good disciplinarians and also good friends to their kids, which I believe is how most fathers would like to be. Because I mean, at the end of the day, when the kids are all grown up, I'm sure there's nothing more rewarding than having your kids visit you and want to hang out with you!

Man, like father like son ha! I mean, it's amazing how much traits fathers tend to pass down to their sons. Because it's like, when it comes to fathers and sons, history tends to repeat itself, you know what I mean? I mean, it's like, for example; if the father happens to be an abuser, then the son will tend to grow up to be an abuser, or, if the father happens to be an alcoholic, then the son will tend to grow up to be an alcoholic, or, if the father happens to be a womanizer, then the son will tend to grow up to be a womanizer also, and or, if the father happens to be lazy, then the son will tend to grow up to be lazy also, and or, if the father happens to be trifling, then the son will tend to grow up to be trifling also, and so on and so on, you know?

And I mean, sure there's always exceptions to the rule, but most often times sons just tend to follow in their father's footsteps. And also too, this is also why if a father happens to be a deadbeat dad, the son will tend to grow up to be a deadbeat dad also. I mean, it's crazy, but sons consciously or subconsciously just tend to follow in their father's footsteps (whether good or bad). And this is why it is very important for fathers to make sure that they set good examples for their sons, because sons consciously or subconsciously tend to copy their fathers behavior, you know, like father like son!

But yeah, it's amazing how much kids just idolize their fathers, I mean, to kids, their fathers are the coolest! I mean we have all done it as little kids (you know, some of us who were fortunate enough to know our dads), remember? I mean remember how you used to imitate how your dad used to walk, talk, sit and or even laugh? Oh, come on, don't tell me that I was the only one who did it, I know you did it too, because almost every little boy does. Because I mean, it's almost like a rite of passage for a little boy to imitate his daddy, because to a little kid, his daddy is the coolest, the smartest, the strongest, and what a real man looks like and acts like. And so, since almost every little boy wants to feel like a real man (you know, grown), they will tend to copy or imitate everything that the father does, you know, from how he walks, talks, laughs, eats, drinks, and so on and so on. And I mean, this is why if you are not careful you can find your little boy in the bathroom with shaving cream all over his face and is about to cut his face off trying to shave, you know, so he can feel like a man, you know, like his daddy. I mean, it's amazing, but it's only right, because a kid's first male role model is usually his daddy, and so, of course he's gonna imitate him, because to him, his daddy is the coolest.

I mean, it's just so funny to me how almost every kid thinks that their daddy is the coolest, because I mean, I too used to think that my daddy was the coolest dude around, and come to think of it, I still think he was one of the coolest dudes around back in those days. Because I can still remember it vividly how he used to like to wear his sun glasses and walk with a confident swagger, you know, and I would be right there beside him with my own sun glasses on pretending to be just as cool as him. And I mean, this was during the time that it was just me and him living together, and so he would usually take me with him wherever he went (if I could go of course), otherwise I would stay with the nuns (who were our next door neighbors), and just wait for him to pick me up when he got home. But yeah, those were the coolest times, because I remember going to the restaurant/bar with him a lot, and every time we would enter, everybody would say hi to us and shake our hands like, "What's up?" Man, I used to think me and my dad were the coolest people in there, you know what I mean? And too I used to feel like I was grown, you know, hanging out with the grown-ups. But of course that feeling wouldn't last long because the waitresses would always come to my little table (because I couldn't sit at the bar, you know, with all that drinking and cigarette smoking going on) and start to squeeze my little fat cheeks talking about, "Oh you so cute, look at you, looking just like your daddy, you cute little sweetie pie!" "Yuck, what do they think they are doing?" is what I would be thinking as I tried to wipe off their kisses of my cheeks as fast as possible as not to be more embarrassed, you know, so as not to mess up my coolness, you know what I mean, ha ha ha ha ha!

But yeah, I loved going to the restaurant with my dad when I was little, because I got to drink up all their sodas, and eat up all their chips. And I mean, I used to drink so many sodas at that place that my belly would be so huge that I would end up having to pee a lot. And I mean, I was only about six or seven years old, and so I mean, if you ask a seven year old kid if they want some more sodas and chips of course they gonna say yes. But I had fun going at that place because the waitresses would always flirt with me and I would be sitting there thinking to myself, "I can't wait till

I'm grown so I can marry all of them!", you know, as I found myself falling in love with each one of them that brought me a soda and flirted with me. I mean it was great, because the way the place was set up (it was one of those out door kind of places), most of the times we would bring our dog with us, and I would just chill with the dog at a table and just watch the grown-ups mix and mingle.

But yeah, I thought my dad was one of the coolest dudes during that time. And also, I remember how he used to like to smoke those pipes, I can't remember what they were called, but they were very popular back in the day, and this was back in the 70s and early 80s. Man, I can't believe I forgot what they were called! I mean, do you remember those pipes that kind of had a bent to them, you know, and was kind of thin and narrow at the tip, and was round at the top of it, you know, were you would put the tobacco and light it up. Man, I can't believe I don't remember what they were called! I mean, they were the kind of pipes that grandfathers liked to smoke, you know, the kinds that would be hanging on the side of their mouths (come to think of it, I think they were just called pipes, with no special name). But so anyway, yeah, I used to love watching my dad smoke them bad boys while reading the newspaper and or watching news on TV.

I mean, I used to think that was pretty cool, and so I couldn't wait to get older so I could get my own pipe and light it up, you know, so I can blow and make that tobacco smoke come out the side of my mouth, you know, so I can be as cool as my dad. I mean, it's amazing what little kids view as being cool, and to me, watching my dad make the tobacco smoke come out the side of his mouth was really cool, and I couldn't wait to get big so I could do just that, you know, make the smoke come out the side of my mouth. I mean it's crazy, but kids just admire their daddies!

I mean, I don't have a lot of memories of me and my dad just hanging out, but those few when I was around six years old are very precious. Because even though I have lived with my dad most of my life, we kind of grew apart during my teenage years (for various reasons, mostly misunderstandings and both of us being headstrong, you know, like father like son). But yeah, during that one or two years that it was just me and him living together when I was around six years old, oh yeah, we got to spend some quality time together. Because he would take me almost everywhere with him, and so I got to know him a lot. I mean, we really become like father like son and I became kind of popular in that little college town. Because I mean, my dad was a college teacher during that time and he was teaching there. And so he used to take me to the campus and to his class a lot (of course I couldn't be in the classroom when he was teaching, usually I would be hanging out at the cafeteria trying to help the food prep guys peel them potatoes or something, but they would never let me use the knife, scared I might cut myself or something, but they would let me wash the potatoes before they peeled and cut them, which was a lot of fun for my six year old self, because I felt like I was grown and doing real work, you know what I mean?). And so, I got to be a little bit popular around there because people got used to seeing me and it seemed like my dad knew almost everybody in that town.

I mean those were fun times, especially hanging out with the food prep guys at the cafeteria. I mean, those guys had so many jokes and stories, I mean, they had me laughing all the time. I mean, I was almost like one of the guys, you know, just hanging out and working and telling stories. And I mean, of course I didn't get most of the jokes, because I think some of the jokes were too mature for me to understand. And so sometimes I would just be looking bewildered or confused as I'm trying to figure out the meaning of the jokes, and they would be laughing even harder at my bewilder ness. I mean, those were good times, I mean, they really looked out for me, as I waited for my dad to finish lecturing to his class. And I remember sometimes sneaking around to my dad's classroom so I could watch him teach (I say sneak around because I wasn't supposed to be around the classrooms while classes were going on), because I used to just love to watch him doing his lecture, you know, using big words and pointing at the board with a ruler or something.

I mean, I used to be fascinated at how those grown looking college students would be just so attentively and intensely listening and watching his every movement and words. I mean, I could hardly understand what he was teaching, but I was just amazed at how serious and interested at what he was saying the students looked. And I remember thinking, "Wow, my dad is smart!" And a few times he almost saw me outside the window, but I tried my best to hide, because I knew I would be in big trouble if he caught me wondering around the place. But yeah, I loved watching him teach, because he looked so cool doing it and I thought he was one of the smartest dudes around. I mean, I used to think about being a teacher during that time, because my dad made teaching look so cool!

But so yeah, it's amazing how much kids admire their daddies, because not only did I think my dad was really smart, I also thought he was really strong. And the reason why I thought he was really strong is because he used to have this exercise bar that he would bend over and over again for his strengthening workout. I mean, that is what you are supposed to do with it, you know, bend it over and over as many times as you can until you feel the burn, you know, till you feel the pump. And so, the reason why I though he was so strong is because, I tried feverishly to bend that darn thing with my six/seven year old Herculean muscles, but I couldn't even get it to bend an inch. I mean I'm telling you, that thing was really hard to bend! And this is why I thought my dad was really strong, because he used to bend it with ease.

And so I mean, of course when I got older (at around fifteen/sixteen years old), I searched for that damn bar at the sporting goods store and tried to bend it again. And this time I could kind of do it, you know, bend it all the way, but to tell you the truth, it was still kind of hard to do still. So, being that I'm a sucker for a challenge, I went ahead and bought that darn thing, took it home and proceeded to work on conquering it, which I finally did after a few years of punishing my arms to total fatigue. I mean it's crazy, but I'm just a sucker for a challenge, and that was a worthy challenge, because not only did I finally conquer it, but I also built some chest and arm muscles along the way.

And so, yeah, I thought my dad was not only cool and smart, but also very strong. I mean, those were some fun times (when I was little and just me and my dad living together), because I actually got to hang out with him a lot, because he would take me with him almost everywhere he went. And I remember he used to like to drive kind of fast, which was cool with me of course. And I remember this one time we were driving back from somewhere (I can't remember from where), and all of a sudden he slowed the car down and asked me if I wanted to drive. I mean I couldn't believe it, my dreams of driving had finally come true (you know how little kids are so fascinated with driving because they think it's so cool, well I was one of them), and so of course I said hell yeah.

And so, since I was too small to reach the pedals, he controlled the gas and braking and I did the steering while sitting on his lap so I could see over the dashboard. And I mean I was so excited and I was actually doing pretty good for a few minutes there until the car started going to one side and for some reason I just couldn't get it to straighten up. And so I kind of started panicking a little because I could see the ditch coming at us closer and closer and my dad was just sitting there calmly. Then I started really panicking because I just couldn't turn the steering wheel fast enough and I could see water by the ditch (because we were by a little bridge by now and the water was really close to the edge of the little bridge). And so, at the last second, and I mean, very last second before I would have crashed the car into the ditch, my dad turned the steering wheel real hard and got us back on the road. And the funny thing is, he was very calm through the whole thing and I was really scared and panicking, you know what I mean? Because I was sure we were about to crash and burn, and it would have been all my fault. But it was fun though, and I would have driven it again if he would have asked me, you know.

I mean it's crazy, but kids just admire their daddies! And this is why it is so important for fathers to be in their kid's lives, because fathers give kids a sense of pride, you know, so they can brag to their friends of how cool, smart and strong their fathers are. And in turn, by bragging about their fathers, the kids will feel a sense of confidence, assurance and optimism that they too will grow up to be cool, smart and strong, you know, just like their fathers, you know, like father like son!

    I mean it's crazy, but fathers just don't know how important they are to their sons. Because the process of going from boyhood to manhood can be as easy or as hard as the environment that the boy is raised in. And when I say environment, I'm talking about both inside and outside the household. Because I mean, you know how they say that you are a product of your environment? Well just imagine how messed up a person can grow up to be having to live in an unstable and or chaotic household and then having to deal with living in a bad neighborhood. I mean, this is why a lot of kids get lost and get trapped into making wrong decisions, which can lead them into dangerous and or unhealthy situations.

    I mean, it's crazy out there in the world already, and so, just imagine how tough it must be for a young person to try and navigate through rough terrains of bad neighborhoods, and then having to come home and navigate through the rough terrains of instability and chaos in the household. I mean, it's crazy out there! And this is why it is very important for fathers to be in their sons lives, because there are just to many traps and bad influences in the streets that a young man who grows up without a father can find himself getting into. Because it's like, peer pressure can be very intense for a young man to handle, you know, because almost all kids want to feel like they belong to something, you know, to have friends. And so, if the kid's environment inside the household is not a positive one, he'll most likely than not fall for the peer pressure and end up in a situation that he probably wouldn't be in if his father was there to tell him and warn him of the consequences that can occur by his involvement in those unhealthy behaviors. And I mean, sure a mother can do the same thing and warn the boy of the consequences of bad behavior and or life style, but it's not the same as a father warning the boy. And this is because fathers tend to have more of a disciplinary influence over their sons than mothers do. And what I mean by this is that, not only can fathers relate more to what a son is going through as he's maturing from boyhood to manhood, but fathers can also explain and mentor their sons by using themselves as an example. I mean you know, because it's like, most fathers have gone through situations in their lives that almost every man has had to go through just as a right of passage.

And what I'm really talking about here is peer pressure, because peer pressure is what really drives boys to get caught up in a lot of the negative behavior and situations that's out there. I mean, almost anything you can think of that a boy gets caught up in has pretty much peer pressure to blame. And I mean, of course that's not a good excuse for the kid to do wrong, but kids are kids, and they want to belong, especially if no one at their household is paying much attention to them. And so, this is why a lot of kids do dumb stuff, you know, like stealing, car theft, joining gangs, drinking, smoking, and so on and so on. And so this is why it is so important for fathers to be in their kid's lives, because mothers just cannot do it alone, because there's just too much peer pressure to trap the kids into misbehaving and getting into negative situations.

Man, it's crazy out there, and fathers just don't know how important they are for their sons! Because I mean, if most fathers knew that just by them being in their sons' lives (even in a part time basis, you know, seeing their kids every weekend or every other weekend), if they knew how much difference they would make in their sons' lives as they are trying to navigate through a rough environment to become a mature and well- adjusted man, I think most fathers would reconsider their decision to be a dead beat dad, unless they just don't care, which I refuse to believe. Because I mean, the reason I think why most men become deadbeat dads is because they just don't think that they have much to offer the kid, you know, financially. And so therefore, they just decide to stay away and let the mother deal with it because they are ashamed that they can't provide for their kid, and so they chose to take the easy way out and not show their face around because they feel like they will be looked upon as being less of a man because they can't provide financially.

Now, of course some men are just irresponsible (broke or not broke), and run away from responsibility. But I believe the majority of the deadbeat dads just don't think they have anything to offer their kid, when in actuality, all a kid wants from their parent is for them to be there, you know, to be there when the kid has a question and or needs a sense of belonging and security. I mean, that's it, that's all a kid wants is to be able to see and talk to their father whenever they want to, because kids love their daddies no matter if the daddy is broke or not. But a lot of men don't get it, until it's too late, you know, until the kid is too old to care or holds resentment that their father wasn't there and took the easy way out instead of sticking in there somehow and be a man about it.

I mean, it's crucial, but many men just don't get it, you know, they just don't get it that it's their presence that the kid requires from them, you know, that money stuff, that is up to him and the mother to deal with. I mean really, I don't think that deadbeat dads just don't care about their kids, I truly believe that they just don't believe that they have much to offer the kid and they just don't think that they are really needed in their kid's life. I mean, it's serious stuff, sons need their fathers, because it's hard for a woman to try to raise a man, because most boys learn from example, and so they need their fathers there to teach them how to be a man by example, you know, to set a positive example so their sons can grow up to be mature and responsible adults. Because I mean, this is where the problem lies, this is why we have so many dad beat dads, because their fathers were also deadbeat dads, you know what I mean? And so when the son grows up, he too ends up becoming a deadbeat dad because he doesn't know and he never had anyone to teach him that being a real man means taking care of your responsibilities, which means taking care of your kids. Because at the end of the day, being a real man means that you do what you gotta do to take care of your family, and your kids are your family, no matter whether you like or don't like your baby mama, that's got nothing to do with the kid, the kid just wants his or her daddy to be a responsible man, as a real man should be.

I mean it's very important for fathers to be there for their kids, you know, so that when the kids grow up, they too can feel a sense of responsibility to be there for their own kids, you know what I mean? And so maybe this way we can also stop the circle of dads abandoning their kids from going around, around and around, you know, maybe we can stop the circle from repeating itself from generation to generation and to generation, you know, and leaving behind messed up kids who grow up to be messed up men, you know what I mean?

And so, it is very important for fathers to be in their sons lives, because like they say, history has a funny way of repeating itself, and therefore, the chances of a son becoming a dad beat parent is very high if his own dad was a dad beat parent. And this is why you will often hear young men use the excuse of their fathers not being in their lives as the reason why they too are not in their own kid's lives, you know? Because it's like, their fathers took the easy way out of the responsibility of raising a kid (them), and so they too decide to take the easy way out, you know (like father like son), even though you would think they would do the opposite knowing how tough and frustrating it was for them to grow up without their father around.

But yeah, like father like son, history just tends to repeat itself! And this is why a lot of times, if the father happens to lead a messed up life, the son will tend to grow up and lead a messed up life. And vice versa, if a father happens to lead a successful life, then too the son will tend to grow up and lead a successful life. I mean, most fathers don't think about it, but yeah, most sons just consciously or subconsciously tend to follow in their father's footsteps. And this is why a lot of times, if the father happens to be an abuser, then the son will tend to grow up and be an abuser also. Because I mean, sons just consciously or subconsciously take a lot of their fathers' characteristics. And so this is why it is very important for fathers to take extra care that they are being good role models for their sons, you know, that way when they grow up and someone says to them, "You are just like your father!", that can be taken as a compliment and not as a negative connotation, you know what I mean?

Well fathers, take care and be there for your sons man (and daughters too for that matter), because they need you desperately, especially in today's crazy world!

Chapter 11

Parenting 101

Parenting is one of the hardest things that any real parent will ever do, especially in today's crazy world! And the reason why I say **any real parent will ever do** is because, there are just so many bad parents out there that it's just so saddening. I mean, there are just so many parents out there that either don't know what the hell they are doing or they just don't care about their kids, which I refuse to believe. But it just never fails, you know, it just never fails for a bad parent to be spotted and to be disbelieved in their lack of parenting skills. I mean for example; how many times have you seen a parent with unruly kids, you know, kids who just don't seem to understand that they can't just behave any which way they want anywhere they are. You know what I'm talking about? I'm talking about kids that think anywhere they are is a playground and insist on climbing, jumping, and running around like they are crazy. I mean, I'm sure you have seen them, because they are not that hard to find, because it's like they are everywhere!

I mean it's ridiculous how so many kids nowadays just don't seem to know how to behave. I mean it's crazy, because it's like, you could be at a doctor's office, and there always will be a kid in there that just insists on rolling on the floor or climbing on the chairs. And so, you will be sitting there (with your kids sitting beside you) looking at the kid and then turning and look at the mother (because it's usually mothers who take kids to the doctor), and then turn and look at your kids, and they turn and look at you with a quizzical look in their face knowing that, that kid's behavior is un acceptable (because you have taught them better). And so you turn back and look at the mother again with a quizzical look that says, "Ain't you gonna stop your kid from rolling on the floor and climbing on chairs?"

But to your amazement, the mother just sits there acting oblivious to their kid's miss behavior. And so, you turn and look at the kid again and in your best attempt to not look or sound impolite, you make eye contact with the kid and tell them to stop climbing on the chairs. And to their shock and surprise that someone actually dared to stop them from their unruly behavior, they stop and look at you, then look at their mother, then look at you again (to see if you are serious or what), realizing you are serious, they move away from the chairs, but, they then proceed to get on the floor and start rolling around. And during this whole time, the mother hasn't said a word to their kid, you know, still acting oblivious, or maybe she's just too used to her kid acting bad that it don't bother her anymore. But anyway, so you just sit there watching the kid and thinking to yourself, "Oh my God, this kid's mother has lost control of her kid!"

And so you just sit there and wonder whom to feel sorry for, you know, you wonder whether to feel sorry for the kid for not being taught proper discipline, you know, or you wonder whether you should feel sorry for the mother for not knowing how to properly teach her kid how to behave in different settings. Because truly, there's a lot of parents that just don't know how to properly teach their kids how to behave. Because I mean really, disciplining a kid is an art form and not a science. And what I mean by this is that, no two kids are the same (in terms of personalities, mental capacity, and or emotional fortitude), and so you cannot just use the same discipline tactics on all your kids. I mean sure, you will use the same kinds of disciplinary styles for all your kids, you know, depending on your disciplinary beliefs (you know, like whipping, time outs, taking away of toys or other stuff that the kids value, you know, and etc.), but the method on how you apply it will have to vary from kid to kid. Because every kid is different, and so, every kid will respond differently to whatever discipline tactic you employ for their punishment. Because it's like, some kids are just so hard headed that, you could whup them all you want, but at the end of the day, they will just end up getting used to the whipping that it won't be a good tool for their disciplinary reinforcement anymore. And this is where a lot of parents go wrong, you know, and start abusing their kids by intensifying the whopping to the point of it becoming harmful to the kid. I mean, some parents just lose it, you know, they just lose their minds and end up whipping their kids like they don't love them or something.

I mean it's crazy, but all this abuse usually happens because there's a lot of bad parenting going on. And there for, since the parents don't know how to handle or discipline their kids in a more effective way, they result into beating their kids, thinking that will straighten them out, which it usually doesn't. Because I mean, there's a method to disciplining your kids by whipping, and this method is, whipping only after you have calmed down, that way you have more control over your emotions. And also by taking the time to calm down you make the kid take time to think about what he or she has done, and you make the kid think about how mad you seem to be and how disappointed you are in them. And also by you taking time to calm down it gives the kid time to think about how intense the whipping might be, which by this time, since you have already kind of calmed down, the whipping ends up being either quick or cancelled, as the kid starts to apologize profusely with a nervous look on his or her face, letting you know that they know and understand what they did was wrong and they will try their best to never do it again, you know what I mean? And so, actually, I like to call this method of whipping (you know, whipping after you have calmed down), I like to call it, "Whipping without whipping", you know, because the fear of getting a whipping can be as effective or even more effective than the actual whipping itself. Because I have come to realize that I haven't had to really whip my kids that much, actually now that I think of it, I haven't whipped my daughter since she was around four or five (she's eight now), and even when she was that young or younger, I never really had to whip her because the threat to whip her would usually do the job.

And as far as my son is concerned (he is five years old), I realized early on that spanking would definitely not work for him. Because I noticed that the first few times that I spanked him when he was around two or three years old (you know, around the terrible twos' time when they just can't seem to sit still or listen), I noticed that he would tense up and get real nervous when I was about to whip him for whatever he did. And so I realized that, I really didn't have to whup him, because he looked really scared like I was really gonna hurt him or something. So this let me know that, just the threat of a whupping could get the job done, and to this day it's still getting the job done.

I mean, it' funny, but I have realized that, most kids don't really want their parents to be mad or disappointed at them, and getting a whipping is the last thing that a kid wants. And therefore, I have come to realize that, if you as a parent learn how to use other disciplinary tactics, such as; time outs, taking away of favorite toys, taking away of video games, taking away TV time, taking away internet usage, and or stuff like that, and then if you as a parent learn how to talk and explain your disciplinary actions to your kids, you can come to find yourself never having to whip your kids, especially if you are one of those parents that refuse or don't believe in whipping your kids (like my wife), but then result to shouting and yelling at them, like that's any better!

But yeah, disciplining kids is a lot of hard work, because you really have to have a lot of patience. Because most kids (depending on how young they are), are just not mature enough to understand or grasp what it is that you are trying to tell them. I mean, sure they hear you, but comprehending and putting to action what you tell them to do or not to do is another thing all together. Because almost all kids' attention span is very short, and so, they can get distracted and forget what you had just finished telling them to do or not to do in just a few seconds. And so this is where a lot of patience and understanding on your part (the parent) comes in, you know, because you are the adult here and your attention span should be a lot longer and sharper. And so, as you recognize the dilemma that you are facing (you know, trying to communicate with a four year old kid), you realize that you might have to tell the kid about ten or more times to either do or not do something before it can really stick in their heads. I mean, this is part of raising kids and this is part of being a parent.

But unfortunately, most parents just don't have the patience or the fortitude to learn patience so they can better be able to deal and nurture their kids. Because I mean, patience is the key to better parenting, because without patience, parents will have a hard time understanding their kids and why they are behaving or acting the way they are acting. Because it's like, kids just don't start misbehaving for no particular reason. I mean, there is always an underlining problem that makes kids behave or act the way they do. Because I mean, most kids just don't know how to express themselves, and so, if the parent doesn't have the patience to take the time to help the kid to learn how to express themselves, the kid is left with no option but to act out, you know, as a way of trying to get his or her parents' attention.

And so, this is why it is very important for parents to take time and be patient with their kids, you know, so their kids can feel free to express themselves and also the parent can feel free to explain stuff to the kid in a more polite and loving manner.

But it never fails, the yelling, the shouting, the cursing and the beating of little kids by their parents. I mean, there are so many bad parents out there that it's just so crazy! And the reason why there are so many bad parents nowadays is because, the parents themselves come from an environment of chaos and confusion themselves, you know what I mean? I mean, what I mean by this is that, most of today's parents were brought up in an unstable home, you know, where their own parents did not know or take time to teach them and or nurture them properly so that they can come to know how to nurture their own kids properly.

I mean it's crazy, but it's not hard to hear or see bad parenting going on, because it's everywhere. And I mean, this is the biggest reason why we have so many kids running around like they are crazy, you know, acting out and getting themselves into trouble, you know, and it's all because their parents have failed to instill respect and discipline into their lives. And the biggest reason why most parents fail to instill respect and discipline into their kid's lives is because, the parents themselves lack discipline and respect in their own lives.

And what I mean by this is, there are just so many parents nowadays that are just plain all trifling, you know what I mean? I mean, from the way they talk, to the way they walk, from the way they look at you, to the way they dress, I mean, just their whole demeanor is just so negative, you know. Because I mean, they look like they are just ready to flip out and curse you out with no warning and no particular reason at all, you know, they just look mad all the time. And so, when it comes to their kids (and since kids learn more from example than from "do as I say"), they find themselves unable to reach and teach their kids proper behavior because they themselves are not practicing proper behavior. Because I mean, kids have a tendency of watching and mimicking how their parents act and or behave. And so, if the parents are not behaving properly, the kids too will not behave properly. And this is why there are so many kids acting out and misbehaving, because their parents are also acting out and misbehaving. I mean, it just never fails, you know, what goes around comes around, you know, like father like son and like mother like daughter, you know, from generation to generation, you know, till someone breaks the cycle, you know what I mean?

I mean, parenting is hard work, especially if you want to be a good parent and raise mature and responsible adults. And this is why it is very important for fathers to be involved in their children's lives, because it's just too much work for the mother to be doing alone, you know? Because raising kids requires a lot of time and patience, which can be hard for the mother to do alone, especially if she has to work two jobs just to maintain a living. I mean it's crazy, but fathers just have to find a way to play a better role in their kid's lives (even if they don't like or want to be with their baby mamas any more), because raising kids is hard work, and a lot of mothers just get tired and let their kids behave and act anyway they want, which tends to lead the kids in the wrong path and force them to succumb to peer pressures, especially if they are living in bad neighborhoods, which a lot of kids of single parents do.

And this is the main reason why I decided to write this book, you know, so I can try to do my best to persuade fathers to participate and be involved in their kid's lives, you know, so they can help out the mothers in the raising of the kids, you know what I mean? Because I mean, I've come to understand how hard it really is to try and raise kids (being that now I'm a parent myself with my wife trying to raise three kids the best we can, you know, so they can grow up to be mature, responsible and successful adults), especially in this crazy society that we live in nowadays.

I mean, I never knew how hard raising kids really was (until I became a parent myself), especially if you want to be a good parent, you know what I mean? Because I mean, there are so many ills in society nowadays that you really have to work extra hard to try and shield your kids from, you know, it's just so crazy! And so, combining the ills of society, together with just the general every day activity that a parent has to do to better care for his or her kids, it all adds up to a lot of work, you know, it all adds up to a monumental task, especially if you want to be a good parent. And then, not only that, if you also add the fact that you have to work two jobs, or work long hours, and then come home and try to properly nurture your kids, I'm telling you, it becomes almost an impossible mission.

And this is why I'm trying to urge fathers to take an active role in their children's lives, because the world has dramatically changed for the worse, and it's getting even worse and tougher and tougher, especially for kids to live in. Because remember how they used to say, or maybe they still say, "It takes a village", you know, to raise a kid. Well, they were right! But, the only problem is, there is no more village, you know what I mean? I mean, what I mean is, people don't look out for each other's kids anymore, you know, because nowadays it's like, every man for himself, you know what I mean? I mean, nowadays people just don't have the sense of community, you know, it's like everybody just minds their own business and just don't feel the urge or obligation to intervene if they see something wrong going on.

And the reason why most people don't intervene is because, everybody has their own problems, and nowadays people don't want other people in their business, even if that person is trying to lend a helping hand of some kind. I mean, nowadays people are just so quick to say "Mind your own business!", instead of accepting the fact that they indeed need help.

And so, this is why a lot of people just don't bother to help or try to intervene when they see or hear a bad situation going down, because most often than not, the person they are trying to help will actually start accusing them of being the problem and actually start to curse them out. And so, this is why a lot of people just tend to mind their own business, even though they wouldn't mind lending a helping hand.

And so, this is also why the sense of community or village has been lost, because we have created a culture of just me, myself and I, you know, instead of a culture of looking out for one another, like how it used to be back in the day. I mean, do you remember how back in the day (and I'm not even talking that long ago, because if you are just a little over thirty years old you should remember), you didn't dare do anything stupid all out in the open, because you knew that someone will see you acting foolish and you knew that someone is going to tell your parents that they saw you misbehaving. And actually, sometimes the adult that catches you misbehaving could whup you themselves and then take you to your parents and let them know that they had whupped you because they caught you doing such and such or you were being very disrespectful.

And then remember how your parents after hearing this would tell the adult thank you for whupping you and then proceed to whup your butt some more themselves for not only misbehaving, but also for embarrassing them, you know what I mean? Because it's like, they knew they taught you better, you know, and so your misbehavior is like a negative reflection on them, you know, their self-respect. And back in the day, parents used to regard their respect in the community or how the community viewed them (as parents) very highly, you know? And so you better not even dare try and drag their good name in the mad by acting foolish and or by being disrespectful, you know, because not only will you get a whupping, but you will get a whupping that you will definitely remember for the rest of your life, you know what I mean, ha ha ha ha ha!

I mean, it used to be serious business back in the day, as far as disciplining kids was concerned, and the whole community was involved. Because I mean, I can remember from when I was little, I can remember all of us kids in the neighborhood would do our best not to get caught acting a fool or using bad language near anywhere adults were present, you know what I mean? Because I mean, they would call you out on it and then ask you your name and who your parents were and then proceed to go tell them what they had heard or caught you doing. And I remember we used to try our best to give them fake names and fake were we lived so they would go to the wrong houses, you know what I mean?

But the problem was, almost everybody knew each other in the neighborhood, so sooner than later they would find out who your real parents were and then proceed to tell them what they had heard or seen you do a few days ago. And also they would tell your parents the fact that you lied about your name and where you lived, and so, not only would you get a whipping for misbehaving a few days ago, but you would also get a whipping for lying to an adult, which back in the day was definitely a no, no. Because I mean, disrespecting an adult was definitely not tolerated, unlike nowadays, where a lot of kids have absolutely no manners or respect for anybody, not even themselves.

But yeah, respect and discipline was taken very seriously back in the day. And not only did your parents expect you to behave and respect yourself and others, but the whole community also expected you to behave and respect yourself and others. I mean, disrespect and misbehavior was absolutely not tolerated, and any adult that saw you or caught you misbehaving would call you out on it and then go and tell your parents. But nowadays, forget it, kids are just not listening to anybody. I mean, they are not listening to teachers, they are not listening to police officers, they are not listening to other authority figures, I mean, they are just not listening to anybody period. I mean it's so bad that some kids are not listening to even their own parents! I mean, it's crazy, it's ridiculous and it's getting out of control, if it hasn't already.

And I blame all this miss behavior, and all this disrespect, and all this craziness in today's kids in the fact that there are just too many fathers missing from the household, you know, there are just too many deadbeat dads. Because I mean, I have tried my best to analyze or figure out why there seems to be so many kids that are just so unruly and or just plain all disrespectful nowadays compared to back in the day. And the conclusion that keeps coming back to me is that, the rate of bad kids that are out there is mostly parallel to the amount of deadbeat dads that are out there, you know what I mean? And of course this is not a scientific analysis or nothing like that, but it's not that hard to connect the two, you know, the more deadbeat dads there are, the more bad kids or undisciplined kids there'll be.

And I mean, sure most mothers do their best to discipline and teach their kids proper behavior, but it's not the same as a father being there and disciplining and teaching his kids proper behavior. Because I mean, even though mothers are seen as authority figures in their kids eyes, their kids see fathers as even more of authority figures. And this is because, fathers are just a little bit more imposing in their kids eyes than their mothers, you know what I mean? And so, when a father says something to his kids, the kids don't dare question it because they do not want the wrath of this big ugly (even if he's really not that big in stature, to them he is big, with his big voice) mean looking giant come down on them, as opposed to the mother, with her small (even if she's big, to them she's small, with her soft loud voice) pretty looking mean face. I mean, mothers are just (well, most mothers anyway) too pretty and just too sweet to dish out threats that will cause a kid to shiver with fear. And I mean, this is why most mothers just leave the extra disciplinary actions to the father, you know, the whipping and stuff like that, because to kids, fathers are more intimidating than mothers (most of the times anyway). And so, this is also why it is very important for fathers to be in their kid's lives, you know, that way the mothers can threaten the kid with the threat of telling the father if the kid keeps misbehaving. Because I mean, threatening to tell the father can be a very effect disciplinary tool, because most kids just don't want the wrath of their fathers to come down on them.

It's crazy, but yeah, absent fathers are making this generation of kids just plain all crazy! Because I mean, parenting is hard work, and so, mothers just can't do it all alone, because there are just too many ills in this society nowadays that kids can fall victim to. And the worst part is, other adults in the community just don't feel like they have the right to discipline anybody else's kid. And so, the kids are just left out there to run crazy and wild, just because the village or the community feeling seems to no longer exist. But yeah, back in the day, it seemed like every adult in the community took it to themselves to watch out for the kids, you know, to make sure the kids are acting and or behaving properly.

And I mean, I can remember this one lady, an older lady (you know, someone's grandma) in our neighborhood where we used to live when I was little (I think I was around ten years old), I can remember how she always used to walk around the neighborhood with a stick. And no, this stick was not for helping her to walk around, oh no, this stick was for putting a whupping on any kid she saw misbehaving. I mean, I kid you not, she would actually hit you with the stick. Because I can remember almost getting hit with the stick a few times myself, and I wasn't even a troublemaker. But to her, I guess, if you are hanging around the troublemakers, then you are part of the trouble and deserve to get a whupping. Because I mean, she would actually come after us with the stick. And so, I mean, even if we weren't doing nothing wrong (maybe just being loud), we got in the habit of running as soon as we saw her.

I mean, it almost started becoming a game, you know, because it's like, someone would spot her coming from around the corner, and as soon as they said, "Oh man, there comes Miss So and So!", all of us kids would just take of running. I mean, even if we weren't doing anything wrong, we would just take off running. And sometimes someone would say as we are running, "Hold on, hold on, hold on, why are we running, we didn't do anything wrong!" And then someone else would say, "Yeah that's true, but you know she can still hit you anyway!", and someone else would say, "Oh yeah, because she hit me the other day and I didn't do nothing wrong!" And with that, like in clockwork, and in unison, we would all say, "She's getting closer!", and just take off running again.

And the funny thing is, it seemed like she knew almost everybody in the neighborhood and also knew who their kids were. Because it's like, whenever she said, "I'm gonna tell your mother!", and she looked you in the face, you could bet your bottom dollar that she knew who your parents were and were you lived. Because I can remember how we would always try to figure out whose house she was going to go to. Because it's like, whenever we were in a group, and we ran from her, I remember we would be debating whose house she would go to, you know, because that person will be the one to get in trouble with their mother that day. And the funny thing is, she would always go to the house of the kid that she made eye contact with and really saw his face. So I remember how we used to do our best to make sure she didn't really recognize us, you know? And I remember how after she had gone ahead and walked pass us, I remember how we would start asking each other stuff like, "Hey, do you think she saw me, do you think she recognized me?" I mean, those were some fun and kind of crazy moments come to think of it. And actually, we started to think maybe she was kind of senile, you know, kind of crazy. But hey, we still didn't dare let her catch us or see us misbehaving, because we knew she would either hit us with the stick, and or go tell our parents.

But yeah, those were the good old days when there really was a village or community of adults who looked out for each other's kids. But nowadays, forget it, it's a me, myself and I kind of culture. And I mean, there are still some old fashion people out there that do try to look out for the youth, you know, and try to get them to behave properly whenever they see them misbehaving, but the problem is, a lot of kids are just so undisciplined and just so disrespectful that instead of listening to the adult that's trying to correct them and to teach them better manners, they instead result to cursing and or disrespecting the adult that's trying to correct them and tell them that their behavior is not acceptable. And sometimes these kids will curse or disrespect the adult right there in front of the adults face. I mean, these kids nowadays think it's funny and cool to be disrespectful. Because I mean, I hear them and see them all the time, you know, laughing and carrying on in a disrespectful manner, thinking it's so cool.

I mean, I'm telling you, we are really failing our kids, us parents and us adults, we are really failing our kids. And the reason why we are failing our kids is because, most adults just don't want or just don't have the time to deal with a disrespectful kid, especially if the kid is not theirs'. Because I mean, it's a lot of work trying to talk to a kid that's not yours and trying to explain to them that their behavior is really not pleasant and that if they continue with the same attitude and or foolishness, they can find themselves in a bad situation one of these days (which they will regret), and it's all because of their trifling attitude. But most kids nowadays just don't want to listen, you know what I mean? Because it's like, there you are trying your best to give them good advice, you know, so they can try their best to avoid the pitfalls of life, you know what I mean? But, instead of listening and taking heed to what you are trying to tell them, they instead are ready to fight you tooth and nail to reject your advice and keep on doing their own thing, you know what I mean?

I mean, it's like, unless you are their mother or their father, they don't really want to hear anything from you, you know? Because I mean, I see a lot of adults who just pass by misbehaving kids without saying a thing to them about their behavior. And I mean I understand why, because most adults know that these kids nowadays are just so out of control that, as soon as the adult says something to them the adult all of a sudden will become the subject of their crude humor and or straight up disrespect.

I mean it's crazy, but a lot of these kids nowadays just don't have any manners, you know, and it's all because there's nobody there in their life to reinforce, and to reinforce, and to reinforce, and to reinforce, and to reinforce good behavior, you know what I mean? Because I mean, it takes a lot of reinforcement for kids to actually get it and for the good behavior to actually become a kid's second nature, you know what I mean? I mean, it takes a while and a lot of reinforcement for a kid to really understand that they are expected and demanded that they behave properly at all times, whether they are in or outside the home. Because I mean, left alone, kids for some reason just tend to gravitate towards bad behavior, you know what I mean?

I mean, I don't know what it is, but for some reason kids just find it easier to act bad than to act good. And actually, I think I know why kids find it easier to act bad than to act good. And the answer is, peer pressure of course! I mean, peer pressure is a monster for kids, because it just has such a powerful peer influence that most kids just can't break away from, you know, because most kids just want to belong or be part of the crowd so bad that they will do anything or act any how just to fit in.

I mean it' crazy, but that peer pressure thing man, that's the monster that parents really have to fight against. Because I mean, kids just don't want to be different, you know what I mean? I mean, kids just don't like the thought that other kids might see or view them as being different or weird, as they like to say. I mean, this is a big struggle for our kids nowadays, you know, because they just don't want to be teased or talked about by their peers, which of course can be very cruel. And so, the toughest thing that a parent will ever have to deal with when it comes to parenting is teaching and helping their kid to learn how to deal with and overcome peer pressure.

And so, this is also why it is very important for fathers to be in their kid's lives, because there are just too much peer pressures out there for the kids to deal with and mothers sometimes are just too tired and or just don't have the time to do it alone. Because I mean, kids require a lot of time and attention, and so, if the mother is the only parent there for the kid, and if she has to work long hours or two jobs to make ends meet, the kid will have no other adult there to supervise him or her, and the kid could end up falling to peer pressure.

And this is the reason why a lot of kids find themselves in trouble doing what they know they ain't supposed to be doing, and it's all because they don't have no adult supervision at home when their mamas are at work. And so I mean, it is very crucial for fathers to be in their kid's lives, because it is just very hard for mothers do it alone, because there are just too many ills in society nowadays that can trap and or badly influence the kids to misbehave and or make bad decisions that can greatly affect their futures!

Chapter 12

Parenting 102

Parenting, one of the hardest things that any parent will ever do, especially if they want to be a good parent. Because I mean, parenting just never stops, you know, it just never ends, you know what I mean? I mean, what I mean is that, once you are a parent, you are always going to be a parent, you know, no matter how old you get, and no matter how old your kids get, you know what I mean? Because I mean, to them, you are always going to be daddy or mommy, and to you, they are always going to be your babies, no matter how old they get. And this is because you are always going to worry about them, you know, you gonna worry about their safety and well-being forever, you know what I mean? Because I mean, they are your kids and you love them dearly. And so I mean, sure parenting can get easier and parents can be more relaxed and not have to worry about their kids too much when their kids are grown and or more self-sufficient, but when the kids are little, forget it, parenting will be head on and at full speed at all times, you know what I mean?

And I mean, sure you might be able to catch a breather here and there (from your kids) every once in a while, you know, like when grandma and grandpa or another relative takes them for the day or weekend, but for the most part, forget it, there will be no break for you, unless both parents are involved in their kid's lives and have learned how to give each other a break from the kids every once in a while. Because I mean, kids are a lot of work, especially the little ones, because they just have so much energy that can force you to have to chase and be at their beck and call all day and every day. I mean, it can really get tiring after a while, you know what I mean?, especially if you have to do it all alone every day with no break. And I mean, this is why a lot of parents just let their kids run around the house like they are crazy, because they just get tired of saying, "Stop, stop, stop jumping, stop running, stop shouting, keep your voice down, stop touching that, why are you rolling on the floor, why are you writing on the wall, why are you playing with the toilet paper, and so on and so on!

I mean, parenting is a lot of work, and it can really exhaust you! And this is one of the reasons why it is very important for fathers to be involved in their kid's lives, because mothers need a break from the kids once in a while, you know, so they can get a chance to relax and to reenergize themselves so that way they can better deal with the monumental task of being a mother. And I mean, this is why I feel sorry for single mothers, you know, because I can just imagine how tough it must be trying to provide a living (you know, working long hours), and then having to come home and try to be the best mother they can be for their kids. Because I mean, most single mothers, if they are not working two jobs, than they will be working long hours (you know, overtime and stuff like that) just to make ends meet, you know, to make sure they have enough money for the bills, food and other stuff.

And I mean, now I know why a lot of single mothers just look tired and mad all the time, and this is because they are just too exhausted to smile. I mean it's crazy, but not only is life getting tougher (as far as inflation and or the cost of living and stuff like that), but it is also getting tougher and tougher to raise kids nowadays, because the world is just getting crazier, crazier and crazier, as far as morality, spirituality, respect, humanity and you know, stuff like that.

I mean it's crazy, but parenting is a twenty four hour, seven days a week, three hundred and sixty five days a year gig. I mean, it's an everyday gig, with no real break in between, unless you have good relatives or a good parenting partner who can give you the break you desperately need, you know, before you go crazy. And so, this is also the reason why I feel extremely sorry for teenage mothers, because they just don't know what they are getting themselves into. Because I mean, most of these little girls run around fantasizing about having babies and they don't really take the time to think and realize the monumental task it may be to take care of a baby.

I mean, these little girls run around fantasizing about having babies like the babies are toys or something to just play with. I mean, they fail to realize the magnitude of the situation that they are fantasizing about until it's too late and they become pregnant and have to be a mother. I mean it's crazy, but for some reason, these young girls nowadays are just in such a rush to become mothers that they don't take the time to recognize the hardship that they will be putting themselves in (as far as having to take care of the baby and also themselves), because you can be sure the baby daddy will not stay with the girl and most likely won't even help the girl with the taking care of the baby (whether financially or otherwise). It's crazy, but more and more young girls are becoming mothers way before they are ready. And I mean, most grown women never really consider themselves ready for a baby, whether because of finance or the lack of a stable relationship. And so, there's no way these young girls could be ready for a baby, because not only are they not mentally ready, but they are definitely not financially or relationship ready, no matter how much they think they are in love.

I mean it's crazy, because it's like, girls see other girls at the mall pushing strollers and they think it's cute. And then so they too start fantasizing about having a baby of their own, thinking it's going to be just as cute. But the one thing that they never figure out is that, even though it might look cute pushing a stroller at the mall and have people (mostly other little boys and girls) admire and compliment you on how cute the baby is, young girls just never figure out or realize how much work it took to get the baby up and read for the trip to the mall. And they also just never realize how much work it is going to be when they get home and have to feed, wash, change diapers, rock the baby to sleep, and if the baby can't sleep, that might turn into an all-night baby crying marathon in which frustration and confusion will set in for the young mother leaving them to question whether having the baby at that young age was such a good idea.

I mean it's crazy, but these young girls just don't get it, for some reason they just don't think about the big picture, you know? I mean, I don't get it, I just don't get it! Because I mean, there's just so many examples of girls that became teenage mothers and have had a difficult time trying to raise the kid (and herself for that matter) for other girls to see and learn from, but it just never ends, you know, it's like they just never learn from others. And the funny thing is, these girls that become teenage mothers actually usually end up having a few more kids even before they have secured a living or finished school.

I mean, I just don't know what they are thinking about. I mean it's like they don't have any guidance, you know, someone to tell them and to warn them that the more kids they have at that such an early age, the harder their struggle of becoming self- sufficient and or successful in life will be. Because I mean, kids require a lot of time and a lot of financial support. And so, by these young girls having babies way before they are even ready (mentally and financially), all they are doing is adding to the amount of obstacles that they will have to overcome in order to finish high school, then go to college and finish that, and then go out there in the market place and secure a good job. Because it's like, truth be told, most girls that become teenage mothers rarely go or finish college. And actually, most of them barely graduate from high school, resulting to having to get their G.E.D years later, when they realize that it's hard to make a living out there in the world without at least a high school diploma.

I mean it's crazy, but these young girls just never learn, you know, they all just think it's all fun and games having a baby, you know, until it's too late to change their minds as the baby is right there staring them in the face and demanding to be paid attention to by crying real loud over and over and over and over and over again. Because I mean, taking care of a baby is no joke, because they demand absolute attention from you from the moment they are born, all the way to the moment they are getting married and or leaving the house to be on their own, you know what I mean? Because I mean, parenting is no joke, especially if you want to be a good parent. Because it's like, from the moment that baby is born, life for you will never be the same, you know what I mean? Because it's like, now, not only are you responsible for your own life, you are also responsible for another life that you have brought into the world that requires your assistance and guidance until they are old and or mature enough to do for themselves, you know what I mean?

But those early years man, those early years that they can't do much for themselves, you know, from when they are babies until they can tie their own shoes, you know, until they can walk, talk, eat and do other small stuff by themselves, yeah man, those are some challenging times, because they need your absolute attention and assistance, leaving you with no room to breath, you know what I mean? Because it's like, when they are babies, not only do you have to be at an alert status at all time, you know, to make sure they are fed, washed, diaper changed, burped, rocked, fed again, diaper changed again (because babies seem to pup almost every time they feed, and they seem to be ready to feed almost as soon as they finish pupping, you know? I mean, that's why babies tend to go through so many diapers a day, depending on how often they feed), you know, and so on and so on until they fall asleep. And then you will have to go through the whole diaper changing and feeding routine again as soon as the baby wakes up (which could be as soon as one, two or three hours later, depending on how well your baby eats and sleeps), you know, before they start crying their lungs out. I mean, it's no joke taking care of a baby, because it's pretty much a twenty-four hour job that requires your full attention. I mean, it's a tough job that really requires two people.

And this is one of the reasons why it is very important for fathers to be involved, because babies require a lot of time and attention which can be very hard for the mother to deal with alone. And I mean, this is why sometimes you will see mothers (especially the young ones) yelling and shouting at their babies to be quiet by telling them to shut up, you know, as if the baby understands. And the reason why these mothers tend to yell at their babies is because they are just really overwhelmed by the baby and it's demand for absolute attention from them. And so, this is why it is important for fathers to be there so they can help the mothers out, you know, so the mothers can catch a breather and rejuvenate, you know, that way they can do a better job of nurturing the baby and so the baby can grow to be a healthy and fit toddler, so that way he or she can terrorize the parents when it reaches the terrible two's, you know what I mean, ha ha ha ha ha!

But yeah, parenting is hard work, especially when the kids are very young, because they just don't understand or seem to grasp whatever it is that you are trying to tell or teach them. And the reason for their misunderstanding is not because they are not smart, oh no, not at all, because little kids are very smart, believe me, kid's brains are very capable of learning anything, just as long as you take the time to teach them, and just as long as they take the time to learn it. And the reason why you have to take time or have patience in teaching them, and the reason why they too have to take time or have patience to learn, is because little kids just don't have patience, you know, I mean, their attention span is almost next to zero.

And I mean, this is why you almost have to tell a kid a whole bunch of times to do something before they actually do it. And this is because they just get distracted so easily, you know what I mean? And the reason why they get distracted so easily is because they are just so anxious and curious about everything that they just can't concentrate on one thing at a time, you know? But the funny thing is, once you do get them to concentrate on one thing, their brains can work wonders on mastering that one thing. And this is how a lot of these child geniuses come to be, because they spend hours on that one subject, you know, the subject that fascinates them. And really, a kid has to be fascinated and or excited about something to really pay much attention to it.

And this is why if you try to force your kid to do something that they don't necessarily find exciting, this is why it will take them a very long time to get to it, and when they do get to it, it will take them an extra longer time to do it. And this is because they are just not interested in doing it. I mean, it's like, for example, if you ask your kids to go brush their teeth (which most kids just find it to be the most boring and tedious thing to do), not only will it take them a very long time to get to it (because they will start playing with something else in the bathroom and just forget what they had gone in there to do in the first place, until you call out to them and remind them by yelling for them to hurry up and brush their teeth), when they do get to it, they will do such a rush, rush hurry up bad job of brushing their teeth, all because they just want to get it over with and so that way they can go back to doing what they deem as being more fun and or interesting. But hey, that's kids for you, you know, kids just wanna have fun, you know? And this is why it is very important for parents to have patience with their kids, you know, because kids just don't understand why they have to do things that are boring and or tedious, you know, like cleaning their rooms or just sitting still without making noise, you know what I mean? But hey, that's kids for you, and kids just want to have fun!

Man, parenting, it's a lot of work, especially if you want to be a good parent! Because kids just have a lot of energy, especially the little ones. And not only do they have a lot of energy, little kids are also just so inquisitive and just want to know everything, you know? And this is why little kids favorite words are; what, why and how come, you know what I mean? And the reason why these are their favorite words is because, they just have to know what something is, they just have to know why something is, and they just have to know; how come they can't have it, how come they can't do it, and or how come they can't be it, you know what I mean?

And I mean, this is also why little kids just like to touch everything, you know, because they are just so inquisitive and want to know what everything is, and why it does what it does, and how come they can't have it. And so, this is why you as a parent can find yourself answering why questions, what questions and how come questions all day long for your kid. And then on top of that, this is also why you can find yourself saying, "Stop touching that, don't touch that, stop touching that, don't touch that, hey, didn't I just say don't touch that?" I mean, it can be very tiring having to answer a whole bunch of questions that follow with more follow up questions just because their little minds just can't grasp or comprehend your explanations. And the funny thing is, I think most parents just don't know how to break down their answers to the simplest form, you know, to where a little three or four year old kid can understand or come close to understanding. And I mean, this is why a lot of parents just result into telling white lies to their kids, you know, because they just don't know how to answer the questions to where the kid can come close to understanding. And sometimes parents tell white lies to their kids because they are just too tired or too lazy to try and answer all of the innocent questions that their kids have.

And actually, sometimes parents just don't know the answer to their kids questions, and therefore result into telling a lie instead of just saying I don't know but I can find out for you. I mean, your kid won't think you are dumb if you don't know the answer to something, I mean, they'll just learn that no one knows everything, which is ok. But then of course, if you have the tendency of saying "I don't know, I don't know, stop asking me all these questions!" Then there you will definitely be living yourself open for your kids to think that you are probably not as smart as they thought you were, you know, because you don't seem to know anything, you know, because every time they ask you a question, you are always saying you don't know. And so, it is very important to try your best to answer your little kid's question as best and or as simply as you can put it, because if you don't, not only are you going to be bombarded with a bunch of follow up questions about the same subject, you are also going to be depriving your kids of essential knowledge and or understanding that they desperately crave at that young tender age.

But yeah, little kids, from when they start to craw, to when they start to walk, to when they start to run, to when they start to talk, all the way until right before adolescence, they are a piece of work, bursting with seemingly endless energy which can leave a parent absolutely exhausted.

And so, this is why it is very important for fathers to be in their kid's lives, you know, so that way their kids can have two parents to try and keep up with them, you know? Because some kids are just extra hyper, you know, requiring that extra attention that one parent (especially a hard working parent, which most single mothers are) just might not be able to provide, resulting in the kid receiving improper nurturing because the mother is just too tired and exhausted from work and other stuff.

And I mean, this is one of the reasons why I'm so glad that my wife is a stay at home mom, because I don't think I would have had the time to try to chase my dreams, work a full time job and also try to be the best father I can be (by helping out with the kids whenever my wife is tired and or just needs a break to rejuvenate herself) if my wife was also working. Because it's like this, kids require a lot of attention, and if both me and my wife were working, that means we would both be coming home tired, and therefore, not only would we both have to be attentive to the kids (you know, with like homework, dinner, bed prep, you know, teeth brushing, bed time story, you know, etc., etc.), you know, because it just wouldn't be fair for just one of the tired parents to do it all. And so, by me working and my wife staying home, not only do the kids get proper attention (because their mother is there for them full time), I too get a chance to work on my Dream of becoming a successful writer and producer with the free time that I get from not having to baby sit and or worry about the kids' daily activities all the time.

I mean, I'm telling you, kids require a lot of attention, because there are just too much stuff that has to be done for them in a daily basis. Because it's like, from the moment you wake up (if it's school days, that means an extra early wake up time), not only do you have to wake them up, but you also gotta get their school clothes ready (if you hadn't done it the night before), then give them a shower (if they are still too young to do it themselves), and then you gotta dress them up, and then you gotta try to get them to eat a quick breakfast (you know, so they don't go to school hungry), and then you gotta fix them lunch (you know, in case they got allergies and can't really eat the school food), and then you gotta rush them to where the school bus picks them up at, so they don't miss the bus again which will force you to have to drop them off at school, which either I or my wife will do on a regular basis. And this is because I insist on making sure the kids eat a little something in the morning before they go to school, which of course causes them to miss the bus more often than not, to the point that now me and my wife don't even try for the bus, instead we just drop them off ourselves. And to tell you the truth, I think the school buses just come to darn early in the morning for these little kids, especially in the winter time when not only is it freezing, but it's usually still kind of dark outside. And so, not only will you have to get the kids ready for school, if you are a working mother, you will also have to get yourself ready for work.

And this is why a lot of parents just don't seem to be able to get to work on time every day, because some mornings it's just a drag trying to get the kids ready for school (which I don't seem to have mastered, because they always seem to be late for school when I'm the one who is handling the morning ritual of getting them ready and dropping them off to school, you know, when my wife is either not feeling well or when I'm just trying to give my wife some rest from waking up early all the time).

But yeah, getting kids ready for school in the morning can be very challenging, especially when they are little and or you too have to get yourself ready for work. And I mean, sometimes the morning ritual can be straight out chaotic, especially when you are running late, you know what I mean? Because it's like, not only are you in a rush to get them ready for school, you are also in a rush so you can make sure that you too are not late for work again, for the third time this week. And so, in like a mad person, you start running around the house making sure everyone is showered, dressed, teeth brushed, hair combed or brushed, and then you dash off to the kitchen and try to make a quick breakfast for them to eat before they go to school, you know? Because I mean, if you have an extremely picky eater like how my four year old son is, you definitely want to make sure they eat something before they go to school, you know, because otherwise they will return home not looking or feeling good because they are starving. And so, me and my wife we definitely try to make sure that he at least eats a little something in the morning, you know, that way even if he doesn't eat or doesn't finish his school lunch for whatever reason, he will still be ok and not starving, which can also make him not concentrate in class.

I mean, I don't know what it is, but both of our kids are picky eaters, you know what I mean? Because it's like, we used to get the same report about our daughter not eating her (school provided) lunch when she was little, you know, when she was around four or five years old like my son is now (my daughter is eight years old now and is not that picky anymore, especially when it comes to junk food, you know, just like any kid, she loves them junk food).

And so anyway, yeah, back to the chaotic morning ritual. And so, as you are preparing a quick breakfast for the kids, you will be dashing back and forth between the kitchen and their rooms, you know, to make sure that they are getting dressed (if they are old enough to dress themselves completely) or to help them finish getting dressed (if they are too little to dress themselves completely), you know? And so, you will be running back and forth and back and forth between the kitchen and their rooms, you know, so you can hurry them up to get ready, because for some reason kids just don't seem to have a sense of urgency, even if you tell them a hundred times, "Hurry up, hurry up, hurry up, hurry up, we are running late, you need to hurry up!" I mean, I don't know what it is, but they will just look at you like, "Gees, what's wrong with him or her!", you know what I mean? Because I mean it's like, there you are running around the house trying to make sure that they get to school on time, and also get something in their little bellies before they go, and what do they do, they take their sweet ass time, that's what they do. I mean, it's crazy, because there you are running around like you are crazy, and there they are taking their sweet ass time acting like they have got all the time in the world to get ready. And I mean, sometimes you can even catch them playing with their toys (as in my four year old son) and or looking at themselves in the mirror singing and dancing and seeing how pretty they look (as in my eight year old daughter). I mean it can be very defeating to your morning energy sometimes, because there you are trying your best to hurry up and get them to school on time and there they are playing around without a care in the world.

I mean it's crazy, and my wife can get really worked up and frustrated at mornings like these, especially when it comes to our daughter. Because my wife feels as though she should at least understand or have a little bit of a sense of urgency when we are running late and be able to hurry up. But you know, I just try to tell her, I just try to tell my wife that, kids are kids, and until they have something that they deem very important to them that they really have to do or want to do and have to be there on time, they will always take their sweet time to get ready. And this is because, kids in general just hate having to wake up early in the morning (hey, most adults hate waking up early in the morning too), and so it takes them a little while to pump themselves up with excitement for the day and get themselves motivated to hurry up and get ready, you know what I mean? But my wife just gets so worked up sometimes over it that I have to remind her that we too used to be unmotivated about waking up early and get ourselves ready for school. And I mean, she understands that they are just kids and that's how kids are, but I guess it just gets to her sometimes, especially the fact that she hates having to shout and yell and repeat herself over and over again for my daughter to hurry up and for my son to sit still and eat his breakfast. But hey, that's what parenting is all about, because leave it to them, they'll never get themselves ready to make it to school on time.

And so anyway, yeah, after getting them dressed, and after you have succeeded in making the little breakfast without burning some of it (like I always seem to do when I'm the one getting them ready), and as they are eating their breakfast, now it's your turn to hurry up and get yourself ready. So as quickly as you can, you jump in the shower (Boot Camp, military style), then jump out and dress up (Boot Camp style again), and then yell for the kids to get their book bags and then off y'all go running to the car as if y'all in a race. And actually me and the kids have turned it into an actual race to where we run and see who can get to the car and touch it first, you know? And since we live in an apartment complex, sometimes we have to park the car a little bit further from out apartment, making the run pretty fun, especially for my kids who swear they are faster than me, because I usually like to let them win, you know? And they love the fact that they beat me almost every time (even my four year old son, who will start to cry if he comes in last, which sometimes I let him come in last just so he can learn that you are not always going to win in a competition, you know, trying to teach them that losing isn't always bad just as long as you do and or try your best).

And then so, as soon as we reach the car, we quickly get in, then we quickly put on our sit belts, and then I quickly start the car, then reverse it, and then screech the tires and off we go in a mad dash trying to get to school on time. And the funny thing is, this is usually the only time that my daughter seems to be more conscience about getting to school on time, as she urges me to drive faster and faster so that she won't be late and have to get a tardy slip. And so as I'm driving, she keeps her eyes on the clock (in the car) and tells me when every minute has passed. But lucky for us their school is only about five minutes away by car, in which I can do in three minutes if I'm really pushing it and if I run a few stop signs (which I don't like to do, but I do, do it sometimes when we are really late). And then so, as soon as we hit the school's front driveway, my daughter jumps out and runs to her class so she won't be late. And then after her, my son jumps out and hurries me to walk him to his class because he's too young to walk to class by himself (school rules) until he's in kindergarten (he is in Head Start right now). And then after I drop them off, if I have to get to work early, I dash back to the car, screech the tires again, and drive off to work like a mad man.

I mean it's crazy how much work it can be trying to get kids to school on time. Because I mean, I have realized that I'm not the only one that is not very good at getting the kids to school on time every day. Because I mean, I see a lot of parents (almost the same parents) dropping their kids late to school all the time, as I'm dropping mine off. I mean it's crazy, because it seems as if everybody is in a rush to go somewhere, because everybody looks frantic and the school parking lot starts to look like a chaotic drive through with a whole bunch of kids being dropped off.

And so anyway, yeah, those morning routines to drop kids off at school can be very tiring and or chaotic. And this is one of the reasons why I'm glad that my wife is a stay at home mom, you know, because she can handle most of the getting ready for school morning ritual without worrying about rushing off to work herself, and I too don't have to worry about waking up so early (especially when I'm exhausted), because I know my wife will handle it. And so I mean, there are a lot of benefits of one parent staying home full time to care for the kids (preferably the mother, because mothers seem to have more patience for nurturing than fathers) than if both parents are working. Because I mean, if both parents are working, this will mean that both parents will be tired after work to really pay attention to their kids properly, especially when the kids are younger and require a lot more attention.

And this is one of the reasons why some couples will make a conscious decision for one of them to quit their job and be a stay at home parent (usually the mother), you know, so they can take better care of the kids. And this is because they understand how much work kids really are, and so they really want to give them the benefit of having one parent there for them at all times. And I mean, of course it's not easy (financially) for most couples to only have one parent working (with how high the cost of living is these days), but more and more couples are making the sacrifice.

Because really if you think about it, the money that most people pay for day care (a good day care) is almost half or more than half of their whole paycheck, especially if they have more than one kid (which most couples do) and or are only making minimum wage or just above minimum wage.

And this is one of the reasons why a lot of households with both parents working still seem to be struggling financially just like the households with just one parent working and the other one staying at home. And it's because the both parents working household has day care expenses that can be very expensive. So really it's like (unless both parents are making way, way above minimal wage), one of the parents is only working to pay for day care expenses while the other parent works to pay for the household and other expenses, you know what I mean?

And I mean, sure the parent that's working to pay for day care might have two or three hundred dollars left from their paycheck (after taxes and day care expenses are subtracted) every month that can indeed help out with extra household expenses, but to me the trade-off of not being able to see and or raise and nurture your kids the way you want to is just not really worth it. Because I mean it's like, there you are, busy working eight or more hours a day, five or more days a week, forty or more hours a week, month after month, year after year, and all you are really bringing home is a meager three or four hundred dollars (after taxes and day care expenses) a month, which to me is just ridiculous. Because I mean, what's the point of working all them hours and not being able to see and or raise your kids your way for most of the day. And also coming back home stressed and tired almost every day, and also, not being able or being too tired to spend some quality time with your love, you know, your sweetie, your darling, your sugar, your honey, your baby, your boo, you know, your significant other, ha ha ha ha, you know what I mean? And also still, what's the point of working all them hours and not being able or being too tired to spend some quality time with your kids. Come on, and it's all for what, an extra three or four hundred dollars a month that will cost you all them hours a week, come on, it just doesn't make sense to me, because that extra money will be gone or spent as quickly as you can say, "I hate my job!"

And I mean, sure that extra money would come in handy, but to me, the trade-off of what you have to give up (in terms of time, which you could use to raise your kids full-time), just doesn't add up, you know what I mean? I mean, to me, it's just not worth it!

And this is the same reasoning that I had to give to my wife when we had our first kid and I was trying to convince her that maybe she should just stay home with the kid, you know, so we won't have to worry about all that day care issues (expenses and what not). And I mean, it took a while for her to get used to the idea of not having two incomes coming in. And to tell you the truth, I still don't think she's totally comfortable with the idea of being a stay at home mom yet, even though it's been almost seven years now. And I don't blame her, because it's hard being broke all the time, you know what I mean? Because it's like, she would always think about going back to work every time we ran out of money, you know, which was a lot of times, you know, the result of living at or just above the poverty line.

And I mean, sure it's tough only having one income coming in, especially with how high the cost of living is nowadays, and especially when you are in the low income earning bracket. I mean, I won't lie to you, it does get a little tough and stressful sometimes, you know, having to live way, way, way, way, way below your means and having to manage every little dollar that we have. But, I wouldn't change anything (as far as my wife being a stay at home mom), because the benefits of having her at home and being able to care and raise the kids properly (you know, by giving them full attention) far out ways the extra money that we might have by her working.

I mean it's crazy, because when people find out that my wife is a stay at home mom, they all seem to ask me the same question, "How can you afford to have your wife be a stay at home mom?" I mean, it almost never fails, man or woman, they all tend to look at me with this serious curious look like I have a secret that they need to know about. And so my answer is usually simple and the same every time, you know, I just tell them that I can't afford to pay all that money for day care. And to my surprise, they usually don't have a follow up question as they nod their heads in agreement and start to tell me they too wish that they didn't have to pay all that money for day care. And then I usually ask them (if they are guys), "Then why don't you just have your wife or significant other stay home and care for the kids so y'all don't have to worry about paying all that money for day care". And it never fails, because I almost always get the same answer, you know, they always say something like, "Nah man, I don't think that will work, I mean, I don't know how you do it, but we need all the income we can get". And the funny thing is, I get almost the same answer from women, you know, they just don't think that they can afford to just have one person work while the other one stays home and cares for the kids full time. I mean, most people think that you have to earn a whole lot of money for one parent to be able to stay home full time and care for the kids. Because I mean, when they find out that my wife is a stay at home mom, the first question or assumption is that I must be making a lot of money. But then when I tell them how much I get paid per hour, they always look at me like I'm crazy or something, and then they ask me if I have a second job or something. And then when I tell them, no, I just have one job, they look at me in disbelief and just say something like, "Man, more power to you, but I just don't think I could do it!"

    I mean it's crazy, but most people just don't think that they can afford to have one spouse stay home and care for the kids full time. And I understand why this is so. And the reason for it is because, most people are just not willing to sacrifice their life style, you know, they just don't want to give up driving nice cars, or, they just don't want to give up going out to eat whenever they want to, or, they just don't want to give up going to the movies whenever they want to, or, they just don't want to give up their shopping habits, or, they just don't want to give up from having their hair done at the salon whenever they want to, and so on and so on. I mean, a lot of couples just get so caught up in their life styles that they just can't fathom losing one income and having to change their life style, especially if it will mean that their standard of living will go down tremendously. But to me, the benefits of having one parent at home full-time to raise and or care for the kids far out-weighs life style changes and or more money. Because I mean, in today's crazy world, if you as a parent don't take extra care and time to teach, supervise and direct your kids in positive and or proper directions, they can easily be misled and or fall for the wrong things that the world thinks or will teach them, even without them or you realizing it. Because I mean, most kids just copy what other kids do or how other kids behave, you know, because they just don't know any better.

And so, this is one of the reasons why kids tend to pick up a lot of their bad behavior or bad languages either at day care or school or playgrounds, and it's because they just don't know any better. And this is one of the reasons why it is so beneficial when one parent is at home full time, you know, because not only will the kid not have too many chances of picking up bad behavior from outside the home, but the stay at home parent will also have plenty of time to instill and to reinforce good behavior, good values, and good morals to the kid, especially when the kid is younger and doesn't know any better.

And so, yes, it can be very beneficial to have one parent stay at home full time to care for the kids, but then of course it will also take a lot of sacrifice. Because I mean, not only is the stay at home parent (usually the mother) will have to quit their job, but they will also be derailing their careers, which can be very hard for them to deal with. And I mean, of course they can resume their careers when the kids get older, you know, but it just won't be the same, you know, because not only might they have to start from the beginning again, but the job market (depending on their field) might just be harder to re-enter because there may not be that many jobs there anymore. I mean it's a tough situation and a tough decision for most parents to make, because there is just no guarantee that your job will still be there for you to regain your position once you decide that you are ready to re-enter the workforce. And I mean, I think this is one of the main reasons why a lot of women don't even consider being stay at home moms, you know, because they just don't want to have to fight or start all over again chasing a career that might be already hard to get into. Because I mean, in today's competitive job market it's already hard as hell to really advance in a career, and so the thought of starting all over again after maybe five, ten, or even fifteen years of being a stay at home parent just doesn't really excite anybody.

And so, this is one of the reasons why a lot of women just don't even entertain the thought of being a stay at home mom, because the thought of losing their career just tends to be too much of a sacrifice for them to make, which should be respected. Because I mean, it does not make any sense for anybody who is not at least ninety percent sure that they want to be a stay at home parent to quit their job and attempt or force themselves to do it. Because I mean, not only will they be miserable and resentful for having to give up their career, they will also be unproductive at home with the kids, you know, because instead of being happy and or joyful that they get to raise their kids full time without having to worry about work, they will instead do a poor job of being a homemaker because they will spend most of the days being resentful and or miserable and may even blame the kids (as if it was their kids' choice) for their own decision to quit their job and become a stay at home mom.

And so, it is very important that the person who is going to be the stay at home parent make sure that they really want to be or really want to try to be a stay at home parent, because I'm telling you, it is a lot of sacrifice. Because it's like, I look at my wife (who has been a stay at home mother for about seven years now), and even though she appreciates being able to be there for the kids full time and not having to worry about day care and all that stuff, I can still sense that she kinds of misses being a career woman, you know what I mean? And so, yeah, giving up a career to be a stay at home mom can be a huge sacrifice, especially for the career minded woman, which is most of the women out there nowadays.

And this is another reason why most women won't even entertain the thought of being stay at home moms, you know, because they are just not brought up that way, you know what I mean? And what I mean is, women nowadays are just not brought up to just be housewives and or just homemakers, you know what I mean? I mean, nowadays women are brought up to be go getters, you know, they are brought up to be career minded rather than being just homemakers. And the reason for this (women being brought up to be career minded rather than just housewives) is because parents have realized that the chances of their daughters finding prince charming who will be responsible enough to take good care of her and her kids and never ever leave her (split, separate, divorce, for whatever reason) is very, very rare nowadays, you know, unlike yesteryears when people rarely divorced or separated. And so, being that parents don't want their daughters to be left out there broke and with no sense of hope if or when their relationships don't work out, parents started pushing and demanding that their daughters get education and get careers of their own, you know, so they won't have to depend on their man fully for financial support, you know what I mean? And so, by the women being able to work and take care of their own selves, their roles as homemakers and or housewives started to diminish because that's not how they viewed themselves anymore, you know?

And I mean, this is why we got all these independent women nowadays, you know, because their careers come first and husbands and or children will just have to wait until mommy comes home late from work again to get that motherly attention, because with her promotion comes more responsibilities and her boss only cares about her getting the job done and done well, especially if she wants to advance in the company, which of course is what every ambitious person wants.

other reason why most women just don't even entertain the idea of being stay at home moms, you know, because they just don't know any better, you know, because their whole life has being geared toward having a career, you know what I mean? And so, when the day comes that they do find that Mr. Right, you know, that Mr. Responsible, you know, that Mr. Wonderful who is more than willing and happy to have his wife be a stay at home mom and wife, you know, so she can have plenty of time to take better care of him and the kids (hey, men need their women to care for them too, you know what I mean guys, ha ha ha ha ha!), she might freak out and not know what to do with herself (with the extra free time on her hand) as a housewife and mother. And this is because being a stay at home wife and mother is usually not in most women's minds nowadays, you know what I mean?

And so I mean, yeah, women nowadays just don't consider being stay at home moms as an option. And of course for single mothers it's definitely not an option, you know, because they definitely have to work so they can take care of their kids. But I mean, even the women who are married and have husbands who don't mind them staying at home full time to care for the kids still find it hard to be stay at home moms. And the reason for this is because, women are not programmed to be just homemakers anymore, you know what I mean? And this is one of the reasons why a lot of working women (women that have jobs outside the home, because stay at home moms do work and do have jobs, which is inside the home, which can be a lot, and really, their jobs might even be a little bit more stressful, because it ain't easy chasing after two or three year olds all day. I mean, trust me, I have done it, and after a few hours, I was ready for my wife to take over, you know what I mean?) tend to look down on stay at home moms, you know, because they just can't imagine not having a job or career. Because it's like, for a lot of these career women, for a lot of them, their self-worth or self-esteem is tied to their careers, you know what I mean? And so, they feel as though giving up their careers is like giving up on their personal accomplishments, you know, they feel as though a part of them will not be fulfilled as stay at home moms, which can be true, all depending on how hard core they are about their careers and how much they really want to be stay at home moms.

And this is why I like to caution any woman who fantasizes about being a stay at home mom, make sure that you really, really want to do it, because it's no joke, I'm telling you, it's not as carefree and or easy like watching soaps on TV all day kind of thing, you know, just relaxing and stuff. Hell no, not especially if you have more than one kid and they are all under the age of eight and one or two of them just cannot sit still for more than two minutes! I mean, I'm telling you, it's a lot of work that just don't seem to have an end in sight!

And this is one of the reasons why I have a lot of respect for stay at home moms, because I know how much work it really is, because I have done it for about six months, not by choice but because I was out of a job and my wife had to work. And I'm telling you, in those six months I grew a new appreciation for what mothers do, and not just stay at home moms, but mothers period. Because I mean, I just never really paid much attention at how much detail goes into the day-to-day chore of taking care of a kid, you know, until I had to do it full time. And let me tell you, it's a lot of work! Because I mean, it starts from very early in the morning, even before they wake up, because as soon as you wake up, it's on, let the parenting begin again, you know, another shift that will go on all day long until night comes and you put the little young'ns to bed. But first, before you send the kids to bed for the night, you will have to go through a morning ritual, which will involve getting the kids ready for the day, which can be very stressful, because you will probably be in a rush and for some reason kids just don't seem to understand what having a sense of urgency is all about. And then after the morning ritual, you will have to go through the afternoon ritual, which can involve changing a lot of diapers and or pull ups, and also feedings, then nap time, then changing clothes again because someone has spilled juice on themselves. Then the numerous doctor's visits for routine check-ups. Then there's laundry, house cleaning, fixing lunch, and then trying to force the kids to finish their lunch so that way they won't bother you an hour later about being hungry, you know what I mean?

And then still, you will have to deal with them being restless and running all around the house. And then, you will have to deal with putting bandages on someone's knee or arm because they won't stop crying because they are convinced that they have hurt themselves because they can see a tiny little red spot on their knee that you can hardly see but they are sure that they are bleeding and since they don't want to bleed to death they demand that they must have a bandage to stop the none blood that they swear is blood and it's coming out. And so, because you just don't have the strength or energy to argue with them anymore, and because you just want a little peace and quiet for just a few minutes (an hour would be nice), you go ahead and put the bandages on them and you put bandages on even the kids that didn't ask for one, you know, just incase they happen to fall and not hurt themselves also but think they did, you know, so you can just tell them to use one of the bandages that they don't need that's on the other arm, you know what I mean?

I mean, the afternoons can be very challenging, especially if you have little kids and they are bored to death, because they will find a way to entertain themselves, which a lot of times will involve running around the house and falling and crying for bandages, you know what I mean? And this is why "Stop, stop, stop, stop running around the house before you hurt yourself!," will be one of your favorite sentences to say when you are a parent and your kids are still little, because you will catch yourself saying this sentence over and over and over again until it becomes second nature. I mean, the afternoon can be very busy also, especially if you have little kids and they just can't seem to sit still and or they just refuse to take a nap (which can be very helpful, you know, because not only will it give the mother a breather and allow her to reenergize herself, but it will also allow her to take her time to prepare for the evening ritual, which can be kind of tiring with all that cooking, homework checking, and getting the kids ready for bed routine).

And so, this is one of the reasons why it is very important for fathers to help out with the kids in a daily basis, even if the mother is a stay at home mom, because towards the end of the day, even stay at home moms get worn out, because really it's a lot of work taking care of kids. And this is why a lot of mothers just get so frustrated when their husbands or their man just won't help out around the house, you know, help out with some of the household chores, you know, like washing the dishes, vacuuming, taking out the trash, and so on and so on.

And I mean, now I know why a lot of women just seem to look so darn tired and or so darn mad all the time, and it's because they just can't seem to get some useful help from their man (you know, help with the kids and some household chores), which could greatly alleviate some of their stresses. Because I mean, think about it, how many women do you know that walk around with smiles on their faces? Not many, right? And I bet you, most of these women with frowns on their faces, I bet you they have kids and I bet you that their man is not doing much to help them with either the raising of the kids and or not much in helping out around the house. I mean, I'm telling you, I have really thought about it, and it's amazing at how much more work there is for women to do (when it comes to raising kids and taking care the house) then there is for a man. And this is because men in general are just not good housekeepers, you know what I mean? Because I mean, leave it up to a man to be the sole responsible for maintaining a clean house, you will for sure be living in a not so clean house.

I mean, I don't know what it is, but us men (most of us anyway, because there are some very clean men out there who are very good in that household stuff, you know what I mean?), we are just not very motivated with all that cleaning stuff. And this is why a lot of college boys' dorm rooms are usually kind of trashy, you know, because they are just not too motivated with putting things in their particular places. Because I mean, for most of us guys, as long as we can find what we are looking for when we need something, then it's cool where it's at. And the funny thing is, we kind of usually know where everything is, just as long as we don't move it when we don't need it, you know what I mean, ha ha ha ha ha!

But yeah, women just seem to have so much more responsibilities than men, in my opinion. Because if you think about it, when it comes to us men, our biggest responsibilities seem to be in paying the bills and only play and or care for the kids when the mother is either too tired or just not available to do it, you know what I mean? But, when it comes to women, not only do they have to worry about the kids on an hour to hour and minute to minute basis, but if they also have to work, they will also have to worry about the bills and on top of that, they will have the house cleaning and other chores to worry about. And so, this is one of the reasons why a lot of women just look mad and or tired all the time, you know, because their men are just not doing their part in helping them out, you know, with the kids and the household stuff.

And so, from that six month period when I didn't have a job and had to be Mr. Mom and take care of our daughter full time (you know, while my wife was busting her ass at work with all them overtime she was doing, you know, trying to bring in enough income), I really learned a lot about what mothers really do around the house and how much work it really is to take care of a kid. Because I mean, there I was, just me and my daughter (she was around two or three years old at that time if I'm not mistaken), looking at each other like, "Ok, so what are we going to do today", you know, not knowing what the hell to do to make the time go by faster. Because I mean, I had already knew about diaper changing and all that stuff, and plus, we were past that stage already, because she was wearing pull-ups by now, but I just did not know how much attention a two year old really needs. I mean, because it's like, when they are younger (before they hit the terrible twos), you can just put them in their play pin or in front of the TV and just let them be amazed with cartoons all day. But, when they reach two and beyond, TV can bore them and therefore they will need more stuff to do so as to keep them busy and to allow their little minds to explore and to discover the meaning of life as they see it, which means a lot of playing. And so, I remember having to play a lot of make believe games, because the park was a little bit too far from the house and I just was a little too lazy to take her, which I try to do more now, because trying to entertain two kids (now that we have two kids) is a lot of work, especially in the summer time when school is out and so they get extra bored.

And so, yeah, when it was just me and my daughter when she was little, all of a sudden I found myself having to do all the morning, afternoon, and evening rituals, you know, bathing her, dressing her, fixing her breakfast, cooking her lunch, putting her for a nap, playing with her (and yes, I even played with dolls and dress up with her numerous times), and then in the evening, fix her dinner and then get her ready for bed. And so I mean, it was kind of tough, especially in the beginning, you know, the first couple of days, you know, when I realized how long and or dragged out a day can be when you are a stay at home parent. Because I mean, the days just seemed to drag on and on and on, you know, without end. And the reason why the days had seemed to go so slow (I came to realize), is because I was so used to being busy with work and other stuff that made the day go by faster. And so, by me not working and having to stay home and care for our daughter, the pace of things just wasn't the same, you know? Because I mean, it's amazing how much time there is during the morning and afternoon hours when you don't have anything much to do beside baby sit your kids. Because I mean, usually after two hours of playing with dolls or something, boredom starts to creep in and you start to look at the clock to see if it's almost time for mommy to get off work and come home, you know, so she can take over the baby sitting and stuff, you know what I mean?

But unfortunately for me during this time, my wife was doing a whole bunch of overtime and or double shifts, which meant that she would be coming home late and most likely she will be too tired to really help out. Because I mean, I remember how a lot of times she would come home from work (after having done some overtime hours) and just pass out on the couch in no time at all, almost like what I do nowadays, you know, after a long day of working, writing and trying to do some music. Man I'm telling you, it can be very exhausting. But hey, that's what you gotta do when you have dreams and or if you really want to get ahead in this world, you know, you gotta work hard!

And so anyway, yeah, those were some long days of baby-sitting, especially when my wife had to do overtime, which was often. And so, sooner than later I realized that I'm gonna have to do something productive around the house with my free time, you know, instead of just waiting for my wife to get home, you know, so I can

No More Baby Daddies

hand over the baby duties to her. And so I tried to do some house cleaning and stuff like that, but to tell you the truth, I don't think I was that good at it, because my wife would always ask me how come I didn't even try to clean the place up, and my response was always like, "What do you mean, I did clean up!" And that's when I realized maybe I'm just not that good at this cleaning up thing. And so I promptly gave it up and decided maybe I should just use my free time to try and write a book (because when I was younger I always fantasized about being a writer).

And so that's exactly what I did with my free time, you know, did some writing in between watching my daughter and especially when she was taking a nap. And that's when my first book "What is love" was written, which I still haven't really promoted yet, and in which I have somehow sold about three hundred copies without even really trying, you know, selling to like friends and whoever else that somehow heard about it and wanted a copy, you know? Because really, I just wrote that first book just to test myself, you know, just to see whether or not I have what it takes to not only have the patience to sit and concentrate long enough to write a whole book, but also I wanted to see if I had what it takes to write a book that was kind of good and that people would actually want to buy it and read it.

And so I was very pleasantly surprised and actually I'm still kind of amazed at how many people actually bought my book and seemed to like it. I mean, don't get me wrong, it's not like I didn't think I had the potential to write a book, oh no, it's just that I wasn't really sure that my writing style and thoughts would be good enough for people to enjoy reading. Well, I guess what I'm really trying to say is that, I was really overwhelmed by peoples excitement and encouragement in my writing career after buying and or reading the book. Because I mean, most people who bought my book wanted me to sign it, you know, like I was a big time writer or something, you know what I mean? And the funny thing is, the few times that I have actually gone out there (in the streets) to kind of promote my book by setting up a table and see if I can sell a few books just for fun, I actually ended up selling at least eight to ten books. And the funny thing about it is that, I'm actually selling the books to none readers, you know, people who are not hard core book readers. Because it's like, I would always get comments like, "You know, I'm not much of a book reader but I think I'mma get yours, because it sounds kind of interesting!" And some people would be like (after flipping and or browsing through the pages for a few minutes), "Oh, I don't usually buy books but I'm gonna buy yours!" And I remember always just standing there and thinking to myself, "Man, there sure seems to be a lot of none readers out here!"

   I mean it was kind of crazy, but the whole thing of people actually buying my book was kind of amazing. Because it's like, I would just set up my table anywhere on the side walk (without being a nuisance of course) where there's a little bit of heavy foot traffic and just kind of show off my book. And most people would just glance over at the table, and once in a while someone would stop and actually flip through the pages and scheme through it and or even actually read a few pages. And the funny thing is, most of the people that actually flipped through it and schemed through it, actually ended up buying the book.

   I mean it was just amazing watching people glance over, scheme over, and actually buy the book and then before they walk off they would make sure that I had signed it somewhere. And I remember this one girl (a young lady), I remember her standing there looking over the book and opening it and start to read it, you know, just taking her time. And then after a few minutes, she stopped reading, looked at me for a few seconds, and then continued reading. And then after a few minutes later, she stopped reading again, looked at me again, then asked me if I really wrote the book, to which I said of-course. And then a few minutes later (which by this time I could tell that she was really digging and or really liking the book, because she had been standing there reading it for almost ten minutes or so by then), she looked up real quick like in a hurry, you know, like she's late for something. And that's when I realized that she was waiting for the bus and was about to miss her bus, you know, because she was too busy reading my book that she didn't notice that her bus was at the bus stop. And so, not wanting to miss her bus, and really wanting the book, she frantically searched her pockets and hand bag for some money, when she found some she hurried up and gave it to me (I think she was a dollar or two short but I told her not to worry about it), and then she ran for the bus.

 The bus driver seeing her running toward the bus (just as the bus was starting to drive off) was good and kind enough to stop and let her in. But, before the driver could close the bus door and drive off, I heard her say to the driver, "Wait a second, I forgot something!" Then in a frantic urgency, she proceeded to jump of the bus, run all the way to my table (I wasn't that far though, but still), and then she started motioning and telling me, "You forgot to sign my book, you forgot to sign my book!" And so I hurried up and singed the book for her, misspelling her name in the process because she was talking too fast and kind of out of breath. And so, even before I could finish putting an exclamation point on my thank you for buying the book part for her, she snatched the book off my hand and started running for the bus again (because by this time the bus driver had blown the horn for her a few times already and was about to drive off without her), in which time I started laughing and yelled out to her, "You know I'm not famous right!?" And she yelled back, "Oh, you gonna be famous, and I'mma have one of your first copies with your signature on it!"

 I mean, it was crazy, and I just couldn't believe how much she really wanted my signature on the book. And now that I think about it, I remember her even making sure that I wrote the date on it. Man, that was funny, but she was just so optimistic in my potential to be a good author I guess, which is very encouraging, because this writing business sometimes can be very intimidating, especially with the amount of authors and books out there that get published every year, you know what I mean? Because it's like, every time I think about how much work it will really take for me to make a name for myself in this deep cut throat business of book selling, I start asking myself whether all this time I'm spending writing will be worth it when it is all said and done. But then I start remembering how many people (the few that have seen my first book so far, especially strangers) actually seem to think that I might have potential as a writer, and who seem to enjoy my writing style and or opinions, then I start to think to myself, "Self, you have no choice but to become a writer, and who knows, maybe you just might become one of them best-selling authors" you know what I mean, ha ha ha ha ha!

And so, anyway, lets continue, I mean, let's go back to our original topic, you know, let's go back to what we were talking about before I started going on and on about my brief first book selling adventure. And so I mean, oh man, I think I have forgotten what we were talking about. I think we were talking something about kids, something about baby-sitting, oh wait a minute, we were talking about me being a stay at home dad and what I did to pass the time as I'm watching or baby-sitting my daughter. Yeah, that's what we were talking about. Ok, so let's continue!

And so anyway, yeah, writing was one of the ways that I found to be very useful and productive way for me to pass the time as I'm doing or trying my best to be Mr. Mom, you know what I mean? And the other way that I would make time go by faster during the day was, I would go to the studio (music studio), and I would take my daughter with me. Because during this time I had become friends with the guy that owned the studio and since I was trying to learn everything I could about the music business and how to produce songs, I used to hang out in his studio a lot, you know, so I could soak up all the knowledge that was there, you know what I mean? And so yeah, me and my three year old daughter would head out to the studio (usually after her afternoon nap), and as I'm watching the producer do his thing, my daughter would either be messing with the broken guitar that no one was using or singing with a fake mike that I had bought for her, you know, so she won't be crying for one of the real mikes in the studio. And so yeah, me and my daughter became regulars at the studio, and sometimes we would even stay a little past her bedtime, especially when her mama was working overtime or double shifts.

But yeah, those were some fun times hanging out with my daughter at the studio. And the fact that we got a chance to do a lot of bonding was great! And that just opened my eyes to how much parents (especially fathers) actually miss out when they don't take active roles or when they just don't make it an effort to actually spend some quality time with their kids. Because I mean, I was actually starting to get used to being Mr. Mom, you know what I mean? Because it's like, I actually got used to being around my daughter all day and I actually got good at answering all of her million questions without flinching or getting irritated, you know what I mean? Because I mean, kids just love to ask so many questions that they can actually wear you out, you know? And this is because they are just so darn curious about everything, and that is because their brains are growing and just need to absorb and understand everything, which is only right.

And so yeah, my short stint at being Mr. Mom just taught me a lot of things about not only parenting, but also about life itself. Because it's like, I came to realize that, life is not all about being rich or having a lot of material things, you know what I mean? I mean, don't get me wrong, there's nothing wrong with being rich (especially with the potential it gives you to be able to help others who are less fortunate than you, which should be every rich person's aim, as the Bible says), but richness alone won't make you happy. Because I mean, how many stories have we heard of people who are rich but just seem to be as miserable as hell. And this is because they never learned or just never understood what the meaning of life is all about. Because I mean, really if you think about it, life really is all about being happy.

And so, if life is really about being happy, then the question is, how do you go about finding that happiness? And this is the biggest quest that every human being seems to struggle very hard in finding. And the reason for this struggle is because, a lot of people spend so much time looking for or searching for happiness every-where else than within, you know, than within their homes, you know, than within their kids and loved ones, you know what I mean? Because I mean, I can't think of anything in this world that can make me any happier than spending time with my kids (and my wife of course) and just enjoy their youthful nature, you know what I mean? Because I mean, I have come to realize that my joy and happiness really lies within my kids, you know what I mean?

I mean, I have come to realize that my happiness really depends upon my kids (and my wife also) being happy also. Because it's like, your kids are a part of you (physically and mentally), and so, if any of them is not happy (for whatever reason), it will be very hard for you to find happiness also. And this is because a part of you will be unhappy, and if a part of you is unhappy, then it is almost impossible for the whole of you to be happy. And this is because you and your kids have an indefinable connection that never ever really breaks (you can call it supernatural). And this is why a lot of parents find it very hard to get over or to heal from losing a child (you know, death), and it's because it's like a part of them has left with the child, you know, leaving them feeling empty inside.

I mean, I'm telling you, this parent child connection thing is very deep, so deep that even death can't stop it. And this is one of the reasons why a lot of women who have had an abortion always seem to wonder and or think about the baby that they had aborted. And this is because, mothers develop connections with their babies way, way, way before the baby is even ready to be born, you know what I mean? I mean it's like, as soon as the mother knows that she is pregnant, bang, the connection with the baby is made right there at that moment and will never really ever be broken even if she has an abortion and or a miscarriage for that matter.

And this is also why a lot of women who have had a miscarriage and or given birth to babies who were already dead in the womb always seem to think about the baby that they never got to know and love, and this is because the mother had already had a connection with the baby even before the baby was born. And also, this is also why a lot of mothers who give up their babies for adoption always tend to wonder and think about their baby that they gave away, and this is because they are still connected to the baby, whether they want to or not. And this is why a lot of mothers tend to start searching and looking for their kids whom they gave up for adoption sooner than later. And this is because they just can't handle the void of not knowing where and or how their kids are doing, because the void of not having their kids in their lives will not allow them to be happy, even if it's been over thirty years later.

And I mean, this deep connection even before the baby is born is not limited to the mother alone, oh no, fathers get it too. Because it's like, even though it don't seem like it by the amount of absentee fathers that are out there nowadays, guys do feel connected to their kids, and this connection usually starts as soon as their woman tells them that they are pregnant, and as soon as the guy realizes that he is about to become a father. And I mean, it doesn't even matter whether the guy really wants to or not to be a father, because as soon as the massage hits his brain that there is a baby in the woman's belly that might be his, bingo, the connection is made right there and then. And I mean, of course the father's connection to the baby is not as deep as the mother's before the baby is born, but as soon as the baby is born, and as soon as the father holds and looks at the baby, forget it, the father's connection becomes just as deep as the mother's.

And this is why a lot of guys who don't want to be fathers usually tend to run away from the pregnancy way before the baby is born, and this is because they know that as soon as they see the baby the connection between them and the baby will be so deep that if they run after that, they know that they will not be able to live without thinking and or missing the baby tremendously. I mean, sure there's still a lot of guys that do abandon their kids after knowing them, but I can assure you that these guys don't always sleep easy, because deep down some-where in their conscious there's a void there that can leave them feeling unhappy. And this is why sometimes you will see guys looking just plain all sad, and if you ask them what's wrong with them, they might say something like, "Man, I haven't seen my kids in a long time!" or they might say something like, "Man, I think I got a kid out there man!" And if you ask them why they think that they might have a kid out there, they might say something like, "Man, I don't know, but I just got this funny feeling man, I just got this funny feeling!"

And I mean, this is why a lot of guys who have never met their kids suffer in silence, because even though they might have run away from their responsibility of taking care of their kids, they will still feel the connection to their kids, whether they want to or not. And so, yeah ladies, guys do feel a connection to their kids too, it's just that the connection is usually way stronger after the baby is born than before it's born, and this is why a lot of guys usually run away before the baby is born, you know, so as to try to not feel connected to the baby, you know what I mean?

And so yeah, it's crazy, but people do spend so much time looking for happiness everywhere else than within, you know, than within themselves and their kids. Because really, that's were happiness really lies, you know, within you and your kids. Because it's like, there's no way that I can picture anybody that has kids ever finding peace and happiness (no matter how much money or material things they might have) in life if any one of their kids is living a miserable life, you know what I mean? Because it's like, most parents live for their kids, you know, their pride and joy is watching their kids lead successful lives. And so, if any one of their kids is not adjusting well to life, and or is struggling to maintain a living, it will be very hard for the parents to find peace and joy, because they will be too busy worrying about their kids well-being. And this is why I truly believe that happiness really lies within your kids, you know, because your kids are a part of you and there's nothing that will make you happier in this world than knowing that your kids are happy and leading successful lives.

But it never fails, you know, people spending so much time and energy looking for or searching for what they think will make them happy than looking for or searching for what they know will make them happy. I mean, people will spend years chasing what they think will make them happy (usually looking outside their homes), but then, at the end of the day, when their kids are all grown and out of the house, that's when they start to realize that they have been searching and or looking for happiness all in the wrong places. And I mean, this is why you see a lot of people who had kids and who did not really spend any real quality time with them just seem to look so miserable as adults. And it's because they have just come to realize that their happiness really lies within themselves and their kids.

And so, this is also why you will tend to hear a lot of parents (after their kids are grown) regretting not having spent a lot more personal time with their kids and enjoying them, you know, because the window of opportunity to really bond and enjoy your kids is really short. Because it's like, before you know it, your kids will be grown and ready to do their own stuff. And so it's like, if you don't take the time to enjoy your kids when they are still young (you know, before they become teenagers and don't really want to be seen with you, you know, because they don't think you are that cool any more) and still think that you are the coolest parent around, before you know it, they will be grown, they will have their own friends, and the only time y'all will hang out again will be either on mother's day or father's day, you know, when they take you out to eat or something, you know what I mean?

And so I mean, it's crazy, but unless you have that super bond with your kids, you know, to where the kids are just so used to you and they just enjoy being around you all the time (which is uncommon, especially with teenagers), you might not really get a chance to really hang out with your kids when they are grown, you know, unless it's your birthday or something and their presence would really be appreciated, you know what I mean? And this is because most teenagers just don't think that their parents are that cool, you know, a myth that I'm gonna try to break by being that cool parent, you know, without being too corny of course, you know, without trying to dress or look cool on purpose, you know what I mean? Because I mean, haven't you seen parents who try just too hard to be hip, you know, parents who not only dress like how their teenagers dress but also try to talk like how their kids talk. And it's funny because, most parents who are in their forties and beyond just don't seem to get the fashion mechanism of today's kids, but they still try so much to be hip, or worse, they still try to be hip with the fashion sense of the sixties and or seventies. And so, if you are one of these trying to be hip parents, your kids (especially your teenagers) will definitely not want to be seen with you, you know, because for some reason kids do expect their parents to dress like and or act like a grown up, you know, and not try to be all cool and stuff, you know what I mean?

And so, yeah, true happiness really comes from your kids, you know, being with and spending time with your kids is truly were happiness really lies. And this is one of the reasons why there's a lot of unhappy parents out there, because a lot of them just don't have that much of a bond with their kids, you know what I mean? And the reason why they never really bond with their kids is because a lot of parents just don't take the time to spend quality and extra quality time with their kids. And so, by not spending quality time with their kids, they end up not really knowing their kids (you know, emotionally and stuff like that) and their kids tend to not really understand their parents.

And this is why a lot of parents tend to clash a lot with their teenage kids, you know, and it's all because the parents just never get to understand their kids. And this misunderstanding of their kids is because the parents just never make an effort to spend quality time with their kids, you know, and get to know them (personality wise) and also get to know what their kids might be going through emotionally. You know, they never get to know whatever stresses their kids might be dealing with, you know, whether from school, the household, or other. I mean it's crazy, but parents just gonna have to make an extra effort to relate to their kids, because if they don't they can run the risk of not knowing their kids, which can result in them having a very strenuous relationship with their kids, especially during their kids teenage years, you know, when they are at their most frustrating time of growing up.

Man, parenting is one of the hardest things that any real parent will ever do! And the reason why I keep saying, "any real parent will ever do" is because, there are just so many lackluster or fake parents out there. Because I mean, there are so many parents out there that just don't put in the work and or the effort to try to be good parents and try to raise their kids right, you know what I mean? Because I mean, parenting really is all about trying, you know, it's all about trying to raise your kids to grow up to be mature and responsible adults.

And so, sure there's going to be a lot of trials and tribulations (tough times), you know, as you are trying to raise your kids properly. But, giving up and letting your kids turn out any which way and how should never be an option, especially in this crazy world today. Because it's like, if you leave kids alone, you know, and never properly try to channel their directions, most likely than not they will choose wrong directions to follow for their lives. And this is because, it generally takes a very long time for kids (people in general) to really know not only what they really want to do or be in life, but it usually also takes a very long time for them to really figure out what they'll have to do to attain their goals and or dreams. And so, this is where parents are usually supposed to come in, you know, to give their kids focus and guidance for their futures, you know, because if they don't, then their kids can find themselves lost in this world of craziness.

I mean it's crazy, but parents really have to make an extra effort to be in their kid's lives, especially in their kids adolescent years, you know, before they become teenagers and start to think that they are grown and don't have to listen to you anymore, you know what I mean? And so, the adolescent stage is where you really want to be extra vigilant in enforcing all of the discipline, behavior and or morals that you want your kids to grow up with. Because it's like, at this stage (adolescence), this is the stage where a lot of a kid's character is formed, you know, this is the stage where kids start to really question who they are, what they are, and what is life all about. And so this is a very dangerous stage for kids, because if their questions are not properly answered, they could end up coming up with the answers themselves and or with the help of their friends, which could be dangerous. Because I mean, most of a kid's friends are kids themselves, and so when a kid goes to another kid for an answer, it's like the blind leading the blind, you know what I mean?

And so this is why it is very important for parents to be available and to make the channel of communication between them and their kids very easy, you know, so that your kids can feel free or comfortable enough to come to you with all kinds of questions that they might be wondering about. Because I mean, at this stage (adolescence), this is the stage that kids start to really notice or become aware of themselves and the world around them. I mean it's like for example, this is the stage that girls start to really notice and wonder about their femininity, and boys start to really notice and wonder about their masculinity. And this is also usually when girls and boys really start to notice each other, you know, girls start to notice boys and boys start to notice girls, you know what I mean?

And so this is where parents definitely need to talk to their kids about sex and sexuality, because if they don't, then their kids will be forced to have to explore and find out what this sex thing is all about on their own. And you definitely don't want your kids exploring sex on their own or to learn about it from their friends or the media, because the conclusion that they will get will definitely be opposite from what you would teach them. Because I mean, in today's mainstream culture, sex is pretty much treated as something to have fun with, you know, instead of something that should be treasured. And so this is one of the reasons why there's so much preteen and teenage sexual activity going on nowadays, you know what I mean? Because it's like everywhere you turn nowadays sex and or sexual images are paraded everywhere, you know, subconsciously pressuring your teens into thinking about engaging in sexual activity, you know, because they think it's cool and they think that everyone else is doing it but them.

I mean it's crazy, but this is one the reasons why it is very important for parents to try their best to get a hold of their kids and instill good morals and positive knowledge into their kid's minds while their kids are still very young, you know, because by the time the kids become teenagers, their minds will have already be made up on what they think or feel about sex for you to try and tell them otherwise. And so this is why it is very important for parents to try their best to get a hold of and guide their kids through the preteen years, you know, so that when their kids become teenagers not only will they be armed with good knowledge of what is really going on in their world (which is the teenage world, which is a very dangerous world, you know, with all that peer pressure and stuff that teenagers have to deal with), but also, when they feel the pressure to have sex, instead of jumping in with blind folds on, their morals, values, and guidance will help them make a more safer and or educated decision, you know, understanding the consequences that can happen, you know, with all these diseases that are out here, let alone the chances of a pregnancy occurring.

So it's like, if you as a parent can really get your kids in line, you know, get your kids to learn good behavior, good morals, good values, good self-discipline, and so on and so on, you know, if you fill your kids (while they are still young) with a lot of positive knowledge, the chances of them screwing up as teenagers and result to making bad decisions that can affect the rest of their lives will be very low, you know what I mean? But, on the other end, if you as a parent fail to instill into your kids good behavior, good morals, good values, good self-discipline and so on and so on, you know, if you fail to instill into your kids (while they are still young) a lot of positive knowledge, then the chances of them making bad decisions that can affect the rest of their lives will be very high. And so this is why it is very important for parents to catch their kids and instill in them all the values, morals and discipline that they want their kids to have, because if you wait until your kids are teenagers to try and teach them stuff, it will be too late, because your kids will have already learned their values, morals and discipline elsewhere (you know, from the streets and or their friends, which is dangerous) and therefore won't be receptive to anything that you might want to teach them, because they will have already made up their minds, no matter how destructive their thinking might be.

Man, parenting, it's a lot of work, and this is why it is very important for fathers to play an active role in their kid's lives, because it's just too much work for the mothers to be doing alone. And this is one of the reasons why there are so many kids out there who are just lost, you know, because their fathers are nowhere to be seen and their mothers are just too tired to keep up with them. Because I mean, most single parent mothers just don't have no choice but to work either long hours or hold at least two jobs, you know, so as to try and provide a good home for their kids. And so as a result in having to work all these long hours, not only is the mother left with no energy to deal with her kids properly, she's also left with no time to properly supervise her kids. And so the result is like we see nowadays, you know, with all these kids running around out here with no supervision at all, you know, resulting in them making bad decisions that can greatly affect their futures.

And so I mean, a lot of men just don't understand how crucial they are to their kids. I mean, a lot of men just don't figure how much their kids really need them, because if they did, they would fight tooth and nail to make sure that they are in their kid's lives, you know, no matter how much they don't like, or how much they despise their baby mamas.

So come on fellas, you've got to be in your kid's lives man, because they really need you, especially in their early years, you know, as they are trying to figure not only about themselves, but also about how the world works, you know, and doing all this while peer pressure is pushing and bombarding them into engaging in activities that they would rather not. I mean, it's crazy, but this is the reason why I definitely had to call this book "No More Baby Daddies", you know, because I truthfully believe that if fathers take a more active role in their kid's lives, a lot of this foolishness that we see kids getting themselves into would definitely reduce tremendously, if not cease altogether. And so, this is why I'm gonna try my best to spread the word and try to get fathers to not abandon their kids, you know, because their kids definitely need them, you know, especially in the first eighteen years of their lives!

Chapter 13

Parenting 103

Education is one of the most important things that parents can ever provide for their kids. I mean it goes without saying, education is so important in today's society that without it most kids will have a very hard time achieving any level of success in life, especially in this very competitive world that we live in nowadays. And this education starts way, way, way back from when the kids are little, you know, from when they are in preschool and kindergarten. And the fact is, preschool and kindergarten is actually the most crucial part of your kid's education. Because I mean, in preschool and kindergarten is usually where most kids learn how to learn, you know what I mean? And what I mean by this is that, besides just learning the ABCs, preschool and kindergarten is where kids also learn how to learn, you know, they learn how to sit still, pay attention and take in what the teacher has to teach. And so this is why early childhood education is very important, because it sets up the framework and mindset for your kid to be able to absorb and digest information, and also it sets up your kid's love for learning, you know what I mean?

But, there's a big problem nowadays (my fellow parents) with early childhood education teaching in the schools. And what I mean by this is that, the school systems nowadays are not doing a very good job of teaching and or preparing the little kids properly for learning in later grades, you know, they are not doing a good job of making sure that the kids have learned the fundamentals (like ABCs, counting numbers, etc.), you know, before the kids move on to first grade and beyond. And so, this is one of the reasons why there are a lot of kids who seem to always be behind their learning curve in every grade level. And this is because the kid that has to play catch up to the other kids that have mastered the lessons from the grade before just never seems to catch up, and this is because they had never really learned how to learn properly, and therefore they are always learning from a disadvantaged position, you know, of missed fundamentals. And so, this is why it is very important for parents to be very involved in their kid's education from the start, you know, from preschool and kindergarten. Because you definitely don't want your kids to not learn the fundamentals of learning. And so by you being involved in your kid's education from jump, not only will you know if your kids are having a hard time learning the basics (by attending PTA on the regular, thereby giving you plenty of time to find out why), but you will also show your kids that you do value education and that they should too.

 I mean, education is very crucial, especially the early part, you know, from preschool to six grade, you know, elementary school. I mean it should almost go without saying, but I truly believe that besides college, elementary school is the most important phase of a kid's education. And the reason why I say this is because, in elementary school is where a lot of basic knowledge and or understanding of different subject matters takes place, you know what I mean? I mean, what I mean is, in elementary school is where most of a kid's learning (that they will actually use in life) that will actually benefit them for the rest of their life takes place, you know, benefits like reading, writing, arithmetic, science, geography, history, etc. and etc. Because I mean, take myself for example (as I'm sitting here writing this book), a lot of what I know about writing (you know, how to write proper sentences and stuff like that) really comes from my elementary school English classes, you know what I mean? Because I mean, I can actual still remember how my fifth grade teacher used to make sure that I not only write a paragraph correctly, but I can also remember all them red marks that she used to put on the paper as she corrected punctuation marks and stuff like that. And I remember how I used to hate all them red marks, you know what I mean? But those red marks truly helped me become more of a conscience and careful writer, you know, as I took my time to make sure that my sentences were proper, you know what I mean? Because I hated those red marks, which were plenty!

And so, yeah, elementary school is where kids learn most of what they will take with them to the world and try to compete. And I mean, of course junior high school and high school also teach a lot, but they are not as crucial as elementary school. Because it's like, elementary school is where you learn all the fundamentals that you will really use in everyday life, you know, and junior high and high school actually is there to reinforce and or to advance what you have already learned in elementary school, you know what I mean? And so this is why parents have to make sure that their kids learn and or master all that the elementary school has to teach, because if their kids wait until junior high or high school to start trying to learn stuff, it will almost be too late. And this is because, the kid will be so far behind their peers that it will be almost impossible for them to catch up.

And so, this is one of the reasons why there are so many kids that end up dropping out of school by the time they get to high school. And this is because they just find themselves unable to catch up to their peers (in learning), and therefore they become so frustrated and just decide to drop out of school, you know, because they think that maybe they are just not smart enough, which of course is not true, because any kid who is taught properly has the capacity to learn and advance.

But yeah, elementary school is very crucial, because this is where most of a kid's learning and learning habits takes place. Because I mean, in elementary school is where most kids learn how to learn, you know, this is where kids really develop their love and interest in education. And so this is why it is very important for parents to be involved and show interest in their kids learning, you know, by checking homework, by going to PTAs, by volunteering, participating and or going to the kid's school activities, you know, like; sports, school plays and etc., you know, showing support in whatever school activities that their kids are involved in. I mean, parental support in a kid's school stuff is very important, you know what I mean? Because it's like, kids really follow the example of their parents, you know, because it's like, if the parent show no interest in the kid's education and or activities, then the kid (no matter how smart and or intelligent they might be) will have no motivation and or interest in school and or the school activities either.

I mean, it's serious business when it comes to kids getting their education, so much so that parents have to really try their best to make sure that their kids have a positive attitude about learning and going to school. And this positive attitude about school really starts at home, you know, by parents properly preparing and reinforcing the good benefits of education to their kids. Because really, most kids in general are pretty lazy when it comes to doing schoolwork and stuff like that, you know what I mean? And so if the parents show excitement every time their kids bring home good grades and stuff like that, their kids will have no choice but to keep trying to bring home good grades. And this is because kids like to impress their parents, you know, kids like to know that their parents are proud of them. And so, if parents show real enthusiasm in their kid's education, then their kids will be excited about education also.

But, if parents don't show any real interest in their kid's education, then their kids will more often than not be uninterested in education also. And so, this is one of the reasons why there seems to be so many kids nowadays that just don't seem to be interested in school, and this is because there are just so many parents out there that just don't seem to care about their kid's education. And the reason why I say this is because, if you go to the PTAs, school activities and etc., (you know, the millions of activities that always seem to be going on in a kid's school), you will tend to see the same ten to twenty parents at almost every event, and this ten to twenty parents is from the whole school. And so you will be left there thinking to yourself, "Wait a minute, where are the rest of the parents at?" Because really, to me, it just doesn't make sense at how very few parents take the time to be involved in their kid's education and school activities. I mean it's almost like most parents treat school as just a baby-sitting place, you know, a place for them to take their kids for about six or seven hours a day, you know what I mean?

I mean it's crazy at how many kids just don't have that parental support when it comes to education. And I mean, sure there will be a lot of parents, relatives and friends coming to support and cheer for their kids when they are involved in a sports activity, but when it comes to actual education, like the PTA, forget it, parents are almost non-existent. Because I mean, it almost never fails at how disappointed my wife looks and feels at the lack of parents that attend the PTA meetings at our kids school. I mean it never fails, because she always almost has the same look on her face (disturbed look) while shaking her head as soon as I ask how the PTA meeting went. I mean, it's crazy, but parents will just have to do better and really make sure that they are involved in their kid's education, because if they don't, then their kids will not be motivated or excited to go to school and learn all that cool stuff, you know what I mean?

And so, yeah man, it's serious business this education thing, especially in this crazy competitive world that we live in today. Because really, it is almost impossible for a person to advance very far in life nowadays without education, you know, unless you have a very special skill or talent that can propel you to stardom or something like that, you know what I mean? And so, this is why it is very important for parents to really be involved in their kids educational process from the beginning to the end, you know, from preschool all the way till they finish college, you know what I mean? Because I mean, if you don't, and depending on where you live, your school system can really let your kid down. Because it's like, a lot of the schools and or school systems in this country suck, you know what I mean? And so, if you as the parent don't take an active role and try your best to make sure that your kid is learning what they are supposed to be learning (either by teaching them yourself or by transferring them to a school that's a little better), then your kid will be academically short changed by your school system.

I mean it's crazy, but I'm just so amazed at how many bad schools and or school systems are out there. Then again, I'm really not shocked at how many bad school systems are out there. And the reason why I'm not shocked is because, a lot of these school systems are run by business minded people instead of educators, you know what I mean? I mean, most of these school systems, instead of hiring educators to develop and run the school systems (with education in mind and being the top priority), they instead hire business minded professionals (with cost cutting in mind) to dictate how the whole school system should run.

And the other reason why there's a lot of sucky school systems around in this country is because the federal government is pretty much holding a lot of these public schools hostage, you know, with that **No Child Left Behind** stuff and it's crazy evaluation standard dumbness that doesn't even take in the consideration of where the school is located and or it's bilingual or population density. Because I mean, truth be told, the environment of the school setting (you know, whether it's in the inner city or not, and whether it has a lot of foreign speaking students or not) will definitely affect the test scores that these so called experts seem to value so much, which I think is very dumb.

I mean, don't get me wrong, I do think kids need to be tested from time to time, you know, so as to monitor their progress in mastering various subject matters, but to test them just for the purpose of deciding whether that school will receive funding based on the number or score that the school gets based on those tests is not only very stupid, but it's also very pathetic to me. Because it's like, now what you are doing is making these schools become more focused on making sure their students pass these tests, instead of trying to teach every subject properly so that the student can become well rounded in their knowledge. Because I mean, most of these stupid tests only tests kids in math and reading. And so I ask myself, what about writing, what about science, what about geography, what about history, and so on and so on, you know? Because I mean, what are they trying to say, that these other subjects are not as important. I mean, this is probably the reason why we have so many dumb kids running around nowadays, you know, because they are just not taught much in school anymore, you know, their minds are just not being filled with different thoughts and ideas, leaving them unable to think and or hypothesize anything.

I mean it's crazy, but this **No Child Left Behind** stuff is really screwing a lot of schools and school systems up. Because I mean, instead of letting teachers teach, and instead of letting school systems set up curriculums based on logic and reason, the school systems are forced to set up their curriculums based on having to focus the kids on passing that darn stupid standardized test, you know, the test that determines whether or not that school system will either get or not get federal money. And this is why I say that the federal government is pretty much holding these school systems hostage, because it's like, everyone is so concerned about passing that darn test so that their school won't be marked as a failure and not receive funding from the government that, instead of taking their time and making sure that the students are learning properly, they rush them through materials that are in the curriculums so fast just so they can have extra time to prep them for the darn stupid evaluation test that only test about two or three subjects, which is so stupid.

I mean, I used to think that the reason why there are so many dumb kids nowadays graduating from high school was because there are a lot of bad teachers, but now I know that it's really not the teachers, it's really the federal government (and States for that matter) that is holding teachers hostage by not allowing them to work their magic and take their time so that they can make sure that every kid in their class has mastered the material in the curriculum before passing them to the next grade.

But, with the federal government demanding a score for each school as a way of evaluating the schools success before distributing funds to them, not only does it make it impossible for a school with a lot of disadvantaged kids from having a high score (designating it as an under achieving school), but it also cheats the teachers from really enjoying their work of passing knowledge and watching the kids become excited about learning. Because I mean, the way they have it now, it seems to me that the system is not doing anything but making everybody stressed, you know? And when I say everybody, I'm talking about everybody that is involved in the school system, you know, from the school president, to the school superintend, to the principles, to the teachers, to the other work stuffs, to the school boards, to the parents, and most importantly, to the students themselves, who are getting very frustrated by how fast they have to comprehend the materials. And I mean, this is one of the reasons why there are so many students that just seem to be so behind in their learning, and this is because teachers are forced to move so fast in teaching the materials that they just don't have time to help the kids that seem to be struggling in comprehending the materials.

And the reason why teachers have to move so fast in teaching the materials is because, the way most of these curriculums are set up, they do not allow time for the teachers to try and be creative with the subject that they are teaching, you know, so as to try and make it easy for the kids that are struggling to better understand. Because I mean, I have looked at a sample of my kids elementary school curriculum, and I have looked at a schedule of how much time each subject is allocated per day for the teacher to teach it, and I kept saying to myself (and a lot to my wife), "How in the hell are these kids supposed to master all these material in such a short amount of time given for each subject every day?" I mean really, I remember looking at the schedule (you know, the schedule that shows from what time to what time your kids will be learning what, you know, like what time to what time is math, reading, lunch, recess and all that good stuff) and then looking at my wife and asking her (like she had the answer or something, which she did, and her answer was something like, "Well, it looks like we are going to be doing a lot of homework checking and a lot of extra teaching of them ourselves!") how the hell are these kids supposed to learn all this stuff in such a short time frame.

I mean it's crazy, and this is why a lot of teachers get so stressed out and just quit teaching altogether, you know, leaving the school systems having to hire fake teachers, you know, teachers who don't even like teaching in the first place but because they can't find any other job they decide to be teachers, you know, because of the job security.

And that's the other thing, how come all these bad teachers just seem to never get fired? Because I mean, even though I truly believe that there are a lot of good teachers out there, I also believe that there are a lot of bad teachers out there, you know what I mean? Because I mean, even from when I used to be in school, elementary, junior high, and high school, and especially in high school, I have run into a few bad teachers myself, you know, teachers who either did not know what the hell they were talking about, or just didn't seem very interested in what they were teaching. And I believe that these teachers are one of the biggest reasons why I never really put much effort in my schoolwork, especially in high school. Because I mean, I used to be very interested in academics, especially in elementary school, where I had my most fun in and out the classroom. I mean, I was even called a nerd a few times by one or two of my classmates, which I took as a complement because I really never viewed myself as being that smart. And so when the few kids called me a nerd, I was like, "Really, thank you!"

And I mean, sure I knew that when most kids called you a nerd, they mean it as a negative connotation, you know, trying to hurt your feelings or something, but for some reason I just never viewed myself as a nerd. Because I mean, not only was I the captain of our elementary school basketball team, but chasing girls and flirting with them was also part of my school fun activity. So by no means did I ever view myself as a nerd, you know, I just viewed myself as an intellectual, that's all, you know what I mean, ha ha ha ha ha!

But, there was one thing that one of the kids did call me that kind of hurt my feelings, especially when he said it in front of the whole class, and especially that he was kind of right, but still, he didn't have to say it like that, or for the whole class to hear, you know? Because I mean, it wasn't really my fault that the teacher kind of took a liking to me, you know what I mean? Oh, wait a minute, I haven't told you what the kid called me ha! Then again, maybe I shouldn't say it, I mean, it's kind of embarrassing, I mean, it might make me look like a punk, you know, it might make me look weak in the eyes of the reader, you know, you, that's right, I'm talking about you, right there, you, the one that is reading this book and this page and this paragraph and this sentence right now, yeah you, stop looking around the room, I'm talking about you, come on, focus, focus, focus, ha ha ha ha ha! Excuse me please, see, this is why it is not good to write when you are half asleep and tired as heck, you know, because you start to get silly, as I am doing right now, you know?

But so anyway, yeah, this is what the kid called me in front of the whole class that made me very uncomfortable for the rest of that day and also for the rest of the days that followed, until I learned how to get over it. And then again, maybe I'm still not over it yet, you know, because why then would I still be talking about it, or maybe talking about it actually means that I'm over it, right? Oh man, I think I'm confusing myself, maybe I should just go get some sleep before this book turns into some kind of organized confusion (if it hasn't already), you know, with me trying to figure myself out, you know, ha ha ha ha ha! So good night folks and I'll talk to y'all tomorrow, when I'm more alert and making more sense, ok, cool, thanks, peace, good night!

Ok, so am, what where we talking about again? Y'all gotta forgive me, because it's been about five days since I last wrote (and I'm still kind of tired but a little bit more alert) and I've kind of lost my train of thought. Oh, wait a minute, yeah, ok, I remember now, we were talking about, I mean, actually I was trying to tell you about what the kid in my six grade class called me in front of the whole class that kind of made me feel real embarrassed and kind of hurt my feelings. And so, this is what the kid called me in front of the whole class, he called me **a teacher's pet.** I mean, come on man, me a teacher's pet! Ok, maybe a little bit, but it wasn't my fault, the teacher just so happen to take favor with me because I think she recognized that I loved to learn, you know what I mean? Because I mean, it's not like I made a conscious effort to impress her (the teacher) or anything. I mean, I was just enjoying learning and it just so happens that teachers kind of tend to like kids that seem to be enthusiastic about learning, you know what I mean? And so, when that kid called me a teacher's pet, I kind of took it very personally, you know, because it's not like I was trying to win the teacher's favor or something like that, it just happened. And I mean, it's not my fault that nobody else in the class liked to raise their hands and answer questions, because I mean, heck, if nobody else is going to raise their hand and I know the answer, then I might as well raise my hand and answer the questions, you know what I mean?

But yeah, calling me a teacher's pet kind of hurt my feelings, especially the way he said it in front of the whole class, you know, because it made me so self-conscious to where I would actually feel embarrassed to answer questions when the teacher called on me. But I couldn't really escape the embarrassment, because it's like the teacher would call on me to answer questions sometimes even when I didn't put my hand up. And the reason why she would call on me to answer the questions so often is because nobody else would either put their hand up or would get the answers wrong, and so I became the turn to student with the right answers, you know what I mean? Because it's like, whenever nobody raised their hand, and or whenever nobody seemed to know the answer, it's like she would automatically turn to me and be like, "Nigel, tell them what the right answer is".

I mean, it was so embarrassing! And the reason why it was so embarrassing is because, as soon as the teacher would turn to me and ask me to give the right answer, it felt like all eyes were on me (and all eyes were on me) and it felt like all the other kids were looking at me while saying to themselves, "Yeah, go ahead teacher's pet, go ahead and give us dummies the right answer, you smarty teacher's pet you!" And so I mean, yeah, that teacher's pet thing did kind of hurt my feelings, more so than being called a nerd, which I didn't mind, because I kind of took it as a complement, you know, because to me (and really), being called a nerd is just another way of saying that someone is an intellectual, which I like to think I am, even if I'm not, you know what I mean, ha ha ha ha ha!

And so, yeah, all this was just to say that, parents really have to be involved in their kids daily school experiences, because there's a lot of factors out there (in the schools) that can really make your kids learning experience not an enjoyable one. Because it's like, besides bad teachers and or bad school systems, the other very negative situation that can cause your kids to really not enjoy school and or learning is, being teased and or bullied by the other kids in school. I mean, it almost should go without saying that being bullied and or teased in school is one of the most hurtful and demoralizing situation for a kid to have to deal with in school. Because I mean, all kids would like to fit in at school, you know, to be liked and or just feel normal like other kids. But of course, not all kids will be able to fit in, you know, not all kids will be able to just act like the other kids, you know, to act like the kids that are supposed to be normal, you know, the popular kids. And this is because, as in life in general, the majority population always tries to put pressure on the minority population to act or behave just like them, whether it be right or wrong. And so when it comes to kids and school, whichever kids that don't seem to fit the so called **normal** stereotype always seem to be the target of bullying and or teasing.

And this is one of the biggest reasons why a lot of kids tend to not like school, you know, because they just don't feel like they fit in, you know what I mean? And it's like, for kids, fitting in is all they really want to do, you know, because kids just don't know how to accept and or to be proud of their individuality, you know?

And so, to be called weird, strange, nerd, smarty, dumb, ugly, bad dresser, and so on and so on (because there are a lot more that kids can call each other to be mean to each other) can really demoralize a kid to the point of taking away their self-esteem, especially if they are also being bullied on top of that. I mean it can get really bad for a kid, you know, to the point of where they don't even want to go to school anymore.

And so, this is one of the reasons why parents have to really be involved in their kids daily school experiences, you know, by asking how the kid's school day went and talking over any negativity that the kid might have experienced that day. Because I mean, being bullied or teased is nothing to play with, because before you know it your kid can become totally shut down, miserable, hating school and you won't even know why. And so, this is why it is very important for parents to make sure that their kids not only are not being bullied, but are also not being teased at school. And if a parent does find out that their kid is being teased or bullied at school, they must at once inform the school. And if for whatever reason the school does not put a stop to it or fails to put a stop to it, then the parent must immediately report it to the police and file a case against the bullying kid and his or her parents if they have to, you know, to make sure that the situation is resolved and the bullying ceases immediately. I mean, I'm telling you, your kid's comfort in school is very important, because without that comfort of knowing that they can be themselves and no one is going to tease them or bully them, their learning can really suffer, resulting in them not only hating school, but they can also result in hating life itself.

And I mean, this is one of the reasons why we seem to have a lot of school shootings nowadays. And it's because a lot of kids just don't feel like they fit in at school because of all the bullying and teasing that they are subjected to by the other kids. And a lot of these bullying and teasing can really be reduced if not stopped altogether by the schools. Because I mean, it's becoming very dangerous nowadays with the bullying or teasing, and this is because kids are just not taking it anymore, you know? And so this is why more and more kids are just deciding to go get a gun and go shoot up their school, you know, because they have had enough of being treated like sh%t, and so it's time for a payback to whomever bullied them and to whomever that participated and or laughed at them while they were being bullied or teased. I mean, I'm telling you, it can get very serious for these kids that are being bullied. And so this is why it is very important that someone intervenes and try to stop the bullying before it goes too far and a tragedy happens.

I mean, it's no joke, especially for young kids (kids in general). And this is because kids are very sensitive and or very emotional in general, and so they view and take everything that is said to them very personally (a lot of adults still do also). And so, when mean things are said to them over and over and over again, they tend to have no choice but to start accepting their lack of worthiness, you know, and this is when a tragedy can happen, because the kid can feel as though they have nothing to live for, you know what I mean?

I mean it's crazy, but kids just like to bully and or tease other kids, you know, they think it's funny, you know, they think it's a game, you know what I mean? But it's not all fun and games, especially to the kid that is being teased and or bullied. And so this is where parents and teachers have to do a better job of paying attention to what might be going on in a kid's life, because it's not hard for a kid that's being bullied to go get a gun (with the easy access of getting guns nowadays) and come back and shoot up not only the kids that have been bullying them, but also whoever else that has ever laughed at them. I mean it's crazy, but parents really have to make sure that no one is bullying their kids, because the bullying can really take their kids interest in school and or joy of learning away, you know, which can be very detrimental to their future. And also, for parents who have kids that are bullies, you really gonna have to make sure that your kid stops being a bully, because one day the kid that he or she is bullying or teasing will have enough of it and just might decide to retaliate by shooting them, you know what I mean? I mean it's crazy, but kids nowadays don't really fist fight anymore, you know, rather they are quick to go get a gun and just shoot their nemesis, you know what I mean?

I mean it's crazy, but kids just think it's funny bullying and or picking on other kids, you know, without even taking in the consideration how the other kid (the kid that's being bullied or teased) might feel, you know what I mean? And this is one of the reasons why I found myself in a lot more than my share of fights back when I was in school (especially in elementary), because I just couldn't stand seeing another kid being bullied or teased that I always found myself coming to the aid of the kid and in a result I found myself having to take on the bully on their behalf, you know what I mean?

I mean it was crazy, but I just couldn't stand bullies, you know, because I knew how bad it felt to be bullied, you know, because I myself had to deal with bullies quite a few times, you know, especially whenever I happened to be the new kid in school or class, you know what I mean? Because it's like, for whatever reason kids just like to pick on the new kid, you know, especially if the kid happens to be a quiet kid and or a shy kid, you know? And so, being that I was an extreme loner (you know, not very good at making friends), kids always assumed that I must be a punk or something, you know, someone who won't fight back and therefore they can use for their own fun and bully them. But, when it came to me, they quickly found out that they had picked the wrong kid to try and bully, because I would quickly, after only two warnings for them to stop messing with me (I never gave three warnings because I didn't have that much patience), I would quickly proceed to whup their butts with a right hand to the mouth and a straight kick to the face. I mean, I didn't play around back in those days, you know what I mean?

And I mean, I didn't have a temper or nothing like that, you know, but I just never had the patience to get to the third warning before I proceeded to whup somebody's ass, you know what I mean? Because I mean, to me, it seemed like a waste of time to be pushing each other back and forth (you know how kids like to push each other back and forth before they actually fight, if they will even fight, because most times they are both scared but they just want to see who will punk out first) and wait to see who will throw the first punch. But when it came to me, a lot of the kids started realizing that I didn't waste time with the pushing back and forth thing. Because it was like, as soon as you put your hands on me (even very lightly), that was it, instead of pushing you back I would be punching and kicking you by this point.

I mean, it was crazy, but I didn't play around back in those days. And so if you managed to get me to stand up and bowl my fists in a ready to swing position, it was almost too late for you to change your mind about fighting me, because I would be roughing you up by now, you know, just to send a message that you messed with the wrong kid this time pal. I mean, it was kind of crazy, but it almost became kind of an unspoken rule in my elementary school (especially when I was in sixth grade) that there will be no more bullying, because if you are caught bullying or picking on someone not your own size, then you will have to face Mr. Nigel, who is willing and ready to give you a fist fight challenge at any time. I mean it was kind of crazy (and you can ask my brother if you don't believe me, because he was there and everybody knew not to even think about messing with him unless they want to face off with me. And by that time my reputation as a hard puncher was very well circulated), but a lot of kids really appreciated me and my coming to their aid. But there were a few kids that kind of resented me, you know, the kids that were supposed to be the bad boys of the school, you know, the kids that weren't really interested in learning and prided themselves in being disruptive, you know, thinking that they are so cool.

And as I can remember, most of these kids were special aid students, you know, the kids that were supposed to be slow. But really what I came to realize is that, most of these kids weren't really slow or nothing like that (because I communicated very well with them in the playground as we played basketball, football or something like that), it's just that most of these kids were just kind of misunderstood and therefore had a lot of behavioral problems, you know, they acted out their frustrations of life by being disruptive. And so, since most teachers and schools don't really know what to do with them, they decide to label them slow and therefore assign them to the special aid class, which frustrate the kids even more by reducing their self-esteem, because now they are viewed as being dumb by the other kids, which causes them to act out even more. And I mean, sure some of the kids in the special aid class had some learning disorder, but the majority of them didn't, and the reason why I know this is because some of them were in the school's basketball team with me. And so I definitely knew that they weren't slow, because they did a pretty good job of following directions from our couch and even from me as I called out the plays.

And so yeah, those were some crazy times, but I just could not stand bullies, because I knew how hurtful and demoralizing it can be for the kid that is being bullied. And really, a lot of times I tried to get the kid that is getting bullied or picked on to stand up for themselves and fight back (because I had learned long time ago that the best way to get a bully off your back is to stand up and punch them in the mouth, which I was always ready to do), but I came to realize that a lot of kids are not fighters, you know, they just don't have the fighting mentality like I did, and so I would just take on the fight for them, which a lot of kids appreciated.

And so, yeah man, school can be very enjoyable or very stressful for kids, and it can all depend on how well they adjust and or get along with the other kids in school. And so this is why it is very important for parents to be very involved in their kids school experiences, you know, that way if there is any negative forces that are trying to impend their kids enjoyment of school, the parent can quickly do their best to remove it so that way the kid can have fun learning without having to deal with too much stress within or outside the school. Because I mean, education is very important, especially in today's society were one world order is definitely in full effect, you know what I mean? Because it's like, not only are our kids going to be competing for well-paying jobs with people from their own country, but they will also be competing with people from other countries for those same well-paying jobs, you know what I mean? Because it's more and more becoming a global economy nowadays that we are living in, and so companies will more and more be looking for employees who are not only highly motivated and educated, they will also be looking for employees who are able to deal with the global market, and this employee can be from any country.

And so it is very important for parents to make sure that their kids get very high levels of education, both in and outside of the school system, you know, you gotta make sure that your kids are worldly, you know, you gotta make sure that they understand how the world works. Because I mean, it is amazing at how many kids nowadays that graduate high school (and some even college) who have no idea what the hell is really going on in the world. And I'm not just talking about political and stuff like that, I'm also talking about economical and historical awareness of how the world is changing right before their eyes, which can greatly affect their futures. I mean, what I'm trying to say is, if we think the world is tough right now, just imagine how much more tougher it's going to be for our kids in about another ten, fifteen, or twenty years from now. And so, if you don't equip your kids with high levels of education (meaning that making sure that your kids not only finish high school, but making sure that they also get a college degree, a master's degree preferred) now, it will be very hard for them to try to compete in the future with the way the world and the economy is going.

I mean it's crazy, but a high school diploma is not enough anymore, you know? Because really there's basically no real jobs for people with only high school diplomas anymore, you know what I mean? And so, nowadays a parent's job of making sure their kids have all the education they can get is not complete until the kid finishes college, you know, especially if you want your kids to have a better chance of competing and surviving in this competitive world. And so, for parents that just absolutely can't send their kids to college, then these parents should greatly consider sending their kids to trade school, you know, so that they can learn a skill that can lend them employment that pays kind of good. Because I mean, with the way that inflation and the cost of living is going up, up and up, pretty soon most people won't be able to afford a living unless they work at least two or three jobs, especially if they are only getting paid at or just above minimum wage, you know what I mean?

And so, yeah man, education is very important, especially in this crazy world today where there seems to not be enough good jobs (or just jobs period) to go around, you know what I mean? So parents, please try your best to give your kids all the education that they can have, because if anything, at least they will be equipped with a degree or a trade skill to take to the world and survive with.

And hey, you never know, maybe your kid can end up being really successful that when you become all old and gray and can barely take care of yourself anymore and there's no one else at home to look out for you, hey, maybe just maybe your kid might hire one of them young and pretty (for the guys) or young and handsome (for the ladies) looking nurses or care givers to come visit you at home, you know, instead of you having to go live in one of those sh%tty nursing homes with nurses that are middle aged and looking mean as hell, you know what I mean, ha ha ha ha ha! Hey, it's a wish right? So who says it can't come true, ha ha ha ha ha!

Well my friends, take care of your kids and give them all the education and skills that they can get, because they are going to definitely need them, especially in this crazy competitive world that we live in nowadays!

Chapter 14

Parenting 104

Chasing dreams and or aspirations is what life is all about (to me anyway). But unfortunately, there are a lot of kids (both talented and not so talented) that just never get a chance to either pursue the career that they really want or to chase a dream that they think they might have a talent for. Because I mean, almost every kid has a dream, you know? I mean, almost every kid has a fantasy or a dream job that they think they would love to do for the rest of their life, you know what I mean? I mean, we have all day dreamed before right, especially when we were kids right? And I mean, there are some adults who are still day dreaming right now, right? And no, I'm not talking about me, cause I'm still going after my dreams baby, hell no, ain't no stopping me, this ain't no day dreaming, cause I'm still going for mines man, that's right, I'm still chasing my dreams y'all, ha ha ha ha ha! Come on, holler at your boy, cause I'm trying to do some big things here man, ha ha ha ha ha, you know what I mean!?

But yeah, we have all got dreams, or better yet, to put it more correctly (because a lot of people do give up on their dreams or have never ever even entertained the thought of chasing their dreams), we have all had dreams of what we would like to be when we grew up, you know what I mean? I mean it's like, we have all day dreamed at one time or another (when we were kids) about what careers or jobs we would like to have when we grew up, I'm I right or wrong? Because I mean, remember when you were little, and how either you by yourself or you and your friends would kind of just sit around and start to think and talk about what y'all would really love to do or be when y'all grew up. And remember how some of your friends (and or even some of your brothers and sisters) talked about wanting to become either lawyers, doctors, nurses, teachers, actors, musicians, models, writers, pilots, astronauts, fire fighters, presidents, businessman, fashion designers, and so on and so on. I mean, do you remember that? And do you remember how you and your friends or brothers and sisters would sit there and be arguing about who's dream job is better and or who's dream job would pay them a lot of money? I mean, do you remember all of that, or am I the only one that remembers all of this stuff. Come on y'all, don't act like I'm the only one that did all this day dreaming stuff when we were little, you know? And I mean, sure I might have done more than my share of day dreaming when I was little, but it wasn't by choice, you know, it's just that, it's just that I found it to be the best way for me to make time past by fast, you know, by day dreaming and living in a fantasy world that I created or made up in my mind, you know what I mean, ha ha ha ha ha?

But yeah man, almost all of us have had a dream before, you know, of what we want to be or do for a living. And actually most of us have had them since when we were little, little kids, you know what I mean? I mean, most of us have had our dreams and aspirations since we were kids playing at the playground or just sitting in our rooms and day dreaming of what we think or know we want to do with our lives, you know, day dreaming of what we want or would like to do or be when we grew up, you know what I mean? And so here is where I have a question, I mean, here is where the question lies; what happens or why is that a lot of kids just never tend to pursue their dream jobs, you know, why is it that a lot of kids never seem to pursue careers that they dreamed of when they were kids and still think of when they become adults. And really, it just amazes me at how many people who just seem to settle, you know, never ever even having tried to chase their dreams and or aspirations, you know what I mean? And so, actually, I think I might know the answer to my own question, you know, to my question of why most people don't pursue or even try to pursue their dreams or aspirations. And the answer for this question is, it's all mostly because of their parents, you know, it's all mostly because of their parents lack of support or because of their parents lack of confidence in their kids potential or in their parents lack of belief in the ability of dreams coming true.

I mean it's crazy, but it just amazes me at how a lot of parents just don't believe in dreams and or the chasing of dreams. And I mean, I have come to realize that, the reason why most parents don't believe in dreams or the chasing of dreams is because that; (1) they either had dreams themselves when they were younger and never got a chance to chase them, for one reason or another, or, (2) they had dreams when they were younger and did get a chance to chase them, but for whatever reason they just never succeeded, therefore leaving a bad taste in their mouths for dreams and their ability to come true, and or, (3) they never had dreams and therefore just don't understand the passion and or the desire that a person with a dream can have. I mean it's crazy, but dreams are something else, I mean, for some people their dreams are so powerful to them that they can't see themselves doing anything else with their lives besides living their dreams, you know, they can't see themselves making a living not doing what they absolutely love, you know what I mean? And I mean, this is why sometimes you will see people spending years and years chasing after their dreams, you know, no matter what or no matter how long it seems to be taking them to make it, they just keep going.

And I mean, this is one of the reasons why there are a lot of starving musicians, actors and actresses, and all other kinds of dream chasers out there. And it's because they just can't quit, you know, because there is something inside of them that just won't let them settle for anything else. But then of course, it comes a time in everybody's life where chasing a dream might not be feasible anymore, you know, it comes a time when real life can come and give you a rude awakening and let you know that hey maybe your dream wasn't meant for you, you know, maybe it's time to give it up or just find another less passionate dream that you might have that might be a little bit more easier or a little bit more suitable for your talents. Because I mean, not everybody that chases a dream actually has the talent for that dream, you know what I mean? And I mean, sure you don't want to give up chasing your dreams so easily, but as the world likes to say, "Reality can be a b$tch!" And so sometimes what you want or think you might have talent for might not be for you to attain or your talents might not be good enough for you to attain that particular dream or aspiration, you know what I mean?

And so, here is where changing a career path or choosing a different dream to chase might be wise, you know, rather than just wasting half or more of your life chasing a dream that you probably don't have the talent or enough of the talent or talents required in order for you to succeed in that particular field or industry. Because I mean, what's the point of chasing a dream that you might not even have that much talent or talents (because most dreams require multiple talents for you to poses if you are really going to achieve it) for, you know? Because I mean, not only will you be wasting your time chasing a dream that you don't have enough talent for, but you will also be wasting precious time that you could be spending with your loved ones, and or your kids, you know what I mean?

And I mean, this is one of the reasons why a lot of people (dream chasers without much talent) tend to get dumped by their significant others. And it's because they spend too much time and energy chasing their false dreams that their significant others just get too tired of waiting for them to wake up and smell the coffee and come to the understanding that maybe their talents are just not good enough to achieve whatever it is that they are wasting precious time on. Because I mean, time is precious, and most significant others will not appreciate you spending all that time chasing a dream, especially if they don't think that you have the talent for it.

And I mean, if you do have a talent for something, and your partner is not supporting you, it doesn't always mean that you don't have enough talent to achieve whatever it is that you are trying to achieve, sometimes it could just be that your partner just doesn't believe in dreams and their ability to come true, that's all. But really and truly, most often than not, if you do have real talent for something (and if your partner really loves you), usually they will stick by your side and support you and your dream for a very long time, you know, because they believe in you and your talent.

But then of course there is a time limit on how long they will be willing participants, you know, there is a time limit on how long you have to start showing some kind of significant progress in becoming a success with your dream, you know, before they too start to question whether or not you should start to think about a new career path, you know, even though they might still think that you have some talents in you, you know what I mean? And I have come to figure out that, five years is the most a significant other will be willing to give the dreamer in support of his or her dream before they start to nag and or try to get the dreamer to change their career path, you know what I mean? And I mean, actually, husband and wives might give each other more than five years (if real progress is being made toward the dream) to chase their dreams, but girlfriend and boyfriends, forget it, five years is the max before they either dump you or nag you or bother you to death about quitting your dream thing and getting a real job, you know what I mean? I mean it's crazy, but besides parents, significant others (you know, boyfriends and girlfriends, or, husbands and wives) are the next most influential people in a dreamer's life that can either hinder or help a dreamer in deciding whether to chase a dream or not and for how long.

But yeah man, all this just to say that, we all have had dreams of what we wanted to be when we grow up. But the only problem is, most people just never get a chance to chase their dreams. And the reason why most people never get a chance to chase their dreams, to me it is because of their parents, you know, it is because their parents never gave them or never instilled in them the positive out-look on life and or the ability of them becoming whatever they want to be, just as long as they work hard for it.

I mean, what I'm trying to say is, a lot of parents just don't give their kids a lot of opportunity and or freedom to chase their dreams, you know, by either supporting them verbally or financially. Because I mean (as I have become a parent myself now), I have come to realize that, even though a lot of kids have dreams, and even though a lot of kids have talent, I have come to realize that mostly only the kids that get support from either their parents or other adults in their lives, they are the kids that usually tend to pursue their dreams and or aspirations. Because I mean, think about it, of all the successful people that you know or hear about, how many of them tend to thank or talk about their parents or an adult in their family as being the reason why they made it, you know, the reason why they have achieved what they have achieved? Most of them right! Because I mean, almost all of the successful people that I have heard or read about, almost all of them give their parents credit as being instrumental in their successes one way or another, you know?

And so all this had me thinking (as I thought about my own situation and wondered how faster might I have achieved my dreams and or aspirations if I too had active parental support behind my dreams), you know what, parents do play a huge role in how their kids future can be shaped, especially when it comes to chasing dreams and or aspirations. I mean it's crazy, but I have come to realize that, kids' lives very much parallel their parent's lives. And what I mean by this is that, not only do kids tend to follow in their parents footsteps (career wise), but they also tend to have the same out-look on life as their parents do. And so, I mean it's like, for example; if a kid's parent is a doctor, a lawyer or an astronaut, then the kid will tend to grow up and become a doctor, a lawyer or an astronaut as well, you know what I mean?

And so I mean, this is why a lot of times kids of musicians tend to grow up to be musicians also, or, kids of actors tend to grow up to be actors also, or, kids of writers tend to grow up to be writers also, or, kids of entrepreneurs tend to grow up to be entrepreneurs also, or, kids of athletes tend to grow up to be athletes also, and the list can go on and on and on. And I mean, it's only natural for it to happen that way, because a kid's biggest influence in their life is their parent, and so if the parent is very active with the kid and exposes the kid to their career in one way or another, the kid will naturally tend to gravitate towards that same career. And the reason why kids tend to gravitate toward the same career as their parents is because, most kids are very intrigued by their parents, and so they get very excited about whatever their parents get excited about.

And so this is one of the reasons why I blame parents as the reason why a lot of kids just never seem to follow their dreams and try to become whatever it is that they think or know they would like to be when they grow up. And the reason why I blame parents is because a lot of parents are just so negative when it comes to their kids and their desires to follow their dreams, you know? And what I mean is, a lot of parents are just not enthusiastic or excited about their kids following or chasing a dream job that is way outside the box of their parent's wishes or comfort. And this is where the problem lies, you know, when it comes to parents and their kids not seeing eye to eye, as far as how they see the world and what their kids want to do when they grow up. And I mean, it can get down-right ugly the misunderstanding or the disagreement between parents and kids in regards to what the parents think their kids should aspire to be when they grow up, as opposed to what their kids really want to be when they grow up.

And I mean, sure there's nothing wrong with parents wanting or desiring for their kids to be something that the parent's wishes or hopes for them, but the problem is that, a lot of times kids have their own dreams and aspirations. And the fact is, a lot of times, in whatever field or occupation that a kid has a dream in, a lot of times that field is where the kid has a lot of talent in. Because I mean, it's like, usually whatever talent the kid has, that's the field that they probably belong in, you know what I mean? I mean, what

I'm trying to say is, usually people receive or get much of their success doing what they really love to do, you know, doing what kinds of comes naturally to them, you know what I mean? I mean it's like, if a kid enjoys computers, then most likely than not their biggest success in life will come from working in the computer field. And, or, for another example; if a kid loves sports, and or if a kid loves singing, and or if a kid loves writing, and or if a kid loves acting, and or if a kid loves biology, then most likely than not, the kid's biggest success will come from either one of those fields that they enjoy the most and or have the most passion for. Because it's like, kids (and people in general) will put the most effort and the most sacrifice only when they are actually doing what they really love to do, you know what I mean?

And this is why a lot of people who seem to be successful in life usually tend to be people who are actually doing what they really love to do, you know what I mean? Because it's like, when people are doing what they enjoy, it stops being a chore or a job anymore and it starts to turn into a hobby, you know, instead of just work, which a lot of people hate, you know what I mean?

I mean it's crazy, but I'm just amazed at how many people just never try to chase their dreams. Because I mean, to me, I believe that before you settle for anything (career wise), you must first try and chase your dreams. Because I mean, to me, life is too short to be working a job that you hate, which a lot of people do. And I mean, of course once in a while you might have to do or take a job that you don't necessarily like or enjoy, but that's life, you gotta survive right? But the problem is, there's too many people out there that have dreams and for whatever reason they just settle for a job they hate even before trying to go after the job that they really want.

And the reason why a lot of people tend to settle for a job that they hate instead of going after their dreams is because, they are afraid, you know, they are afraid of failure. And the reason why a lot of people are afraid to fail is because they lack the confidence that they might actually have what it takes to succeed in whatever it is that they want to do in life. And the reason why a lot of people lack a sense of confidence in themselves is because their parents or other adults in their lives have never instilled in them the confidence that they can be anything they want to be in this world. And so this is why a lot of kids tend to grow up not having the confidence that they can achieve their dreams, and therefore never really even try to chase their dreams.

I mean it's crazy, but parents just don't understand how much power and influence they have over their kids. I mean parents just don't understand how much their own negativity or positivity for that matter can greatly either hinder or encourage their kid's confidence in their ability to succeed in whatever they want to do. And this is one of the reasons why a lot of kids never go after their dreams, and it's because their parents have such a negative outlook on life that their kids become paralyzed to even think about trying to chase their dreams. And this is why a lot of kids just settle and never go after their dreams, and it's because they know that their parents won't support them, and so instead of going at it alone, they just decide to settle.

I mean it's crazy, but it's just amazing at how many parents just don't support their kids and their dreams. And the reason why a lot of parents don't support their kids and their dreams is because, a lot of parents just don't believe that their kids can actually attain or achieve that dream, you know what I mean? I mean it's like, for a lot of parents, chasing a dream is like wasting time, because they just don't believe in dreams coming true. And the reason why a lot of parents don't believe in dreams coming true is because a lot of parents have read or heard of so many sad stories of people chasing dreams and not making it that they just don't want their kids to be one of them. I mean it's almost like parents are trying so hard to protect their kids from failure that they won't even give them a chance to even try and see if they can succeed in going after their dreams. Because I mean, you never know, your kid could actually have the talent for what they want to do. And so stopping him or her, or not giving them the freedom to even try can do nothing but harm not only their talent, but also their chances for attaining the ultimate success in life, you know, living their dreams.

So parents, try your best to support your kids' dreams man, because you just never know, they might actually achieve them. And wouldn't that be so sweet, you know, your kids being successful doing what they actually love, and you getting all the credit for helping them to achieve their goals, dreams, and or aspirations. Because I mean, I don't know about you, but for me, I believe that seeing your kids being successful doing what they love is the greatest joy that a parent could ever have, you know what I mean? And so to me, I believe that before a parent can allow their kids to just settle for anything (you know, settle for any nine to five job that they probably won't even like), I believe it's a parent's job to try their best to recognize any passion or dreams that their kids might have and to try and help them attain that dream, you know, before their kids have to settle for something else in life (as a career).

And I mean, I'm not talking about being stage moms or over-zealous sports dads here (you know, the parents that tend to push their kids so hard just because their kids might have some kind of talent but don't really want or have the passion for whatever the parent is trying to get them to be or to do for a living), oh no, not at all. I'm talking about just recognizing what your kids like or dream of becoming and instead of just sitting by idly and watching to see whether they'll either make it or fail, I'm talking about actually making an effort to support your kids and their dreams, not only verbally but also financially if possible and or necessary. Because I mean, dreams sometimes (and actually a lot of times) cost money to attain. And this is one of the reasons why a lot of kids just don't go after their dreams, because they just don't have that extra little (or big) money that it might take for them to chase their dreams.

And so this is also why you will tend to see that a lot of kids that actually tend to make it or chase their dreams, you will tend to see that these are the kids that usually have their parents supporting them, you know, because a lot of dreams kind of cost money to chase. And this is another reason why a lot of parents tend to not support their kids and their dream chasing ideas, and it's because a lot of parents are scared of losing their money in an un guaranteed adventure that is a dream, you know what I mean? Because I mean, dreams are not guaranteed, you know? I mean, there's no telling whether someone will actually make it or not, in whatever field that they are chasing. But, like they say, you will never know until you try. And to me, I would rather try and fail, and or I would rather have my kids try and fail in trying to reach their dreams than never having tried at all. Because I mean, to me, there's nothing worse than having some kind of talent or passion for something and never ever having tried to chase it. Because to me, at the end of the day (when you are old and gray), there's nothing that I think will be more satisfying or that will make you more content with how you lived your life then knowing that, not only did you live your life doing what you loved to do for a living, but your kids are also making a living and being successful doing what they too love to do with their lives.

And really at the end of the day it is not all about the money, you know, it is not all about how much money you are making or earning at your job. Because I mean, how many people have we heard of who seem to be making a lot of money in their fields but for whatever reason they just don't seem to be happy or even enjoying their jobs. And the reason why they might not be happy at their jobs, even though they are making good money at it is because, they probably just took the job just for the money, you know, something a lot of people tend to do. But at the end of the day these people usually tend to find themselves being miserable with their jobs, and some even decide to quit and take a job that will pay them a little or a lot less but they know that they will really enjoy that job. So you see, it's not all about the money at the end of the day, because you could make a lot of money and still be miserable doing what you are doing, because at the end of the day, it's all about enjoying what you do for a living that will bring you great joy and satisfaction in your life.

So parents, try your best to support your kids man with their dreams, because you definitely don't want them going through life wondering what if, you know, what if they had tried to chase their dreams, you know, what if they had tried and made it, you know, how much more wonderful would life have been for them, you know, if they had gotten a chance to live their dreams, you know what I mean? And I mean, of course not everybody that chases their dreams will make it, but as the saying goes, "Trying is half the battle!"

And so parents, don't be afraid to let your kids try, because I mean you never know, your kids could be one of the lucky ones and make it, especially if you are taking an active role and supporting them with their dreams. Because you know what, it is amazing what kids can accomplish when they have support. Because it's like, when a kid has support, not only will their self-confidence rise, but their focus in what they are trying to accomplish will increase as well. And when a kids focus and self-confidence increases, forget about it, because nothing will seem impossible for them to accomplish. And so this is when parents need to just sit back and watch and remove some obstacles that might be in the kids' way and just let them spread their wings and fly, you know, fly like an eagle and go for their dreams. And for whatever reason if your kids' dreams don't seem to be coming true, you will be right there to lend them a shoulder to lean on, you know, as they dust themselves off and gear up for plan B, you know, this time with a college degree, if they didn't have one already, you know what I mean?

Well my fellow parents, take care of your kids man and don't be afraid to let them spread their wings and fly, because at the end of the day, to me, there's nothing more enjoyable in life then to watch your kids being successful at what they love to do, you know, especially if you were instrumental in their success and they in return are giving you all the credit, in which you can use to brag about among your friends, you know, as how a proud papa or a proud mama should, you know what I mean, ha ha ha ha ha! But yeah man, don't be afraid to let your kids fly and chase their dreams, because they just might amaze you at what they can accomplish, especially with your help and or support!

Chapter 15

Child Support

Child support, a guy's worst nightmare, you know what I mean fellas, ha ha ha ha ha! I mean it's crazy, but guys just don't like paying child support, you know? I mean guys just hate having to give money to their exes, you know, guys just hate to give money to their baby mamas. And the reason why guys hate to give money to their baby mamas is because, hey, just that, it's their baby mama, it's their ex, you know, they are no longer dating them, you know what I mean? I mean, guys just don't see why they should have to give money to a girl that they no longer like, you know, a girl that they no longer want anything to do with, you know, a girl that they had no intention of having a long term relationship with, you know, a girl that they had no intention of having babies with. But, that's the problem (fellas), if you get a girl pregnant, it don't matter whether you like her anymore or not, because at this point (where there is a baby to be cared for), it's not about you and or the baby mama anymore, now it's all about the baby and the baby's needs, which requires a lot of financial support.

And this is one of the reasons why ladies tend to give guys a lot of baby mama dramas, and it's because guys tend to not put paying child support at the top of their priorities (by paying it promptly every month), in which case ends up forcing the ladies to have no option but to harass their baby daddies in the attempt to get the child support money that they desperately need in order to better care for their kids.

And so this is one of the reasons why there are so many baby mama and baby daddy dramas out there. And it's because the ladies are trying to get financial help from their baby daddies and their baby daddies are constantly refusing or neglecting to financially help out with the baby's financial needs. And one of the reasons why guys don't like to give money to their baby mamas is because, a lot of guys just don't trust that their baby mama will actually spend the money on the baby instead of on herself. I mean, guys just tend to think that their baby mamas will most likely spend the money going shopping for themselves instead of actually spending the money on what the baby actually needs.

And this is one of the reasons why a lot of guys tend to be hesitant in giving their baby mama money for child support, and it's because they just believe that their baby mama is lying about needing the money for the baby, you know, they think their baby mama is using the baby to actually get money for their own use, you know, like using the money to get their hair and their nails done, you know, stuff like that. But truth be told, I truly believe that a lot of guy just don't know and or just don't understand how much money it really takes to properly take care of a child. I mean I truly believe that guys (either consciously or subconsciously) just don't take into account how many things there are to be bought and or paid for each year that a kid requires. I mean, some of these things like; baby food, diapers, baby cloth, cribs, car seats, and other small stuff like that don't seem that expensive, but believe me or not they do add up to being very expensive if you actually calculate how much has to be spent on them every month or every year.

And then there's the big ones, you know, the health insurance and the day care expenses. Man I'm telling you, guys just don't understand how much these expenses really are. Because I mean, if they understood how much just day care expenses alone really is, I don't see how they can either play games with child support, or play stupid with helping out with babysitting duties for their own kids. I mean it's crazy, but I just don't really think guys actually get it as how hard it really is for the ladies trying to properly raise children with little or no support from their baby daddies.

And so this is why I would like to (in the ladies behalf) beg and or ask the fellas to please do not neglect your financial responsibilities to your kids man, because your kids will tremendously suffer for no fault of their own. Because I mean it's like, if the mother doesn't have the finances to better care for the kids, then the kids are the ones who will suffer, you know what I mean? Because it's like, if the mother doesn't have the money to buy the kids knew shoes, then the kids will have to wear the same old shoes that are too small for their feet, you know, causing the kids to not only have feet pain, but they can also be the joke of misery from their friends in the neighborhood, which can greatly affect their self-esteem. And also too, if the mother doesn't have enough money to take the kids to day care, then the mother will not be able to maintain any sort of full-time employment, which will further complicate her financial abilities to properly care for the kids.

And so this is why I would like to beg and or implore for guys to step up their financial responsibilities to their kids and help out, because the kids are the ones that will suffer. Because believe me or not, most ladies are very responsible and will use the child support money to better care for the kids. Because really, at the end of the day, it's the mothers who actually usually shoulder the majority of their kids financial needs. And so whatever money the baby daddy might give to the mother will by no means come anywhere close to the amount of money that the baby mama will be spending from her own earnings.

I mean it's crazy, but guys just don't seem to be that motivated in their financial obligation to their kids. I mean it's so bad that the government actually has to threaten jail time for guys who are either extremely late on their child support payments or who haven't paid anything at all. I mean it's crazy, but I guess the government is just too tired and too financially broke to keep having to take care not only the kids (which it doesn't mind doing from time to time, as in; day care supplemental support, child health and dental support, free school lunch, and other governmental children services), but having to take care of the baby mothers as well, you know, like providing welfare, food stamps, subsides housing, and etc. I mean the government is just too broke to keep shelling out money like that, that it just decided to start putting guys in jail for not paying their child support. And really when this law passed a few years ago (I don't remember the time frame), I didn't think it was such a good law. And the reason for this is because (as I was thinking about the law as it passed), what good will it do to put guys who don't pay or are behind on child support in jail? But then when I thought about it some more, I realized that there are really no good solutions that the government can come up with that will for sure increase the number of guys that will do their best to try and pay their child support.

And I mean, even though I know that most irresponsible guys will continue to be irresponsible no matter whether you lock them up or not (because most irresponsible guys are not scared of doing jail time), I wish instead of locking them up, I wish maybe a program could be developed where guys who are behind or haven't paid any child support at all (for whatever reason), maybe instead somehow these guys could be sentences to babysitting duties to their kids as a punishment, you know, instead of going to jail. I mean I don't know, but I just think that locking them up won't really solve much of the real problem, which is guys not being involved in their kid's lives. And so, as I was thinking about the law of locking up child support neglectors, I thought maybe sentencing the guys to baby sit their kids for whatever hours that would be almost equivalent to the amount of child support money that they owed would be a better idea than putting them in jail to do nothing. But of course implementing any new ideas takes a lot of effort and dedication and even money, which at this time I don't think the government will be willing to take on, not with all that financial mess that it's in.

But so anyway, yeah guys, come on man, we can't neglect our kid's financial needs man. I mean we can't just let the ladies bear the brunt of the financial obligation that is necessary for better care of the kids. So come on guys, let's not make excuses and let's be there for our kids financially. And so even though it pains you to give your baby mama money for child support, you still gotta do it, you know, because you really don't want your kids to suffer and you really don't want to go to jail and waste your time when you could be out there working and making sure that all of your kids are taken cared of to the best of your abilities. And also, if you definitely think that your baby mama will miss use the money that you will give her for child support, then you can actually just buy most of the stuff that the baby needs yourself and just keep all the receipt, you know, that way in case your baby mama tries to send you to court for child support all you gotta do is show the judge all the receipt that should prove that you are actually are helping to pay for your kids' needs on a consistent basic, you know what I mean? And so really there's no excuse to not do your best in helping out financially for your kids well-being, because kids do require a lot of financial support, which is too much for the mothers to be doing alone.

And so come on guys, I know it's hard, I know it's financially tough (especially if you can't stand your baby mama and or, especially if you have more than one baby mama and or, if you have another girlfriend who is also demanding your time and finances), but that's your kid, your know, that's your flesh and blood. And so I mean, you don't really want him or her to grow up hating you for not helping his or her mother financially in trying to better care for him or her do you? Because I mean, that's usually what happens to guys who don't help in taking care of their kids, you know, their kids grow up and don't want anything to do with their fathers, you know, they just can't put behind the struggle that they and their mothers had to go through to make it while their fathers were out there somewhere not helping out, you know, their father being out there taking the easy way out by acting like he has no kids to worry about.

And so this is one of the reasons why you will tend to see athletes and other famous people not wanting anything to do with their fathers, and it's all because their fathers were not there during all those years of difficult struggles and sacrifices that their mothers had to make in order for them to become successful adults. And so guys, I'm telling you, don't think that just because your baby mama has stopped harassing you for child support that means you have gotten away easy, oh no, not at all. Because it's like, if karma doesn't get you, and if the government doesn't get you, then your kids will get you when you get old and gray and wonder why none of your kids are coming to visit you at the shady nursing home that you somehow ended up in, you know?

I mean it's crazy, but a lot of old guys tend to find themselves by themselves at that golden age where they should be playing with grand-children and stuff, you know? I mean, a lot of old man just find themselves by themselves feeling and looking miserable all the time, and it's all because they were too selfish as fathers when they had kids and now none of their kids want anything to do with them.

So guys, come on man, let's not make excuses and lets start handling our financial obligations like how real men should, you know what I mean? And so go ahead player, go ahead baller, go ahead shot caller, you know, go ahead and handle your business of taking care all of your kids, because at the end of the day (when they are all grown and successful), not only will they thank you for always being there for them, they will also have no choice but to try to be the best parents they can also be for their own kids, which is what you want (so you can relax and have fun spoiling the grand-kids), and which is how it should be!

Chapter 16

Where's daddy?

It is amazing to me at how many kids nowadays are growing up without their fathers. I mean, it is amazing to me at how many fathers out there who are not involved in their children's lives. I mean, it is very disappointing to me at how many men out there who are running away from their responsibilities of being fathers to their kids. I mean, it is very disappointing to me at how men nowadays don't seem to take pride in their manhood by manning up or owning up to their seeds and taking care of their kids.

I mean, it's just amazing to me at how many baby daddies are out there nowadays, you know, men who don't take care of their kids. And I mean, sure baby daddies have always been around, but it just seems that nowadays it is becoming almost an epidemic, if it isn't already. Because it's like, everywhere you turn nowadays, there goes another kid without a father wondering who their daddy is, you know what I mean?

I mean it's crazy, but it's just amazing to me at how many kids nowadays are being raised with just their mothers, you know, because their fathers weren't men enough to deal with or weren't men enough to man-up and be responsible for their actions. And I mean, sure there are a lot of scandalous and or trifling women out there, but that's no excuse, because a kid is a kid and they need both parents to be in their life in order for them to get properly nurtured so they can increase their chances of growing up to be mature and successful adults. Because I mean, with all this craziness that's going on in the world today, it doesn't take much for a kid to get lost because of the lack of parental supervision and or direction in the kid's life.

I mean it's crazy, but I see kids running around aimlessly all the time, you know, not knowing what to do with themselves. And this is usually when a lot of them end up finding themselves in situations that they would rather have not gotten themselves in. But you know, kids will be kids, and most of them are just not strong enough to overcome peer pressure, which is usually why they tend to do the stupid stuff that other kids are doing, which ends up getting them into trouble. And so this is why parental supervision and or parental involvement in your kids' lives is very critical, because even the well taught or the well- mannered kids can end up finding themselves in trouble, and it's all because of the peer pressure thing.

And so, here is where I would like to ask (because I know where the mothers are, and it's usually at work), where is daddy? I mean, I'm serious, where are the fathers to all these kids out here who are running around like crazy with no direction and no manhood training? I mean, where are the fathers to all these kids out here who can't seem to stay out of trouble in one form or another? Because I mean, to me, the majority of the problems that kids tend to find themselves in is all because of a lack of that strong male figure in their lives that can demand proper behavior from the kid. And the father is usually the best person to do it. Because I mean, sure step-fathers and other male adults that are close to the kid can try and discipline or demand proper behavior from the kid, but after a while, or if the kid is very rebellious, the kid can easily dismiss their step-father or another male adult figure in their life by saying stuff like, "You can't tell me what to do, you are not my father!", you know what I mean? And this is what a lot of kids like to say to male adult figures in their lives that they don't want to listen to. And this is because, to kids, only their biological fathers (or biological mothers for that matter) have the right to rule over their lives and or discipline them. And this is also why it is very hard for step parents (mothers or fathers) to really try and discipline their step kids the way that they would their own biological kids, and it's because they just don't feel like they have the power or freedom to discipline their step kids the way they see fit.

And so, this is why biological parents always must make sure that they are involved in their kids' lives even if the kids have a good step-father or a good step-mother in the household, you know, because they just might not be able to discipline your kids properly, you know, therefore needing you to come in and help out with the disciplining of your kids, especially if your kids happen to be very rebellious, you know what I mean? And the reason why I say this is because, a lot of kids just tend to not like their step-fathers or step-mothers, especially if the kid is already a teenager when they meet them and have to live with them.

And so this is where it is very helpful to the kid if he or she can have their other biological parent (who is not living with them) available at all times just in case the kid feels frustrated with the situation and needs someone they trust and love there to talk to them and explain whatever situation the kid might be going through. I mean it's crazy, but kids go through so much bull just because their parents aren't responsible enough to make sure that their kids come first, you know? I mean it's crazy, but parents (especially fathers) will just have to do a better job of making sure that they make themselves available to their kids at all times (even if they are not living with their kids), because you just never know when your kid is going to desperately need your attention in one way or another, for whatever reason.

And so, this is where I would like to beg or ask the question again, where is daddy? Well my friends, I actually think I know the answer to this question. And the answer is, and no, they are not in jail or prison as a lot of people tend or like to think. Because I mean, most of them do get out of jail don't they? And I mean, sure the majority of them do end up going back to jail for second and third offenses, but that's only about five percent of all of the baby daddies that are out there, according to my estimation. And so where are all the other baby daddies at? And so, once again (drum roll please), and the answer is; most of the baby daddies are right there in your neighborhood running around hiding and dodging from not only their baby mamas, but also from their kids, you know, being straight out trifling.

I mean it's crazy, but most of the baby daddies live right there almost in the same neighborhood, or the same city, or the same county, or the same state as their kids, but they will still not make an effort to be in their kids' lives. I mean it's sad that men will actually avoid being in their kids' lives even though their kids are right there within their neighborhood, you know, just because they don't want to be responsible (financially) in having to help with the raising of the kids (their own kids). I mean, it is very sad nowadays that a lot of men don't have enough pride in their manhood to where they can force themselves to man-up and own-up to their responsibilities and do whatever it takes to take care of their kids, you know, as what a real man should.

I mean, it is very disappointing that a lot of men nowadays don't know what being a man or a real man is all about. Because I mean it's like, for a lot of guys nowadays, being a man to them is when you can grow a beard or mustache and be able to talk girls into having sex with them. I mean it's crazy, and it's so pathetic that a lot of guys equate macking a girl down into giving them her goodies as being a real man, when in actuality being a real man means a lot more than being a smooth talker, which actually just makes you a player, and most players just end up being baby daddies and not real men. Because I mean, to be a real men, not only will you have to make sure that all of your kids are taken cared of financially, but you will also have to make sure that your kids emotional, spiritual, educational and future outlook are headed in the right direction to the best of your abilities, you know what I mean? And so being a real man actual means being willing to do whatever it takes (legally of course, because there's no point in you chancing going to jail by engaging in illegal stuff to make money, because then you will definitely not be able to take care of your kids when you get caught) to make sure that your kids are taken care of both financially and emotionally. And so I mean, being a real man will definitely require a lot of sacrifices and a lot of hard work from you, you know, because that's what being a real man is all about, you know, taking care of your responsibilities with pride, you know what I mean?

I mean it's crazy, but a lot of guys nowadays just don't take pride in being a real man, you know, they just settle for being boys trapped in a man's body, you know what I mean? Because I mean, just because you have a beard and a mustache and look and talk and walk and can sex a girl down pretty good, it all doesn't mean a thing (as far as being a real man is concerned) if you are not taking care of all of your kids, which will just mean that, you are just a boy trapped in a man's body. I mean it's crazy, but there are a lot of men out there nowadays who are nothing but little boys trapped in a man's body.

And this is one of the reasons why a lot of women nowadays are having such a hard time in finding a real man, because they constantly run into boys trapped in a man's body but for whatever reason fail to realize it before it's too late, you know, before they get pregnant and the guy runs away from the responsibility, leaving the woman to have to raise the baby on her own. I mean it's crazy, but ladies, I think I have just helped y'all out some more in your test in trying to decide whether your guy or the guy that's trying to get with you is a real man or not, you know, by finding out whether he's taking care of all of his kids or not. And if you run into a guy who doesn't have kids, you can still find out if he is a real man or not by checking to see if he seems to be a responsible hard working guy with goals or not, you know, because real men always have goals or plans on how they are going to succeed in life. And when I say goals and plans, I'm talking about actual goals and plans that not only have they written them down somewhere, but they are actually actively pursuing them with purpose. So ladies, stop getting caught up with boys trapped in a man's body, because all they will do with you is play, you know, because that's all what boys really want to do anyway, you know, play. And I mean, it doesn't even matter if they are thirty, forty, or fifty years old, you know, because a boy will be a boy until he decides to be a man!

But yeah man, a lot of guys nowadays just don't know what being a man is all about. And the reason why a lot of guys don't know what being a man is all about is because, they just never had a father or an adult male figure in their own life that they trusted and respected enough that could sit them down and tell them or show them by example what being a man is all about, you know what I mean? And the reason for this lack of adult male figures or male role models in a lot of guys lives is because a lot of fathers just take it for granted or just don't realize how much their kids really need them. And so instead of them manning up and owning up to their responsibilities, they run like cowards and leave the mothers to try and raise a man (you know, their sons), which can be very tough for a woman to do.

And the bad thing is, a lot of kids that grow up without their fathers usually tend to grow up and become deadbeat dads themselves, you know, like father like son. And so it's like, the circle of kids growing up without their fathers tends to go from generation to generation without an end in sight, which can be very dangerous, because before long (if we are not there already), we gonna have an epidemic of kids running around crazy with no direction and or purpose in life growing up causing mayhem because they don't value anything, not even their own lives, let alone others. And I mean, this is one of the reasons why there is so much violence and homicides nowadays, and it's because there are so many kids out there that just don't value life, and so they have no problem killing people. I mean it's crazy, but fathers just don't understand what kind of damage they are doing to their kids by abandoning them. I mean it's serious stuff, because a lot of kids who grow up without fathers tend to feel very incomplete, you know, they tend to feel as though they are not as special as other kids that have fathers in their lives. And this is one of the reasons why a lot of single mothers tend to have such a hard time in trying to instill self-worth and or self-esteem to their kids, because for some kids, the void of not knowing or not having their fathers in their lives is so huge that they just can't shake it, you know, leaving them feeling depressed and or despaired.

I mean it's crazy, but fathers just don't know how important they are to their kids. Because I definitely believe that if the majority of the kids out here had their fathers in their lives, I believe a lot of all this violence and mayhem that kids get themselves into would tremendously reduce. Because I mean, most kids get themselves into trouble because of desperation, you know, desperation for attention, you know, to feel loved and or wanted. And this is one of the reasons why a lot of kids end up joining gangs, and it's because they are desperate to feel wanted and loved.

And this is also why a lot of girls tend to cling to these little boys and even let them impregnate them, and this is because they are searching for love from a father figure, you know, they are searching for a male figure in their lives. And so it's like all these kids are running around searching for love all in the wrong places and or wrong faces, and it's all because their fathers are not there to guide them and give them that belonging love that kids desperately need. Because I mean, kids usually get their strength of knowing who they are from their fathers, you know, by knowing and or understanding their roots or family tree, which in turns fosters a strong sense of pride in their last name, you know what I mean? And this is another reason why nowadays you don't tend to see a lot of family reunions going on, and if you do see them, they tend to have very few people and mostly women and children. And this is because a lot of families are broken up and or missing strong men who can carry the family name forward, you know, with pride.

I mean it's crazy, but I don't know what men are thinking by abandoning their kids. Because I mean, at the end of the day, when they are all old and gray, having their kids there gathered together at a picnic or family reunion talking about how their daddy is the greatest man they know, and having their father there to hug and show their appreciation for all that he had done or tried to do for them as they grew up, to me that is the greatest joy any father could ever have. I mean, I think this is what most parents live for, you know, to watch their kids become mature and successful adults with a wife or husband and kids enjoying life. I mean, I just don't get it, you know, I just don't get how a man can abandon his kids and just think that everything will be cool. No, not everything will be cool, not everything will be cool in their life, and not everything will be cool in their kids' lives either. Because I mean, I fail to believe that any father who abandons his kids does not get hunted by the thought of his kids in his mind from time to time.

And I mean, I think this is one of the reasons why a lot of fathers who have abandon any one of their kids just never seems to get any real peace or happiness in their lives. And it's all because deep down inside of them somewhere (consciously or subconsciously), their brain keeps reminding them of a part of them (their kids) that is not settled, you know, a part of them that might be wondering around out there in the world looking or searching for daddy who ran away from his responsibilities. I mean it's crazy, but this is one of the reasons why I think that a lot of deadbeat dads just don't seem to prosper in life, you know, because they have abandon a precious blessing that could have been a part of their lives and could have even been a source of great joy and inspiration to motivate them to make a success out of their lives.

But no, they missed out, and now they find themselves all alone at their old age, and it is all because they were too selfish to sacrifice their little bachelor lifestyle by not making any time for their kids. And I mean, this is one of the reasons why a lot of men tend to grow old all alone with no one to come visit them (besides their mamas, if they are still alive), and it's all because they were too selfish to make time to visit their own kids, better yet take care of them.

I mean it's crazy, but I truly believe that if fathers took more ownership of their kids and made sure that their kids knew where daddy was and they can call him and talk to him any time they want, I bet you there would be less confused kids walking around today than ever. Because I mean, it is scary at how many kids are out here nowadays that are straight out confused, you know, that have no sense of direction or purpose in life. And I mean, you can see it in their eyes, just straight out lost, you know, they don't know whether they are coming or going, you know, they just seem to be wondering aimlessly in the streets while their youth (you know, their young life) is passing them by. I mean it's very scary and sad, because I see them all the time, you know, just chilling, in the middle of the afternoon, with blank stares in their faces (as if they have lost all hope for humanity or for their lives to be better) that to me are crying out for help, you know, crying out for someone to come and guide them or show them how to improve or how to better their lives.

    I mean it's crazy, but it's just amazing to me at how many confused young people are out there running around crazy and or misguided nowadays. And the thought that always comes to my mind is, "Where is their daddy?" I mean, it's like, when I see a teenage girl walking around with like two or three boys around her flirting and giggling like it's all good, the question that comes to my mind is, "Where is her daddy?" And it's like, when I see a teenage boy dressed in gang colors and acting all thuggish and stuff, the question that comes to my mind is, "Where is his daddy?" And it's like, when I see a young girl dressed like a prostitute (you know, wearing very little clothing as to show as much skin as possible without being totally naked) trying to be sexy, the question that comes to my mind is, "Where is her daddy?" And it's like, when I see a young man walking around aimlessly with his pants half way down his legs (making him unable to walk straight because his pants keeps falling down to his knees) showing his boxers thinking that is cool, the question that comes to my mind is, "Where is his daddy?"

    And still, it's like, when I see a young girl with her belly all big (obviously pregnant) standing at a bus stop looking all tired and miserable, the question that comes to my mind is, "Where is her daddy?" And still yet, when I see a young man or a young lady walking around looking confused about their gender, you know, boys walking, talking, and acting like girls, and girls walking, talking, dressing and acting like boys, the question that comes to my mind is, "Where is their daddy?" And yet still, when I look at magazine covers, or when I watch music videos, or when I see TV shows with half naked girls in them posing very provocatively, the question that comes to my mind is, "Where is their daddy?" And yet worse still, when I see young girls out there in the streets prostituting themselves, or when I see young girls out there dirty dancing or stripping in the clubs, the question that comes to my mind is, "Where is their daddy?"

And I mean, the list can go on and on and on, because I truly believe that a lot of these situations that a lot of girls and boys find themselves in can be avoided, especially if their fathers take an active role in their lives, you know, so they can help guide and encourage their kids to take the right path for their futures. Because I mean, it's crazy out there in the world, especially for young people with no proper direction.

And the bad thing is, for a lot of kids with no proper guidance in their lives, when they find themselves in desperate financial situations, selling something (usually illegal stuff) always tends to be the only option that they see. And this is why a lot of boys tend to turn to drug dealing as a way to make ends meet or to survive. And this is also why a lot of girls tend to turn to stripping or prostituting as a way to make ends meet or to survive. But I truly believe that if more fathers took an active role in their kids' lives, a lot of these drug dealing and prostituting or stripping could be avoided as being the only option for survival. Because I mean, an active father in his kids' lives will definitely go way beyond the call of duty just to make sure that his kids are doing fine at all times, even when they think they are grown and are ashamed to ask for assistance from their parents. And I mean, what I'm trying to say is, a true father will tend to know if his kids are in need of his assistance even if the kids don't ask for it. Because I mean, some kids have too much pride and don't want their parents to think of them as being failures even if their hardship is not of their own making, you know, like a loss of a job or a bad break up from a relationship that has left them financially desperate.

I mean it's crazy, but a true parent never leaves his or her kids out there in the wilderness (called the streets) to fend for themselves. Hell no, that's your baby, and they will always be your baby! And so you might as well help them in their time of need, even if you have to drag their butts back to you kicking and screaming while you try and redirect their lives, if for whatever reason they ended up getting lost even though you did your best to guide them properly. Because I mean, truth be told, sometimes kids just go astray for no damn good reason at all, you know what I mean? And I mean, even kids who might come from a two parent home can seem to get lost or lose their focus on what is important and what is just a waste of time (like partying instead of studying, or becoming a teenage mother instead of waiting until marriage to have children).

But that's kids for you, you know, and some will drive you crazy before it's all said and done or before they start to understand that what you were trying to teach them was for their own good. Because most likely than not, you yourself have been there and done that and nothing good ever came from that except a lot of headache and pain, which you were trying to spare your kids from having to go through or deal with. But hey, like they say, sometimes kids will just have to go through the rough experiences of life for themselves before they can really appreciate your wisdom as a parent and what you might have to offer them as real life lessons.

But yeah man, fathers are definitely needed in their kids' lives, because there are so much ills in this world today for mothers to be raising the kids alone. Because I mean, mothers sometimes just get so tired and so frustrated by having to raise the kids by themselves that they just can't do it anymore and just give up, you know, especially if the kids are very rebellious. And so this is one of the reasons why it is very important for fathers to take active roles in their kids' lives, you know, so as to balance out and help out the mother whenever she needs a break from the kids so she can rejuvenate, you know, so she can re-energize and refocus herself before having to deal with the kids again. Because I'm telling you, taking care or raising kids is no joke, especially if you want to be a good parent and nurture your kids properly, which a lot of parents fail to do. And so this is why fathers are definitely needed in a kid's life, because it's just too much work for mothers to be doing alone.

And so here is where I would like to beg all the fathers out there who are not involved in their kids' lives to try their best (actually don't just try, do it) and make sure that they get involved in their kids' lives. Because your kids need you man, I mean, I'm telling you (and I'm sure you know it), trust me, they desperately need you! Because I mean, I can't tell you how many kids I see who don't have their fathers in their lives and how I can tell that they wish that they had their fathers around, even if it's just for the weekends. Because I mean, I can't tell you how many times when I go to the park to take my kids to play that I end up becoming a coach to a whole bunch of other kids who want to participate in whatever I'm trying to teach my kids to play.

I mean it almost never fails that a few kids will be drawn to where me and my kids are doing some kind of practice drills, you know, just trying to teach my kids how to play whatever sport they want to learn that day, and sometimes we will do more than one or two sports, you know, just having fun. And it's like, because I'm a sports playing junkie, my kids find it kind of cool that I'm kind of good in a whole bunch of sports, and so they too want to learn how to play almost every sport that I might know how to play. And so every time we go to the park (especially on weekends), I end up becoming like a coach of some sought as other kids start to gravitate to what we are practicing (whether it's basketball, football, soccer, tennis, baseball, etc.).

And at first, when this used to happen, I used to try and brash them off, you know, because I really just wanted to concentrate and just have fun with my kids, you know, just enjoy spending time with my kids alone. But, as time went on, I started to realize that most of these kids that come to the playground they are brought there by their mothers, and most mothers don't really like to run around and get sweaty and all that, oh no, most mothers just sit down somewhere and just watch their kids run around until they get bored and or until the mother gets bored and it's back to the house to watch more boring TV. And so I started to let the other kids practice with us (after asking my kids if they didn't mind, which they didn't, because actually that just increased participants for them to play with, and all kids like to play with their peers, you know, it makes playing more fun) after realizing that most of them probably don't have fathers in their lives to play with them and or to show them how to play some sports.

And so, after a while, it just became a regular thing for me to have a bunch of kids lined up in a ready practice drill and start teaching all of them how to play whatever sport we are playing that day. And I remember one time we played like three sports with like ten or fifteen kids of various ages (between four and ten years old, and that's my kids age group) and gender, and I remember having a hard time trying to control all of them (especially the boys who want to do everything rough, but I had to keep reminding them that there are ladies here gentlemen so try to take it easy).

But that was fun, and I could see that the kids enjoyed having fun playing with a grown up. And that's when it downed on me that, most of these kids are missing that father to kid enter-action, you know, chasing your father around kind of stuff. Because I came to realize that the kids in the park usually have a lot more fun when they are either chasing me around the field (along with my kids chasing me too), or playing me against all of them, or playing the boys against the girls plus daddy, you know, me, Imani's daddy (that's my daughter's name). But yeah man, it has become a regular thing for me to find myself teaching a bunch of kids how to play something that my wife thinks that I should definitely become a coach, because kids seem to respond well to me and she knows that I love playing sports and I love teaching kids how to play sports.

And so, yeah man, all this just to say that, come on fathers, we gotta do better, you know, we gotta be involved in our kids' lives, you know what I mean? And really, it's not even about the money, you know, it's not about whether you have money to give to your kids or not. Because at the end of the day, all your kid really cares about is love, you know, knowing and feeling loved by his or her father. And showing love to a kid is very simple, it doesn't even require money, all it requires is a little bit of your time and presence in a consistent basis, you know, for you to be there when the kid needs to talk to you, or for you to pick him or her up and take them to the playground on a regular basis. And I mean, that's it, that is all that a kid really wants from his father, you know, to make the kid feel like he or she is very special, which all kids are.

And I mean, sure it would be nice if you contributed financially for the expenses of taking care of the kid, but if for whatever reason you can't right now (and see how I said right now, because sooner than later the mother is going to need some financial help, especially as the kid is growing bigger and older and will require a lot more to not only feed and shelter them, but also to cloth them and to sign them up for extra-curricular activities like sports and stuff, you know, as a way to keep them busy so they don't just hang out in the streets or the malls wasting valuable time and energy), then you should at least make a consistent effort to spend some quality time with your kids by either taking them for the weekend or just taking them to the playground for the day so they can have fun playing with their father, which every kid would love, because it would definitely make them feel very special and very loved?

Chapter 17

No More Baby Daddies

"I can see the head, I can see the head, push, push, push (the doctor says to the mother), come on, give me two more pushes, the baby is almost out, one more push, one more big push, good job, here it comes, here it comes, it's out, it's out, good job, congratulations, it's a boy!

Man, there's nothing more amazing and joyous as watching your kid being born. I mean, the whole process from the mother carrying the baby in her belly for nine months, all the way to the day the baby is born is a very humbling experience, especially the delivery part. Because it's like, there you are (with your wife or girlfriend) at the delivery room, finally, after nine long months of patiently waiting for the due date, and after going through two false labor episodes (you know, when your wife demands that you take her to the hospital right away because she is convinced for sure that her contractions are strong enough and the baby might come out any minute now, but, when you get to the hospital the doctor sends y'all back home because not only are the contractions not strong enough, but she is not even dilated at all), finally the day has come.

And so there you are, standing right beside your woman as she lay on the hospital bed screaming like a mad woman, as the contractions start to get stronger and stronger (signifying that labor has truly began). And then so there you are, anxious, nervous, half confused, doing your best to comfort your lady as she screams in pain every other minute or so as the contractions get stronger and stronger. And then so, finally, after sixteen hours of torturous labor (leaving the both of y'all exhausted), finally the doctor walks into the room and says, "Ok, she's fully dilated now, come on, it's time to push the baby out." And then so, after sixteen hours of exhaustion, you now finally get to witness the most awesome, amazing, magical wonder you will ever experience, which is, the birth of your precious baby.

I mean, I'm telling you, there's nothing like it, there's nothing more amazing than seeing your child being born. Because it's like, that whole process, from your woman pushing, to the baby's head crowning (you know, when only the baby's head and hair can be seen), to the baby's face sticking out (looking like an alien), to when the baby's whole body comes out (looking like they have been playing in some slimy liquid stuff), to the cutting of the chord, to the hearing of the baby's first cry, to the doctor handing you the baby and saying, "Congratulations daddy, make sure you take good care of this precious baby!" And then so, after nodding and saying, "I sure will" (promising to take good care of the baby), you can't help but be overcome with joy and pride as you hold and stare at your little "mini me", you know, fruit of your loins, you know, a part of you, you know, your precious offspring!

Man, it's an amazing thing having a baby. Because it's like, there they are, in your arms, calmly staring at you with their little eyes, barely blinking, you know, as if they haven't seen you in a while, or, as if they are studying every feature of your face, or, as if they are trying to say, "Hi, daddy!"

Man, what an awesome experience watching your kid being born is. But, what's even more awesome is watching them grow up, you know what I mean? Because it's like, from like when they first learn how to crawl (leaving a proud look on your face, as they enjoy the freedom of movement), to when they first learn how to stand (leaving a proud look on your face, as they proudly showoff how long they can stand before falling back down), to when they first learn how to walk (leaving a proud look on your face, as they showoff how far they can walk without falling), to when they first learn how to run (leaving a proud look on your face, as they proudly showoff how fast they can run), to when they first learn how to talk (leaving a proud look on your face, as they do their best to form words and sentences), you know? And then, yet still, to when they first learn how to tie their shoes (leaving a proud look on your face, as they do their best to make rabbit ears with their little fingers without getting frustrated), and to their first day of school (leaving a proud look on your face, as they wave you goodbye as they get on the school bus, leaving you fighting back tears of joy, pride, and nervousness as you start to realize that your baby is not a baby anymore, they are a big kid now).

And then still, there are a lot more proud moments to look forward to, you know? Because it's like for example, another proud moment can be when your kid first joins their little league sports team and ends up being one of the best players on the team (leaving a proud look on your face, as you start to fantasize and or day dream about them being the next Michael Jordan, or the next Tiger Woods, or the next Venus and Serena Williams, you know, and so on and so on). Because I mean you just never know, your kid could actually end up being one of the greatest athletes in the world, a proud moment for any parent, but more so especially for us parents who used to be former wannabe athletes who never made it and are kind of still not over it yet, you know what I mean? Ha ha ha ha ha, or well, that's how it goes sometimes right? Hey that's life, right? Sometimes your plans and dreams just don't happen or just don't happen the way you planned them, right?

But yeah, there's a lot of proud moments for parents to enjoy and cherish as they watch their kids grow up. And some of these proud moments can include for example; (1) watching your kid learn how to skate, (2) watching your kid learn how to swim, (3) watching your kid learn how to ride a bike, (4) watching your kid learn how to play sports, (5) watching your kid make the Honor Roll, (6) watching your kid win the Spelling Bee, (7) watching your kid win an Essay Contest, (8) watching your kid graduate from High School, or better yet, (9) watching your kid graduate from College, or better still, (10) what about watching your kid get that dream job that they always wanted, and then, better, better still, (11) what about watching your kid getting married to that wonderful person that they are in love with.

Man, I'm telling you, there's a lot of joy and pride to be had for parents from their kids. Because I mean, you just never know, your kid could actually end up being the next Oprah Winfrey, or the next Michael Jackson, or the next Michael Jordan, or the next Denzel Washington, or the next Tyler Perry (of Medea fame), or the next Bob Johnson (founder and former owner of BET), or the next Bill Cosby, or the next Beyonce, or the next Condoleeza Rice (the first black female Secretary of State of the United States), or the next Colin Powel, or the next Ben Carson (one of the best neurosurgeons in the world, the doctor that other neurosurgeons seek after when there is a severe or delicate brain surgery that needs to be done), or they could end up being the next Barack Obama, you know, President of the United States.

I mean, picture that, the President of the United States, that could be your son or daughter. I mean, how proud would you be? Because I mean, there's no more excuses, Barack has broken the glass ceiling. And so now saying the Man is holding me back won't work anymore, because a black man has actually made it to the White House, and has made it as the President of it. And I mean, how great is that! Because it's like, now when black folks tell their kids that they can be anything that they want to be just as long as they work hard at it, now their kids won't have to ask them whether or not they can actually be President of the United States. And if they do ask, they won't have to just take their parents words for it, because the answer will be staring at them right there in their faces, you know, whether through the television screen or the history books, you know, "Yes You Can", Barack Obama, the 44th President of the United States (who happens to be black).

Man, I'm telling you, there's a lot of proud moments to be had for parents from their kids. But then of course all of these proud moments don't just happen by chance, I mean, all of these proud moments don't just come easy, or for free, or by accident, or by luck, or by a miracle, hell no, there's a lot of hard work and sacrifice that the parent will have to make and or do before all of those proud moments can be enjoyed. And this sacrifice and hard work is what will separate the good parents from the bad ones. And this sacrifice and hard work is what will separate the real men from the boys. And this sacrifice and hard work is what will separate the real fathers from the baby daddies, you know what I mean?

Man, I'm telling you, "fatherhood" is one of the most important and one of the most challenging rewarding jobs that any man will ever experience, especially if they want to be a good parent. And the reason why I say "if they want to be a good parent" is because, unlike the ladies, who pretty much have no choice but to be there for their baby (because they are the ones who have to carry and give birth to the baby, therefore by default have no choice but be stuck with the baby), guys on the other hand pretty much have a choice on whether or not they will man-up, own-up, accept their responsibilities as fathers and help take care of their kids. I mean, I know what y'all thinking ladies, "that, that is not fair", and y'all are right, a man shouldn't be able to just walk away from his parental responsibilities just like that. But think about it ladies, because truth be told (unless the mother is married to her baby's father), it's just so easy for a guy to walk away from his responsibilities as a parent than a woman can. And I mean, sure marriage doesn't truly guarantee that the guy will never leave and end up becoming a deadbeat dad, but marriage is what usually forces a guy to step up his game as a father. And this is because most guys are not usually ready to become fathers unless they are married. And the reason why I say this is because, most un-married guys are never totally sure whether the girl that they are dating is really the one they want to spend the rest of their lives with or not. And so if their girlfriend does end up getting pregnant, the guy usually will start to feel like his girl is trying to trap him with the baby (whether it's true or not).

And then so, this is usually the time when most girls end up getting dumped, you know, between the time that they tell their boyfriends they are pregnant and before they give birth to the baby. Because I mean, why do you think most girls end up going through their pregnancy alone, you know, without their soon to be baby daddy? It's because the guy done split, you know, not wanting the responsibility of raising a kid, the boy done ran. I mean, instead of manning up to being a real father to his kid, he has instead chosen to settle for being just a baby daddy. I mean, instead of standing up for fatherhood, he has instead chosen to be another deadbeat dad, you know what I mean?

See ladies, this is why I say most guys are not really ready to be fathers unless they are married to their baby's mother. And the reason why I say this is because, most guys don't totally commit themselves into their relationships (you know, work hard to make it work) unless they are married to their woman. And so, likewise, most guys don't totally commit themselves to their kids (you know, embracing fatherhood) unless they are married to their baby's mother. And this is because, guys generally just don't like to be tied down. You know, guys just don't like their freedom of movement and or libido (you know, their ability to chase other skirts, you know, their ability to get down and dirty with any woman they want) to be limited and or hampered. And so likewise, most guys tend to view kids just like how they view marriage, you know, as just another way to tie them down, which most guys don't like, and therefore tend to reject, and in which case end up forcing them to except the lousy, careless, and useless position of being just a baby daddy.

Now, you are probably asking yourself (ladies), why, why if guys don't like to be tied down, why then do they continue to get girls whom they have no interest in marrying pregnant? Or, to say it in another way, why do guys who don't think or know that they are not ready to be fathers continue to end up impregnating girls that they have no intention of marrying? Well my friends (ladies), I have two simple answers for you; (1) guys just wanna have their cake and eat it too, and (2) guys are not good at thinking straight when they are horny. See, I told you I had two simple answers for you. What, why are you shaking your head? Or, you don't think the answers are simple enough? I mean, you actually want me to expend on them some more? Ok, fine, you win, I'll expend on my answers, gee wiz, y'all so demanding, my goodness, ha ha ha ha, just kidding!

See, this is why I don't like to write when I tired, because I quickly lose focus and start getting silly and end up making a fool of myself. So word to the wise, don't work on your book when you are really, really tired, unless of course you got something to say that you might forget the next day (which I won't), or unless you got a dead line to meet (which I don't), or unless you are having a hard time falling asleep (which I'm not), or unless you want to make a fool out of yourself (which I don't), or unless…, you know what, I think I should just go to bed now, so good night and we will resume our baby daddy discussion tomorrow when I'm more alert and focused, alright, thank you and good night!

Hello my friends, it's the next day and I'm still a little tired, but I'm a lot more alert and ready to continue our discussion on lousy guys, you know, guys who keep impregnating girls that they have no intention of marrying. And so on answer number (1), what I mean by guys just wanna have their cake and eat it too is, guys like the idea of having kids, but without having to deal with the responsibilities that come with having kids. And also, guys like the idea of having kids, but without having to deal with having to commit to their baby mothers, you know, without having to give up their freedom of being a player, you know what I mean? And so this is why I say guys like to have their cake and eat it too (you know the saying). Because it's like, the kids are the cakes (which the guy can show off his offspring to his friends from time to time) and the guy's freedom to chase other women is his "eat it too", you know what I mean? I mean it's like how the other saying goes, "Why buy the cow when you can get the milk for free!" You know the saying right? And so likewise, most guys just figure why give up their freedom of being a player when there are plenty of ladies out there who are willing to give them babies without demanding any real sort of commitment from them. And so, this is also one of the reasons why most un-married mothers tend to find themselves having different baby daddies for their kids, and it's because they allowed themselves to give kids to some of the guys they have dated without first demanding true commitment (marriage) from them. And this is one of the reasons why there are so many baby daddies nowadays, and it's because a lot of guys just want to have their cakes and eat it too, and there are a lot of women who are more than willing to oblige.

Ok, I think I have answered answer number (1), now let's go on to answer number (2), which is, guys are not very good at thinking straight when they are horny. And the reason why I say this is because, I mean think about it, why would a guy allow himself to impregnate a girl that he doesn't even really like, or he doesn't even really know (like a one night stand), or he doesn't even really find her that attractive, or a girl that is known for sleeping around, or a girl that has three or four other kids by different men? I mean, think about it, why would a guy allow himself to get pregnant a girl that he shouldn't even be messing with (underage girls, mistresses, etc.) in the first place. It's horniness my friends, it's all horniness!

And the bad part is, the more the younger the guy is, the more horny he is. And the more the younger the guy is, the less control he has over his horniness. And this is one of the reasons why there are so many baby daddies nowadays. And it's because there are a lot of girls nowadays who become sexually active from a very young age, you know, who end up getting pregnant from young horny boys who are not yet ready or willing to take up the responsibilities of fatherhood. And so, this is also why there are so many pregnant teenage girls out there, and it's because in their quest for love, they end up giving their sex to horny boys whose only mission is to score and to score with as many girls as they can get with. See ladies, I'm telling you, most guys are not thinking about making babies when they have sex, hell no, they just want to satisfy their sex drives. And so, if you are ready, willing, and able to help them with their horniness problem, you are good to go, you know, no matter whether they really like you or not.

See, I'm trying to tell y'all (ladies), most guys (whether consciously or subconsciously) are not really ready to be fathers unless they are married to their women. And this is why there are so many baby daddies out there, and it's because women continue to give babies to guys who have no intention of marrying them. And so anyway (ladies), don't get me wrong, I'm not at all trying to put all the blame on y'all for why there are so many baby daddies out there, oh no, not at all. Because the truth of the matter is that, there is really no excuse for any guy who has fathered a child to not be a real father to that child. I mean, there's really no excuse! Because I mean, when you father a child, that child is yours, you know? Because it's like, not only does that child carry your DNA, but that child is really a reflection of you. You know, not only is that child carrying your genes, that child is really a part of you, you know what I mean? And so, really, if a guy rejects that child and decides not to be a part of that child's life, what he is really doing is, he is really rejecting himself, you know, he is rejecting a part of himself that is very precious. Because I mean, truth be told, every kid is precious, you know, no matter what circumstances they happen to be conceived at. And I mean, it don't matter whether they were the result of a one night stand, or the result of a weekend affair, or the result of someone cheating on their mates, or the result of the guy forgetting to use a condom, or the result of the woman tricking the guy by lying or pretending to be on birth control. I mean it don't matter how the kid was conceived, that kid is precious.

And this is one of the reasons why I decided to write a book on fatherhood, and it's because kids are very precious. But it's just so sad that too many of them are out there wondering around aimlessly not knowing or not feeling like they are worth anything. I mean there are just too many kids out there who don't feel special at all, you know, and it's all because their fathers are not in their lives and or are not taking the time to tell them and to show them how special they really are. And this is what leads most kids to not value their lives and therefore end up choosing wrong destinations for their lives.

Man, I'm telling you, guys just don't understand how important fatherhood is, especially in these days of so much peer pressure and traps that are out there just waiting to victimize kids who have no proper guidance and or direction for their lives. I mean it's crazy, but guys just don't understand how important they really are to their kids. I mean guys just don't understand how much their kids really need them. Because I mean, if guys really knew how important they were to their kids, and or how precious their kids really are, there would not be that many kids out there that have to grow up without a father. And this is the other reason why I decided to write this book, and it's to try and inspire, encourage, and or beg guys to own up to their responsibilities as men and be fathers to their kids. Because I mean, that's what being a men is all about, you know, taking care of your responsibilities. And there is no greater responsibility than that of raising a child. Because raising a child is really a twenty-four hour, seven days a week, twelve month, three hundred sixty five days a year for at least eighteen plus years of that child's life. And I mean, the job should get easier as they get older (if you are raising them right), but until they are grown and living on their own, a parent's job is really never done.

And so this is the other reason why I decided to write this book, and it's to expose or explain to guys how much work raising a kid really is, you know? And this hard work should start before the baby is even born, you know what I mean? Because it's like, there are diapers to start saving for, there are baby food to start saving for, there are baby cloth to start buying, there is the baby crib to be bought, there is the car seat to be bought, there is the day care to figure out, and the list goes on and on and on. And then there is the hospital bill to consider, you know, that huge delivery charge that has to be paid. Hey, who said having babies was cheap! And so all this is before the baby is even born. And then so after the baby is born, that's when the real fun and hard work of raising a kid really begins. And it begins as soon as you bring the baby home from the hospital and you lay them down in their crib and you get in your bed trying to get some well-deserved sleep so you can rest up from the eighteen hours of labor. But then so, right before you hit that important deep sleep that determines how well your body and mind will be rested and or alert, right before that good peaceful dream starts to formulate in your sleep, right before you start to snore, that's when you will suddenly, without no notice or warning, without any consideration for your need of rest and relaxation, you will suddenly be awaken by a very determined screaming and crying baby who desperately needs your attention. And this is just day one, there's three hundred and sixty four more days like this to go, you know, until the baby gets used to sleeping for at least four or more hours straight at a time, you know what I mean?

    Man, I'm telling you, it can be very tiring, stressful, and even a little frightening to deal and or take care of a baby, especially if you have no one else to help you. And this is because babies pretty much totally depend on you for everything, you know? I mean, since they can't do anything but lay there, they pretty much need you to tend to them at every minute and or hour of the day every day for at least the next three hundred sixty five or so days of the year, you know what I mean? And so this is why the first year of taking care of a baby is usually the toughest, and it's because it demands a whole lot of time, energy, and patience in order to take care of a baby properly at this stage in their life. And so, this is why the first year of parenting can be very exhausting. Because it's like, until the baby is old enough to walk, talk, eat and play by themselves, you know, until they are able to talk (so they can let you know how they feel, making your job of taking care of what's bothering them easier), and walk (freeing you from having to carry them around all day), you are pretty much stuck having to do everything for them, which can be very tiring, especially if you don't have anybody else to help you.

    Man, I'm telling you, taking care of a baby can be very challenging, especially at that early stage. And this is one of the reasons why I feel sorry for single parents, because they pretty much have to do the whole baby caring thing by themselves. And this is one of the reasons why a lot of single mothers tend to be very resentful towards their baby daddies. And this is because they hate the fact that, while they are stuck to have to struggle, sacrifice and work hard to take care of the baby, they hate the fact that their baby daddy is out there running around acting like he has no responsibilities towards the baby at all, you know what I mean? I mean, it's like, they hate the fact that, while they have to deal with a crying baby all day, they hate the fact that their baby daddy is probably out there hanging out with his friends doing nothing in particular. I mean, they hate the fact that, while they have to deal with sleepless nights because the baby has a hard time falling asleep, they hate the fact that their baby daddy is probably out there chasing skirts, you know, looking for other women to sleep with. You know, they hate the fact that, while they have to be stuck in the house on weekends (because of the baby) instead of going out partying with their friends, they hate the fact that their baby daddy is probably out in the clubs bump and grinding with another girl.

And still, they hate the fact that, while they have to rush in the morning to take the baby to the baby sitter or day care so they can go to work, they hate the fact that their baby daddy is probably just chilling at his mama's house playing video games all day, you know what I mean? I mean, they hate the fact that, while they are working so hard to make sure that their kids are well taken care of (financially and or otherwise), they hate the fact that their baby daddy don't seem to have the same sense of obligation (financially and or otherwise) towards their kids.

And this is one of the reasons why a lot of single mothers tend to walk around looking mad, angry and or cranky all the time, and it's because they hate the fact that they have to raise their kids by themselves (which can be very overwhelming) while their baby daddies are out there running around being irresponsible.

And this is one of the reasons why I decided to write this book, and it's because the task of raising kids nowadays is very monumental. And this is because, you know how they used to say "It takes a village to raise a child", well my friends, there's no more village. That's right my friends, we have lost that sense of community feeling towards each other, you know, where neighbors actually felt obligated to not only look out for each other, but to especially look out for each other's kids. I mean it's crazy! But nowadays not only do neighbors hardly know each other, but they hardly trust each other, you know what I mean? And so, this is why I say there is no more "village", and it's because people are not really looking out for each other anymore, you know? I mean, nowadays it's like every man for themselves, you know, it's like, it's all about me, myself and I, and you, yourself and yours, you know what I mean? I mean it's like, don't bother me, and I won't bother you. And so, this is why it is so hard to raise kids properly nowadays, and it's because with people so concerned with minding their own business, it pretty much leaves the parent to be the sole protector and or supervisor for their kids, which can be a monumental and almost impossible job for single parents to do, especially with the fact that most single parents have to work either long hours or at least two jobs just to make ends meet.

And so this is why I decided to write this book man, you know? And it's just to try and encourage and or beg guys to take more responsibilities for their kids, you know? Because I mean, the task of raising kids nowadays is just too monumental for the ladies to be doing alone, you know? So come on guys, we got to do better, you know what I mean? I mean it's time for us to stand-up, man-up, own-up, be fathers and take care of our kids. Because our kids need us man, our kids desperately need us. I mean, I don't have to prove it to you, you see the evening "News". Because you know, those are our kids who end up in jail, those are our kids who end up dropping out of school, those are our kids who end up being teenage mothers, those are our kids who end up being strippers, those are our kids who end up being drug dealers, those are our kids who end up being in gangs, those are our kids who end up being thieves and robbers, those are our kids who end up feeling like failures, those are our kids who end up feeling like their lives are worthless, you know what I mean?

So come on guys, we can do better, you know? So let's stop making excuses (because really there's none) and let's start acting like real men. Because I mean, that's what real men do, you know, they take care of their responsibilities. And plus, there's a lot of joy to be had from taking care and watching your kids grow up, you know? Because I mean, there can't be any more of a joyous occasion than knowing that you the "parent" was very instrumental in helping and raising your kids to being successful and mature adults. And so I mean, sure there's a lot of sacrifice and hard work that goes with raising kids, but at the same time there's a lot of joy to be had while raising them, you know what I mean? And this joy can start as soon as the doctor says, "I see the head, I can see the head, push, push, push, come on push, good job, here's the baby, congratulations, it's a girl!"

Well my friends, I think this is it, I mean, I think I have done my best to try and explain why I truly believe that fathers are very important in a kid's life. And so, with all that's said, I would really like to thank everyone who will be reading or has just finished reading this book, and I hope that it was very inspirational to you that you will share it with someone else, especially someone who you think might benefit tremendously from it. Because I mean, that is what inspired me to write this book in the first place, you know, to try and encourage fathers to get involved in their kids' lives, because Lord knows there are just too many kids out there running around confused and depressed because they don't know who their fathers are, and so are desperately longing for their father's love.

I mean, a lot of men take it for granted, but your kids need you man, so go and see them. And I mean, what's the worst that could happen? And I mean you just never know, having your kids in your life could be the greatest joy that you will ever find! Because truly and honestly, life is all about enjoying your loved ones, and there is no greater joy (if you have kids) than the joy and happiness you can get from watching your kids grow up to be mature and successful adults with their own families. I mean that is it, because really, think about it, there is nothing in life that can be more satisfying than knowing that you the parent were very instrumental in your kids becoming what they are in life, you know, knowing that they made it, and not just made it, but they thrived and you the father was there to land a helping hand any time they needed it. And that to me is what life is all about, you know, being the best parent you can be (if you have kids, and if you don't, then you can be the best uncle or aunt to your nieces and nephews, because a kid can never have enough adult role models in their life, so the more the better), by being there for your kids, you know, from birth to college and beyond if need be. Because to me, once you are a parent, you will always be a parent, even if your kids are grown and out the house, you know what I mean? Because I mean, you just never know when they are going to need you again, because in this crazy world, sometimes things don't go according to how you and or they might have planned it, and therefore a restart or a new plan might have to be made later on in life, you know, when sh%t happens that's out of any ones control. But hey, those are your kids, and as a parent you should always be ready to have your kids' back, you know, be ready to help and or support your kids as they try to spread their wings and fly on their own.

    Well my friends, thank you again for reading my book, I hope you enjoyed it as much as I enjoyed writing it. And I want to say much love to all the real men out there who are taking care of their kids, keep up the good work man, your kids will definitely benefit tremendously from your guidance and your love. And to all my baby daddies out there who are kind of slacking off on their responsibilities, hey man it's time to own-up, stand- up, man-up, and be a father to your kids, you know, as how a real man should. So come on player, get yourself together and go ahead and be an active participant in your kids' lives. Because trust me, as you bless them with your love, they will in turn bless you with their love, and your life will start to be more joyful as you are filled with blessings, because believe me or not, kids are a blessing.

Ok, well that's it, take care y'all, be good to each other (baby daddies be good to your baby mamas and baby mamas be good to your baby daddies, because your kids need all of you for their proper nurturing). And just remember, don't have the babies, if you can't take care of the babies (remember Michael Jackson's song), ha ha ha ha ha, yeah, peace, I'm out, and God bless!!!

www.ingramcontent.com/pod-product-compliance
Lightning Source LLC
LaVergne TN
LVHW051545070426
835507LV00021B/2415